THE Wilderness Paddler's Handbook

ALAN S. KESSELHEIM

RAGGED MOUNTAIN PRESS / McGRAW-HILL

*Camden, Maine ▪ New York ▪ Chicago ▪ San Francisco
Lisbon ▪ London ▪ Madrid ▪ Mexico City ▪ Milan ▪ New Delhi
San Juan ▪ Seoul ▪ Singapore ▪ Sydney ▪ Toronto*

Ragged Mountain Press 🌀

A Division of The McGraw-Hill Companies

2 4 6 8 10 9 7 5 3

Copyright © 2001 Ragged Mountain Press

All rights reserved. The publisher takes no responsibility for the use of any of the materials or methods described in this book, nor for the products thereof. The name "Ragged Mountain Press" and the Ragged Mountain Press logo are trademarks of The McGraw-Hill Companies. Printed in the United States of America.

Library of Congress Cataloging-in-Publication Data

Kesselheim, Alan S., 1952–
  The wilderness paddler's handbook / Alan S. Kesselheim.
    p.   cm.
  Includes index.
  ISBN 0-07-135418-2
  1. Canoes and canoeing—Handbooks, manuals, etc. I. Title.

GV783.K46 2001
797.1'22—dc21   00-045691

Questions regarding the content of this book should be addressed to
Ragged Mountain Press
P.O. Box 220
Camden, ME 04843
www.raggedmountainpress.com

Questions regarding the ordering of this book should be addressed to
The McGraw-Hill Companies
Customer Service Department
P.O. Box 547
Blacklick, OH 43004
Retail customers: 1-800-262-4729
Bookstores: 1-800-722-4726

This book is printed 55 lb. Sebago by R. R. Donnelley, Crawfordsville, IN
Design by Shannon Swanson
Production by Deborah Evans and Dan Kirchoff
Edited by Tom McCarthy and Alice Bennett

All photos courtesy Alan S. Kesselheim and Marypat Zitzer unless otherwise noted. Photo page 127 by Mark Jordan/oi2.com; photo page 86 courtesy Craig Kesselheim; line illustrations by Elayne Sears.

Band-Aid, Battleship, Capilene, Cordura, Cream of Wheat, Deks Olje, Fastex, Frisbee, Kevlar, Malt-o-Meal, Outward Bound, Royalex, Scrabble, Steri-Strip, Subaru, Suburban, Thorazine, Tupperware, Velcro, Watco, Winnebago, Yahtzee, and Ziploc are registered trademarks.

Contents

Introduction

I need to come clean from the get-go. I own very few how-to books, and I hardly ever look at the ones that do sprinkle my bookshelves (mostly presents from well-meaning aunts and uncles). More than that, I tend to be skeptical of people whose shelves are jammed with technical, jargon-polluted, list-littered outdoor tomes. I'm skeptical the same way I am of someone whose bedside table is stacked with self-help or dieting books.

My experience has been that it's easy to confuse reading a book with doing something. You finish the last page feeling that flush of expanding awareness, that opening window of possibility, but it fades with time. A year later you're still overweight, still hounded by neuroses, and you still haven't gone paddling. So maybe you buy another book, and you slide a bit further into the dark tunnel of informational addiction. How else to explain the popularity of those things? There just can't be that many new ways to become better people, thinner people, or people who go off in canoes.

You don't pull off a great canoe jaunt because you finally get hold of a spiffy equipment list, or because some gearhead elucidates the nuances of Kevlar and ABS. No. We go on trips because we've latched on to a great paddling companion, that rare and precious treasure. Or because one day we're sucked in to a quadrant of blank map with a blue squiggle running through it and get so infatuated with the idea of that country that we can't stop thinking about it. Or because we read an intriguing explorer's journal . . . or get ambushed by a slide show full of wild, intense, sun-soaked river along about mid-January, just when the straitjacket of cabin fever is getting snug.

If I had to come up with a pithy summary of my canoe tripping philosophy, it would be something like this: Get in the boat and go! Things will work out. If they don't, figure out how to adapt. My bias is heavily in favor of inspiration over information. I'd go so far as to say that trips are nine-tenths inspiration and one-tenth information.

Along that line, I'm not an obsessive, techweenie gear hog. When the discussion starts heating up about the degree of bend in a bent-shaft paddle or the latest wrinkle in global positioning system displays, I get weary. My head droops. I find myself wearing that stand-and-nod, cocktail-party smile and peering around for something to lean on so I won't fall down with boredom.

I'm blissfully content with the humble, tried-and-true package of canoe tripping stuff I've amassed over the years and with my tidy bundle of trip-planning axioms. It might be that if my paddle were four ounces lighter or the tumblehome of my canoe hull were a tad more pronounced I'd get a more efficient stroke. My shoulders might be a bit less sore after a day of fighting headwinds. I might be able to cut two minutes off the stretching routine to work the kinks out of my back. But you know what? I don't care. It doesn't matter to me. What I have seems to work fine. I'm happy on trips. A slightly lighter paddle isn't going to make me appreciably more so.

I feel the same way about my tripping outfit as I do about the cars I buy. The simpler the better. Given a choice between hand-crank car windows and the electric variety, I'll wind it down every time. The simpler something is, the less likely it is to break down. More than that, the simpler the system, the less time I'll have to spend tinkering with the campsite, reading instruction manuals, and duct taping failed gizmos.

All that said, I understand the impulse to buy these how-to guides. They have that information-rich tone of certainty that is so reassuring when you first start out. Starting out, with only a blurry and romanticized vision of trip lore, *is* daunting. Where to begin? How to find maps and route descriptions? What food to bring? How to avoid being seduced by outdoor salespeople who only want your credit card number? All of it—from what kind of boat to buy to how to read a map—looms like a mountainous, crippling ordeal.

Never mind that once you start in hardly any of it is really that mysterious or difficult. I admit that a good part of my reluctance to produce this book arises because I keep saying to myself as I write, "They can figure *that* out!" Or I'll hear my first-grade son and sometime bow paddler saying, "Duh, Dad!"

Well, anyway, somewhere on the rather short list of things I know how to do is canoe tripping. I've gotten in boats and gone places, a lot. In the past quarter century I've paddled ten thousand miles or more. I've tracked upstream and paddled down, stroked across expansive bodies of water and along streams so tiny I couldn't turn the boat around. I've paddled north of the Arctic Circle and down in Mexico. I've gone on solo trips, with a partner, with a bevy of strangers, and with three toddlers crammed in among the load. A couple of times I've loaded up and not come back for more than a year.

I've figured out what works for me; my packful of essentials, the things that keep me content on an outing and safe for the next one. I also have some strong opinions about what isn't worth the trouble or is downright silly.

Along the way I've had my share of ignoble moments, the type not generally brought up by someone setting out to offer sage advice. I've learned how to do a few things right, mostly by not doing them right the first time or two. And I've imposed a rather quirky and marginally rational method on this lovely madness of putting people and boats and water together and starting up the music.

Finally, I've got a few stories to tell. I believe that a good yarn is worth a chapter full of lists. Besides, I've figured out that honesty, coupled with an absolute lack of pride, makes you pretty well invulnerable as a giver of advice. Those stories, I hope, will help with the truly important inspirational part of canoe tripping. Then the rest of it—the lists and addresses and charts—can be relegated to its place, in the margins and at the back, where it belongs.

NAVIGATING THIS BOOK

I put this book together in a way that made sense to me. I hope I won't be alone. There are inescapable gray areas when it comes to assigning topics to one section or another. There are almost always pretty good arguments in favor of moving things elsewhere, but life is like that.

The discussion is divided into six parts, followed by two appendixes and an index. It will help if you browse through the table of contents, go to a few chapters that seem of particular interest, and get a feel for how the text and sidebars and illustrations work together. You might find yourself reading all the way through, or you might want to flip to the sections most pertinent to your paddling life—the chapters on family canoeing, for example, or the pages devoted to trip food.

Part 1 starts with that ethereal moment of inspiration when the idea for a trip germinates and begins to work its way toward reality. Subsequent chapters deal with researching trip information, handling travel logistics, and coping with the myriad details, from trip budget to roof racks to group makeup, that can be the most obstacle-strewn part of a journey. At the end, you're presumably standing at the put-in, ready to launch your adventure.

Part 2 takes on the techniques and issues that crop up on the water. Chapters focus on partnership, the rewards and challenges of going solo, strategies for travel against the current, reading and reacting to moving water, portage techniques, and the like.

Part 3 covers living in the wilds: camping tips, packing the boat, setting up the camp kitchen, dealing with first aid and sanitation. Coping with critters and bugs, selecting a home for the night, and keeping up group morale all shuffle into place here.

Part 4 is all about gear and food—the trip outfit. Look here for the complete gear list, a discussion of canoes, a menu plan, how to calculate your daily metabolic needs, gear that isn't worth the hype, and perhaps most important, how to gain control of the pile once you have it all amassed.

The kids come along for part 5. This section is dedicated to convincing you that going paddling as a family is one of the best ways to enjoy wilderness adventure with children. Here you'll find strategies for different ages, trip activities, tips on safety and gear, and a discussion of the way your paddling point of view necessarily shifts when offspring clamber aboard.

In the final section, part 6, I finally let loose a bevy of cherished trip destinations. Look there for eight canoe trip suggestions, some easy, some difficult, some accessible, some remote, some perfect for quiet solo paddles, some ideal for the family, and each with a trip-planning section to get you on your way.

PART ONE

FROM IDEA TO PUT-IN

How Trips Get Born

Some memories float unrooted in time, sharp and vivid as yesterday. They leap across decades with a clarity as startling as lightning. Like the April morning some fifteen years ago when Marypat and I were hunkered down over our camp breakfast in Chesler Park, in the Canyonlands of Utah.

The spring sun colors the fantastic minarets of sandstone and pools in the clearing like liquid warmth filling a basin. We sip our second round of coffee—a lazy desert morning in that early period of our relationship when we savor everything together. The arid panorama sweeps around us, but our talk is of the Far North and of our budding passion for canoe tripping in the Canadian wilderness.

"The trips are just too short," Marypat complains. "Just when I really feel centered there, really in the trip rhythm, it's time to come out. Even a thirty-day trip is over too soon."

"It sounds pretty ridiculous," I say, "when most people would be elated to get two weeks of that kind of immersion, but you're right. It's almost painful to leave, as if we've just gotten to the threshold of great awareness and have to turn back."

I notice a raven rowing through the sky, its shadow flickering across a sandstone wall. To the west, across the Colorado River, the layers of rock lead my eye off to the distant float of the Henry Mountains. I settle in against the broad trunk of a juniper tree. Space hums around us.

"What if we took a really long trip?" I break the spell. "Not just a week or two longer, but really long. What if we went off for a year? The whole cycle. It would be like the old-time explorers who wintered over between travel seasons."

We're silent for a long moment, as if we both know that the next thing we say will set the tone for how we take this outrageous suggestion. The turning of mental gears is damn near audible.

"Wow," Marypat finally breathes, "that would really be something, wouldn't it!" When she looks at me her blue eyes crackle with that light that I already recognize as her pure, fierce joy in the face of a grand and daunting and slightly crazed challenge.

Uh-oh, I think. Here we go.

The rest of the morning, as the sun climbs over the desert world, we spend talking around the edges of this seed of a plan. We grow so animated at times that we pace around our camp, thinking out loud, figuring potential routes, worrying at the obvious logistical problems, calculating how much a trip like that might cost, weighing the names of people who might come along. More coffee goes down the hatch. The desert is only a backdrop for our scheming. We could be in an office cubicle for all the impact our surroundings have on us.

What an idea!

It was two years between that heady morning in the desert and the morning we set our canoe in the glacial meltwater of the Athabasca River

and paddled away on that "really long trip." We gave ourselves to the wilds of Canada for the next 420 days, and the moment we stroked away into the unknown, our self-contained world funneled down to the confines of that 17-foot red canoe.

I'm still stunned that we pulled it off. We weren't all that experienced—our paddling résumés included a couple of monthlong Canadian trips with groups of friends and lots of generic camping. We were absurdly optimistic about working out winter arrangements en route. We were competent paddlers, but not highly skilled. We took a flying leap into the abyss, trusting that things would work out. We just got in the boat and went.

When I think about the key ingredients in pulling off that adventure and many others, it's our partnership that stands out. On that desert morning, it was our joint enthusiasm that stoked the fires of excitement and commitment. Either one of us alone would have been hard pressed to get beyond the initial idea. With different companions, the same spark might have flickered and quietly died—another scheme in the dustbin of abandoned ambitions.

And it was our partnership that kept us on task. When we couldn't infect any of our friends with enough trip fever to commit to joining us, together we had the confidence to settle back to a single-boat expedition. When one of us periodically fell prey to the many handy doubts that hovered over our plan, the other would push on with blunt-headed enthusiasm.

We talked about our plans with that fabricated certainty that all crazed endeavors require, and told enough people that after a while it would have been an embarrassment not to try. At some point it became obvious that at least part of our commitment to going through with this was to avoid getting a reputation for big talk and no action.

The bulky atlas at home was opened so often to the map of northern Canada that the spine finally broke. Often enough that we eventually worked out what seemed a feasible route, more or less the right length, that wouldn't break our meager budget with expensive fly-ins.

We picked up a food dehydrator on sale and started drying food. We knew we couldn't afford packaged camp food, so we just dried everything that went on sale at the grocery—hundreds of pounds of it. Eventually we sorted out a menu that would fit the food we had piled up. The dehydrator hummed, essentially nonstop, for a year.

We sent out letters soliciting equipment sponsorship. We tried out recipes and bagged food. We cried through dehydrating a fifty-pound sack of cheap onions. We ordered maps and pored over the difficult portions of the route. We bought a used shotgun for protection from bears. We saved all the money we could and then outlined a budget to fit. We paid our bills, moved everything we owned into a tiny storage shed, and on an arbitrary day in June, packed up our gear and drove north.

Did we make mistakes? Of course. Were we lucky? Hell yes. Did things go according to plan? Only loosely. But 420 days later we had put a remarkable trip in our canoe wake, a trip that changed our lives.

Expeditions, even weekend adventures, are the products of inspiration. By definition, the source of these lightbulb epiphanies is elusive, mysterious, fantastic, unpredictable. You can't go out and plan to conjure up an inspiration on your lunch break—but it's entirely possible that the next great trip concept might smite you between the eyes midway through your pastrami on rye. Or one afternoon on a bicycle ride, or walking home after work on a snowy Friday afternoon when you thought your mind was stuffed with details, or in the middle of reading a novel about a relationship gone sour. Who knows where these things pop up from? They're like dreams, sudden stabs from the subconscious.

There are, however, things you can do to prime the pump of inspiring adventures.

The most important one is to view the world as a paddler, to see it through the filter that highlights paddling potential everywhere, like putting on 3-D specs. We already have practice at this with a range of other filters we employ in life. I encounter the world as a writer much of the time, and it turns the landscape into one made up of images and dialogue, mannerisms and vivid scenes. Photographers frame their view in mental camera lenses. Painters see color and texture. Musicians hear rhythm and sound patterns. Builders see structure and the integrity of shape. Farmers see soil and weather.

Looking at life as a series of canoe trips connected by other, peripheral events opens the floodgates. Boat trips are everywhere. Trust me. They don't have to be elaborate or extended or hair-raising or exotic or written up in a guidebook. They just need water and you in a boat.

Some of my best trips have been unglamorous neighborhood jaunts on pretty plain pieces of water. I have a favorite stretch of a local creek, for example, that I've paddled dozens of times. Much of it never leaves the city limits of my home town, but it's a refreshing, renewing escape. I go there the way people go to the health club, and I feel pretty smug about it.

Last summer I was looking at the state highway map and I noticed that the main stem of the Jefferson River, one of the three forks of the Missouri, is only eighty-three miles long. I bet I could zip down that in three days, I said to myself. About a month later I did just that, all alone, and I didn't see another boat the whole time.

Marypat and I paddled almost six hundred miles on the Yellowstone River with our first son when he was eight months old. Our put-in was two hours from home. We loaded up and headed across the state for almost a month. A friend came and got us where the Yellowstone and Missouri come together in North Dakota. The whole deal probably cost us $200. Now we go back and revisit favorite sections every year: two-day outings, week-long expeditions in search of agates, afternoon whitewater thrill runs.

One of the corollaries of seeing the world as a paddler is that every trip spawns more trips. I can't think of a single canoe journey that didn't spark ideas for several more. I want, sometime, to extend my run on the local exercise creek, just to see where it goes. I'd like to do some of the main tributaries of the Yellowstone, and I've been dreaming of circumnavigating Yellowstone Lake, near the headwaters in Yellowstone National Park. Our long Canadian trip added a dozen or more parallel routes to the wish list. Pretty soon it's not coming up with trip ideas that limits you, but how to set priorities for the ones that are jumping up and down on the mental periphery like a kindergarten class trying to get your attention.

Some props are useful in the quest. Maps, for one. I spend a significant part of every winter crawling around the living-room floor on top of the maps I have spread out. There's nothing like it to stimulate the imagination glands, especially when it's been twenty below for two weeks and it gets dark at four. I start following a blue trail through empty country, linking drainages, crossing lakes, finding connections, seeing what access comes near, and pretty soon I've gone deep into a virtual landscape created by the spell of flat sheets of colored paper.

On trips I spend more time studying maps than I do reading the books I bring along. "Look at this little river over here," I'll call to Marypat. "We'd just have to hop over this neck of land and we'd be in a new drainage." Maps, in my experience, are inexhaustible sources of possibilities. Just when I think I've wrung every trip out of a quadrangle, another route unfurls itself across the worn creases and squashed insect stains.

Books are good too. Not the how-to books, for the most part, but explorers' journals, trip accounts, narrative treatments of historic trails. I got the idea for a monthlong expedition above the Arctic Circle in Canada from a one-page aside in a book about the fur-trade routes of the North.

Hmmm, I thought, that looks neat. I'll bet not many people try that one. And look, there's a road to the start. We could drive up there in a week or less, be on the water a month, and get back in another week. Pretty soon I'm writing away for topographic maps and testing the interest level of potential partners. A year later we put in on the Peel River and paddle off.

A lot of water has gone downstream in the years since our inspired morning in Chesler Park. A lot of trips have piled up in our wake, too. Things have changed. We have kids now. We're older and slightly less crazed these days, though I hope we aren't any less susceptible to the whiff of a great paddling notion when it comes wafting up from wherever those things do.

SOURCES OF TRIP NOTIONS

FRIENDS AND PADDLING PARTNERS

Some strange, magical chemistry occurs when several people start focusing on trip ideas—a kind of heady alchemy that makes schemes crystallize and grow. Many of my canoe trips have had their source in innocent statements like "I heard of a little river down in Colorado that's supposed to be a great family float" or "I've been thinking about that country north of the Boundary Waters" or "I'm considering applying for a permit to float the Smith this year; would you be interested?"

MAPS

Atlases, highway maps, topographic quadrangles, maps drawn on napkins, city street maps. . . . Follow where they lead. There's nothing so fundamentally evocative as landscape rendered two-dimensional. Mapmaking has to rank up with the internal combustion engine as one of the salient accomplishments of our kind.

BOOKS

Spend an afternoon at the library. Browse the sections with outdoor writers, water adventure books, explorers' accounts, regional histories, archival collections. Pick a few and start reading. Before long the trip ideas will ripen like zucchini in August. Pretty soon you'll be leaving them on friends' doorsteps to get rid of the excess!

THE WORD-OF-MOUTH SMALL WORLD

Open the door by taking a trip or two and the paddling world blossoms, full of its own magazines and newsletters, paddling clubs, Web sites, symposiums and workshops, slide shows, and lunatic-fringe hairball boaters. Even if you choose to be a wallflower in this subculture, you'll absorb trip ideas through your pores. It's the adventuring form of osmosis.

The life list of trips hasn't shortened up any, despite my determined efforts to knock off the ones at the top. More keep crowding in, like a spring bubbling up from some subconscious groundwater source. It's reassuring, because that's one of the lists I hope never to see the end of. That would really be scary—crossing off the last great journey on the life list of canoe jaunts.

I have every intention of passing that particular to-do list on to my kids, an inheritance of sorts, no less important than whatever real estate or bank accounts I can muster up at the end. Maybe I'll even include it in my will, written on a tattered piece of journal page smeared with food stains and folded up small, a legacy of routes, bloodlines of water pulsing on, generation after generation, trips without end.

Now there's a concept.

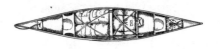

TWO

Square Peg, Round Hole: Making a Trip Fit

I would rather be in bed, nursing my cold, than in this drafty gym/auditorium with forty college students who are my responsibility, the lot of us about to be regaled with a canoeing slide show. When the lights snap off I slouch down in my chair and wad my jacket into the crack between seats. My only worry is that my snoring will get so loud I'll wake myself up. Canoeing is all well and good, but not tonight, thanks.

An hour later, when the lights come on, I'm sitting up straight, haven't honked out loud once, and have managed to ignore my sore throat for the first time all day. For that hour I've been transported to northern Manitoba, to a river called the Seal, and at the end of it, despite myself, I'm inspired.

It helps that it has been thirty below zero for the better part of a month in northern Wisconsin (where I lived then) and that I've had a bellyful of shoveling my driveway only to find that my car won't start, or returning from vacation to find burst water pipes and a skating rink in the crawl space.

When I clump out into the bitter cold and my car battery does that "don't wake me up now" routine before the engine turns over, I barely notice. I'm aflame with trip fever.

Over the next couple of weeks I find myself standing at windows looking north with no idea how long I've been there. I'm embarrassed at a faculty meeting when the discussion comes around to me and I haven't a clue to what the topic is. More than once I'm roused by some disturbance and discover a companion staring at me with that solicitous look we use around the sick, infirm, or not altogether present.

About midwinter I get serious. The trip shouldn't be that big a deal—a month on the water—but the expanse between concept and real journey is a minefield. I enlist Grant, my best friend and paddling partner. He's an easy mark.

"Sounds great," he says. "Count me in."

But in the next breath he deflates the trip balloon I've filled with romantic hot air with a few innocent and entirely reasonable questions. How will we get to the put-in? Can we afford being flown in? Who else will go? What about that forty miles of ocean paddling at the end to get to the nearest town?

REASONS NOT TO GO

There are always more reasons not to take trips than justifications for going. Not enough money. Not enough time. Not experienced enough. Too much work to do. Course work to finish. Gaping holes in the equipment list. Yada-yada-yada. . . . Some of them may even be pretty good, altogether solid, reasons. There is, after all, life outside adventure and times when it plain isn't a good idea to head off. Fair enough.

But there is also a weasely tendency, from time to time, to take refuge in these rational-sounding arguments when in fact they could all be overcome and what you're really doing is caving in to the bountiful unknowns in the plan and to the admittedly unappealing mound of work that is the precursor to adventurous exploits.

Whenever I find myself teetering on the edge of talking myself out of a trip, I remember a college professor who knocked on my door one weekend while I was working on a research paper for his class. It was a warm fall Saturday, and he wanted to go on an all-afternoon bike ride.

"I'm working," I told him. "On a paper for you!"

"It can wait," he said. "Look at this day. How can you stand being inside?"

"I don't have much choice. It's due this week, remember? I've barely started."

"Look," he said. "Do you want to be sixty-five and looking back on life and all you can remember are the things you didn't do?"

He was a persuasive son of a gun. I went riding that Saturday. I must have gotten the paper (which I have absolutely no memory of) done on time. But you know what? I remember that fall bike ride, twenty-five years ago on the country roads of rural Indiana, like yesterday.

There's a brief moment, in the face of all that, when I almost close the door on the whole endeavor. He's right, I think. What about all that stuff? It's a great temptation, just then, to give in. Life would be a good deal simpler without northern Manitoba in it.

THE PARTY LIST

If you're lucky, you won't have to go through this business. Deciding how big the canoeing group should be, then soliciting candidates, and finally nailing down commitments can be the most worrisome and anxious part of the pretrip grind.

If you're lucky, the group makeup is a given from the top. If you paddle alone, for instance, or with your partner or your family. Or perhaps you're blessed with a cadre of paddling buddies who are committed to yearly reunions on the water—a group of women, old college friends, your former rugby team, whatever.

If not, prepare for the angst of creating a group of water partners out of the ether of past connections, current candidates, and the luck of the draw. Some guidelines to consider:

- Think about a one-boat trip (either solo or with a partner). Safety is the obvious caveat and a cautious travel style the obvious strategy, but one-boat trips are quiet and contemplative, decision making is clean and crisp, and the goals and expectations are easy to negotiate.
- In the case of larger groups, start by inviting the people you really want first, well ahead of the journey. Often they'll have ideas for other compatible candidates.
- Consider a theme for the invitation list: all women/men, extended family, old workmates.
- Set a deadline for committing to the trip and nail it down with a financial contribution to the group fund.
- Beware of overbooking. Out of nervousness that you won't get enough takers, it's tempting to invite too many. Then you might face having to uninvite a friend who's eager to go.
- From the start, clearly communicate the demands of the route and your expectations for the journey. Unclear communication always seems to haunt you on the trail.

Then Grant goes on, with excitement in his voice. "Let's look at maps," he says. "I've only been as far as Winnipeg!" He isn't undermining the idea at all, just thinking it through, a process I've pointedly avoided to this juncture. And maps, it turns out, are the antidote to trip doubt, the fastest way to transform anxiety and frustration back into enthusiasm.

A month later we nearly have a quorum, almost enough paddlers for the three boats we've decided are a good safe number. Several of the worrisome details have fallen into place. One of the trip members has connections at a nearby Outward Bound school and has negotiated buying trip food from their warehouse, along with a place where we can pack it up.

Someone else has been working at travel logistics. With the kind of trip serendipity I now recognize as common to almost all these endeavors, she stumbles on a fishing camp owner who agrees to split the expense of a DC-3 flight so he can get camp supplies flown in at the same time we get our boats, gear, and bodies to a lake from which we can, theoretically, connect to the watershed of the Seal. It requires a few leaps of faith across blank sections of map, but we're told it can be done.

There's a good deal of wrangling over trip dates—weddings to attend, a graduate course that doesn't finish until July, a job with a start date in early August. It takes about $50 worth of heated long-distance exchanges, and some fast talking about the value of independent study in graduate course-work—before we have brackets around a month in midsummer. The Manitoba month.

That spring there's another sag in commitment. The fervor that burned in the dark heart of winter has waned to a more feeble energy. Everyone is busy with other things. The weather is lovely. There's open water to paddle. Other possibilities for summer diversions have come up.

Besides, we still haven't roped in the final paddler. More than that, we have no reliable vehicle to transport us to the airport in central Manitoba where the flight originates.

Grant's old pickup is more duct tape than metal. My compact Mercury is too small to begin with and prone to side-of-the-road mishaps. Nobody has a rig, or a combination of rigs, that will do.

Four of us get together for a disheartening session over happy hour in a dark bar on the shores of Lake Superior, sometime in May. Forty-five minutes and a couple of drafts later, we've circled back to the same bleak place in the discussion. Grant plunks quarters into the jukebox and asks a woman at an adjoining table to dance. Our table is littered with maps, a scribbled budget on the back of a menu, and a list of the crossed-off names of everyone we can think of to invite.

TRIP TASK AND TIME LINE

First Things First
(Sometimes a Year or More Ahead)

The route. The trip is still miragelike, but start playing with the route.

The group. Imagine yourself on the water and picture the ideal group in the scene. How many people and boats are there? Does anyone have a face yet?

The itinerary. How much time does the dream trip require? How much time do you have?

The budget. If it all comes together, is there money in the bank, or is it time to start buying lottery tickets?

Getting Serious
(Six Months Out)

The route. Order some maps, research other information sources, and start shaping that dream route into something with a beginning, middle, and end.

The group. Finalize the invitation list, send out feelers, and then start nagging for commitments.

Travel. Figure out access points and the need for shuttles, then inventory the available vehicles (or other forms of transport).

Jobs. As the group gels, start delegating—travel manager, menu organizer, gearhead . . .

Goals. Have at least one meeting, even if it's by phone, to blab about group goals, expectations, and trip resolutions.

Food. Discuss the menu and cooking style.

So, We're Actually Going
(Final Month or Two)

Food. Get that grub and put it in bags.

Gear. Jury-rig—er, I mean customize—any gear that needs it.

Travel. Fine-tune the logistics. (What do you mean, there's no bridge there?)

Route. Finalize the route and itinerary and gather last-minute information for those unsettling dubious sections.

Details and expectations. Have one more meeting to compare notes and make sure somebody will remember the matches and can opener.

Packing. Gather for the final pack-out before seeing if you actually fit in the vehicle.

We're in the parking lot, about to head home, when Sherry remembers her friend Larry, who's just back from a construction job in Alaska.

"He's not much of a paddler," she says. "I don't know for sure if he's ever been in a canoe, come to think of it. But he's got a killer truck!"

The final piece to the trip puzzle: a rig up to the test.

And Larry it is. Not only does he have a big new truck with a camper shell, but he contributes a spiffy trailer that can carry all our gear. Most important, he's willing. He commits to the trip within hours. It's true that his paddling technique is a long way from accomplished, but we get him on the water a few times before our departure, and he seems to make up for his lack of skill with brute strength and a good attitude.

Larry gets us over the hump. He's that single interlocking contribution that takes our plan from the bog of uncertainty to the solid ground of final commitment. There are lots of details yet—food to pack, routes to figure, spray decks to install on boats, the flurry of equipment customizing—but they're simply the drudgery that will get us to departure, nothing fundamentally threatening.

The day before we leave, we're still pop riveting snaps on boat hulls and buying insect repellent, but the next morning all three canoes are stacked, pyramid-style, on top of Larry's truck, all of us have piled into the cab or are taking our turn under the camper shell, and the engine fires right up.

TRIP BUDGET

Trip expenses, with a few exceptions, fall into three general categories: travel, food, and equipment.

Travel. (See chapter 3 for more details.) It isn't uncommon for travel expenses, including the vehicle shuttle to the take-out, to soak up a third, or even half, of the budget. Once you're on the water, it hardly costs anything. It's getting there and back that kills you. That said, there are some ways to cut costs.

Look for trips that are conveniently accessed by road, bridge crossing, rail track, or town. Even if the trip you initially identify doesn't have a road to it, maybe a navigable tributary stream or connecting chain of lakes does.

Get past the obvious, superficial travel contacts. Dig beyond the glossy mainstream brochures and you'll find the resources like the fishing-camp owner who helped get us to northern Manitoba cheaply. By the way, that trip had a logistically sweet ending as well. We paddled to Churchill, then took the train right back to Larry's truck! Call up outfitters or park rangers, find out about local paddling clubs, contact river guides . . .

If the vehicle is the problem, consider pooling your money to buy a used rig, then sell it when you return (see pages 23–24). Shorter trips can sometimes be shuttled by bicycle. Lock your bike to a tree at the take-out, paddle down, and ride back to the car.

Food. (See chapter 30.) If money is no object, buy packaged camping food and be done with it. But beware of skimpy portions and meals with a tendency to all taste the same after a while. Drying your own food is far and away the cheapest way to go and the best way to build variety into the menu. It won't take long to pay back the purchase of a dehydrator. It is, however, the labor-intensive road to food supplies. Check the mainstream grocery store for camping food too. You'll be surprised by the variety of quick-cooking, lightweight meals—entrées based on beans, noodles, and rice, noodle soups, and so on.

(continued next page)

A round **dehydrator** with a built-in fan and thermostat, and capacity to add extra trays, is ideal.

TRIP BUDGET

(continued from previous page)
For longer trips, try to avoid expensive fly-in food resupplies. Pack efficiently, and if you have to replenish supplies, check into mailing packages general delivery to post offices along the way or caching food en route ahead of time.

Equipment. (See chapter 26.) Well, this depends. Starting out, or if you feel compelled to keep pace with "new and improved" gear, it can be expensive. But later on equipment becomes a relatively minor expense, even if it's still a significant part of the budget.

Maps, first aid kits, cooking utensils, fuel, repair kits, and the like all need to be replaced or maintained regularly. It's a good strategy to establish a group fund to cover these one-trip supplies.

Don't automatically get duped into top-of-the-line gear, with corresponding top-of-the-line price tags. Some things—life jackets, for example—aren't worth skimping on, but do you really have to buy the nesting titanium cook pots, or can you squeak by on the army surplus mess kit?

Finally, add 25 percent to your estimated equipment budget. It always costs more than you expect.

THREE

Getting There and Back

FIVE FLATS TO THE ARCTIC

Vehicles. Always vehicles. Along about February it became clear that the wheels to get us to our put-in, above the Arctic Circle in Canada, were the logistical stumbling block that might founder our adventure. One person's car was brand new and not big enough anyway. The rest of the fleet was too old, too small, too beat, or otherwise unfit for the challenge. We certainly couldn't all fly. No train went where we were heading. We had a plan, we had paddlers, we had the gear and the wherewithal to get food, but it didn't look good for getting to the riverbank.

Sometime around Groundhog Day I was driving past a gas station on the outskirts of town that sold used cars on the side. In the front row sat a behemoth Suburban that looked a little the worse for its life on Montana roads but still proud. Hmmm, I thought.

Three weeks, half a dozen test drives, and a flurry of long-distance calls later, I was the owner of a vehicle half the size of my rental house. Everyone in the group kicked in a share of the $1,800 purchase price, and we were in business. We'd sell the beast when we returned and absorb whatever we lost as part of the trip expense.

Not long afterward, still months from departure, I discovered that the Suburban drank oil almost as fast as it drank gas. Every time I filled up, I needed to pour in another quart. A couple of cases of 10W30 got added to the trip supply list, along with two good spare tires and a couple of gas cans. The crux of the drive would be a 500-mile round trip on a gravel road above the treeline: a road with a reputation for inflicting flat tires by the score; a road with one gas station in 250 miles.

One morning near the end of June we drove off—the Suburban crammed with six adults, gear, and food for a month in the wilderness and with three canoes strapped to a homemade boat rack bolted together out of two-by-fours. It took us five days just to get to the beginning of the infamous dirt road. Five days, more gas money than we're likely to admit, the better part of a case of oil, and a certain tarnishing of the group euphoria from almost a week of thigh-to-thigh existence.

Not ten miles down the shale dirt road, when we stopped for a photograph, somebody noticed the right rear tire going down into a puddle of rubber. Hours later, we got it patched at the midway gas station. Perched there on the edge of the Arctic Circle, this was a gas station with no competition, plenty of tires on hand, and no mercy when it came to pricing.

The next afternoon, on the ferry crossing the Peel River, I was feeling pretty cocky just before I saw the other rear tire settling into itself. Another patch job at the Fort McPherson gas station. Another bill that would buy a new tire back home. Then, while we reorganized gear around the picnic table at our mosquito-ridden campsite that night, I saw the front driver's

A one-trip vehicle.

side tire assume that familiar sagging look. Change the tire, decide to fix the flat *after* the trip.

A month later, after another Fort McPherson repair special, we started back home. Two more flats on the way to pavement. One spare absolutely trashed. All of us fully qualified for jobs in the pits at the Indianapolis 500.

But the Suburban got us to the northern fringe of the continent with our gear and all our boats. Several weeks later we sold the old girl for $1,700. What's a couple of flat tires and a barrel or two of crude?

FLEXIBILITY AS A TRAVEL VIRTUE

At the take-out of that same Arctic canoe journey, we found ourselves in the little bush town of Old Crow, Yukon, on the banks of the Porcupine River. Before leaving home we had set up a charter flight to get us back to a town along the tire-eating dirt road where the Suburban waited. It was expensive, but it was the only way out—at least the only way we knew about from afar.

It turned out that between our making the flight arrangements and pulling our canoes up near the airstrip, things had changed. Once at the airport, we found out there was now passenger service to the same town, at a fraction of the cost, and that we could send our boats and heavy packs out to Whitehorse as cheap cargo on a freight plane.

It didn't take a pocket calculator to figure out how much money we'd save, even though we lost our deposit with the charter service. A few days later, we picked up our boats and gear at the freight hangar in Whitehorse and were on our way south.

Years later, on another northern canoe trip when it looked like a charter flight was the only option to get us and our boat back to civilization, we decided to hang loose and see what developed on-site. Sure enough, within two days of arriving at an Inuit community along an exposed stretch of Hudson Bay, we were able to finagle our canoe onto an oil tanker, to be picked up later in the Montreal harbor, and then get ourselves aboard a small bush plane that had flown in a load of dynamite for a construction project. On twenty minutes' notice, we jounced up to a tiny tundra lake on the back of one of those awful four-wheel contraptions and climbed aboard the little float plane. Half a day later, nearly deaf from the engine roar and decidedly green with airsickness, we stumbled back into civilization. But hey, the price was right.

THE SHUTTLE GAME

One rule of thumb becomes clear early on in the shuttle scenario. Shuttles always take longer than you think they will. Always. You never, ever, return from driving a shuttle to find a happy group waiting at the put-in, friends who say, "Wow, that didn't take long at all!" No. You return to disgruntled companions who had the boats rigged and ready hours ago, who have exhausted every distraction imaginable at the boat launch, who have already devoured most of the trip snacks, and who are openly wondering how many pit stops you made en route.

A survival tip for those returning from a shuttle to such a welcome: make sure you bring a little treat with you—ice-cream bars, a six-pack, something to mollify the crowd.

In many cases shuttles are the bane of water trips. If it's a matter of an hour or two, no big deal. Longer than that and it's time to think about alternatives.

Paying for a shuttle looks better and better the longer the trip. What might seem like an exorbitant fee pales by comparison to wasting the better part of a day either behind the wheel of a car or hanging around a desolate put-in. Once everyone chips in, it starts looking more and more worth it. Check with outfitters, fishing shops, or tourist information offices to get names and numbers.

In some cases leaving your vehicle at a take-out for days and days is not the best idea anyway, if you want to find a rig with wheels and windows intact. I had a shuttle driver in Texas once demand that I give him a precise time for our take-out along the Rio Grande. He didn't want any part of leaving the car unattended for more than an hour or two.

On shorter trips, or when the roads provide a shortcut between put-in and take-out, consider doing a bicycle shuttle. I'm serious. Leave your bikes chained to a tree at the take-out. When you arrive by boat, lock the canoe up by a thwart and then pedal back upstream to your vehicle. Think of it as a kind of cross-training trip. On the first stint your upper body gets buff, on the second it's time to tone the lower half.

PLANNED-IN ACCESSIBILITY

Next to food, travel to and from a wilderness destination is likely to be the most expensive item in the trip budget. By the time you count fuel, repairs, shuttle expenses, parking fees, and the rest, the figures after the dollar sign can really mount up. Add in a couple of fly-ins and you'll likely need a bank loan to pull off the trip.

Travel will be expensive. Start with that expectation, but then work on some angles to reduce the burden.

- Use circle routes. Making a loop out of your journey is the sweetest way to economize on the time and expense devoted to travel. Look for chains of lakes that can be connected by portages or short stretches of rivers and that allow you to come back to the starting point. Circumnavigating large bodies of water can also make for surprisingly rewarding trips. Yellowstone Lake inside Yellowstone National Park comes to mind in that regard, or Lake Athabasca in northern Alberta and Saskatchewan (see page 264). Both are large, beautiful bodies of water with varied shorelines, and the travel logistics would be dead easy. Many wild areas are brimming with circle routes. Study the Boundary Waters or Quetico region, for example. Geography with lots of lakes almost always can be massaged into a loop or two.

- Research other transportation corridors. Train spur lines some-times penetrate wild country, and you can arrange drop-off and pickup at rail crossings at each end of a water journey. Once I drove to a parking lot at a train station, took the train to my put-in on a lake, and paddled back downstream to a river mouth not five miles away from the railroad and my waiting car. Ferry or barge service sometimes provides access to remote coastline communi-ties. Other trips have been through really quiet country, but a cou-ple of dirt roads and bridges provide access for vehicles. Even if you require a fly-in for one leg of the trip, you can almost always find an alternative, and cheaper, way to the other end.

- Don't forget the lost art of hitching. Carry along a life jacket or paddle when you stick out your thumb, and motorists will see that you're a river person. It usually doesn't take long to snag a ride.

ROOF RACKS AND TIE-DOWNS

I miss the days when vehicles had rain gutters. Life was simpler. You could make your own rack for $20 and switch it from car to car with no trouble. These days most cars don't have rain gutters, and roof racks have become the province of yuppie companies. Each cartop carrier is made to fit a specific model and year of car, and each part costs hun-dreds of dollars.

I still have the old rack I cobbled together from two-by-fours almost a generation ago. It's riddled with holes drilled to fit the six or seven vehicles it's been mounted on. I'm fortunate enough to still own a car old enough to have gutters, and every so often I get to use the old rack. It clips on with those Quick n' Easy towers, bolted through the board. I made the crosspieces long enough to fit two canoes side by side, and a

(continued next page)

ROOF RACKS AND TIE-DOWNS

(continued from previous page)
third boat can be centered on top, pyramid style. Works slick. The only drawback is that I've got a couple of permanent knots right by my temple from ramming into the rack getting in and out of cars.

I've thought periodically about covering the boards with carpet scraps to cushion the boat gunwales and my forehead. It's another in the long list of perfectly good ideas that I haven't gotten around to.

Lacking gutters, you pretty well have to get a part-time job so you can afford the yuppie rack and whatever gizmos go with it to cradle your canoe, bike, skis, and snowboard.

As far as tie-downs go, I used to be a master of the trucker's hitch and butterfly knot, those handy quick-release, loop-making rope tricks that give you a bight to run the rope end through and tighten down against. They still work great, and I use them once in a while, but I've been converted to the raft strap crowd.

You know what I mean—inch-wide webbing with a cam lock on one end to tighten it with. They almost never break. You can get them tight as you want, they won't loosen up, and there isn't a knot to learn anywhere.

Using webbing straps, I often don't bother tying down the bow and stern to the car bumpers, especially for a short drive. In a bad wind, on longer trips, or if I'm driving a Volkswagen bus, I'll certainly tie the front

*An **extended roof rack** can carry two or three canoes.*

of the canoes to a solid part of the vehicle chassis under the bumper, and about half the time I tie down the stern for good measure. Then I stop once or twice near the beginning of a trip to check whether the boats have shifted and tighten things up if they have.

Occasionally I've used the marginal technique of laying a boat right on the vehicle roof, buffered with those foam blocks made to fit a canoe gunwale. It works for a short jaunt, if you tie the bow and stern down tight as all get out and maybe run a rope around the whole deal and through the car doors.

For a long journey, get a rack.

Raft straps with cam lock for canoe tie-down.

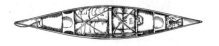

FOUR

Mining for Information

I f you ask me, trip-planning packets take away all the fun of research. People who put those things together are well meaning, I suppose, but getting your adventure in a bundle, with campsites identified, maps enclosed, information phone numbers listed . . . Where's the joy?

OK, sometimes it's a relief to have all that logistical navigation taken care of. It makes things easy and linear and predictable. Boring, but easy. There must be some people who like it that way. Probably the same folks who have those car computers that tell you when to turn left.

What trip packaging eliminates is that lovely process of discovery, those moments of brilliant connection between you and some far-off, yet-to-be explored segment of water. Now that is a satisfying thing—exhilarating even, in its own way.

Take the weeklong spring family trip I took down part of the White River in Colorado and Utah. I heard about it one morning in the hallway outside the office where I go for my writing time. A guy a few doors down mentioned an out-of-print river guide that had a little description of a great family float. The next day he brought in the book. On the surface it sounded promising. About the right length, nothing very difficult in the way of rapids, enough current to keep us awake. The write-up extolled the remote, quiet, and beautiful qualities of the desert. Along about February in Montana, a little desert float over spring vacation sounded downright titillating.

OK. Next I went to the highway map. It so happened that my folks' house lay just about halfway there. We could stop off and give the kids a little grandparent time, break up the drive, then carry on. An easy two-day drive would do it.

The description mentioned the seasonal nature of the river flow. Spring would be good for runoff, but too early and the snowmelt would still be locked up in the high country, too late and we'd be dragging boats over shallows. Also, we needed dates that worked with the school break.

Turns out that the United States Geological Survey maintains readouts of all its river gauging stations from all over the country on the Internet (see appendix 2). I got into the Web site, found gauging stations on the White as well as other area drainages, and pulled up the historical record of average flows for the week in April we had targeted. Plenty of water. In fact, the danger was that the flows might be too high during a big snowmelt year—a chance we'd have to take.

So far, everything looks positive. Time to get a closer view. I go to my map file, fish out the index of topographic maps for Colorado and Utah, and order the large-scale (1:250,000) quads for the river. The bummer is that now I have to wait more than a week before that cardboard tube arrives on the front porch and I can start unrolling quadrangles in the living room.

GETTING TRIP IDEAS FROM HIGHWAY MAPS: AN EXERCISE

Some of my nicest floats have been inspired by highway maps. I'll be gazing at a map of Montana that I've looked at dozens of times, and suddenly a length of river through quiet country will leap out at me. Pretty soon I'm studying topographic maps and looking into details. They don't always work out, but at least half the time something I've seen on a road map has eventually led to putting a canoe into the flow and heading off for a few days.

Try it with your state or province. Get out a road map and start looking it over. This time, instead of concentrating on towns and highways, focus on the blue squiggles that writhe across the page. Find the sections of water that pass through the least populated quadrants of country. Look for bridge access points, state or federal land, signs of dams or falls.

See if you can come up with half a dozen potential trips at least a day in length, and preferably longer. Once you've got a handful of candidates, look them up on large-scale topo maps or in regional guidebooks. My guess is that three out of six will be viable canoe destinations.

Once that happens, the country comes looming up out of the shaded sheets. Sure enough, some great deep canyon walls, neat-looking tributary canyons to hike up, no roads crossing the river in sixty miles. I search for the hash marks in the river that indicate rapids, look for narrows or sections of steep gradient, sharp bends, access points. The more I get lost in that high desert terrain, the better the whole thing starts looking.

At this point the trip feels 80 percent there. What I really need now is some local information, someone knowledgeable who can fill me in on the details of car shuttles, drinking water, put-in and take-out, camping areas, likely weather. What I need is an on-site source, or at least someone who knows the area firsthand.

On a whim, I decide to call the chamber of commerce in Rangely, Colorado. These general information calls are worth a try. They don't always help, but a surprising number of them are more fruitful than you'd expect. I get the number through information and dial it. A pleasant-sounding receptionist listens patiently to my explanation. I'm thinking, no way this lady knows anything about paddling. Dead end for sure. When I'm through she doesn't even hesitate.

"You need to talk to our mayor," she says. "He's quite the canoeist. Been down the White River I don't know how many times. He even coordinates a race down the river each summer. He's in a meeting with the city council right now, but give me your number. I'm sure he'll want to call you."

And damned if he doesn't call back as soon as his meeting's over. Sounds pretty relieved to talk rivers and paddling logistics rather than parking lots and library fines. Turns out he does know everything I need to learn about the river and then some. We even realize we've paddled a couple of the same places in Canada over the years. Pretty soon we're trip pals.

Bingo. About as sweet as expedition logistics ever get. There's nothing like having the mayor tell you it will be fine to park behind the police station and that he'll personally keep an eye on the vehicles. He even insists we stop at his house for a visit.

Finally, right at the end, he confirms his stature by saying, "Don't worry about the shuttle, we'll get you at the end."

The mayor is even better than advertised. After a prolonged visit at his home, he ferries us all to a riverside camp near the put-in. Before he leaves, he huddles with us over the maps and points out some potential problem areas on the river, places where snags tend to hang up, some good side hikes. Then, a week downriver, he's there as promised, waiting at the dirt road take-out to shuttle us back.

Now, not every trip research project goes as slick as that one did. Hardly any have a prize along the way like the mayor of Rangely. But mostly the process is surprisingly easy, and the investigative steps are pretty commonsensical. The information leads naturally from one piece to the next. A couple of trips under your belt and you have collecting trip information down to an art.

Just please, please don't succumb to the temptation to start publishing your own spiffy trip guide packets. Leave the fun for others to experience. As for the folks who don't have the perseverance or wherewithal to find their own way into a trip, who needs them cluttering up the place anyway?

TRIP INFORMATION IN 1:250,000 SCALE

When I did the exercise described on page 31 for Montana, one spot that caught my attention was the Judith River. Now it's time to go in closer, get some topography, and come to grips with the lay of the land with a 1:250,000 scale map (see illustrations pages 34–35). On many trips I've made do with this scale of map in the field.

First I'd check out the shuttle and road access. The put-in looks great—not far from Lewistown on a paved two-lane road. The take-out looks a little less good. The road is fine to Winifred, but there it turns to a pretty long stretch of dirt leading to the bridge across the Missouri just downstream of the confluence with the Judith. Still, it's marked on the highway map, so it must get regular use. But it might be muddy and impassable after heavy rains. Even so, given the remoteness of the area, and roads in Montana, the shuttle looks pretty straightforward.

Next, look at the surrounding topography. It's country chock-full of coulees, which should give the trip a kind of scenic, badlands quality and perhaps allow for some side excursions. The valley bottom itself seems well defined and fairly broad in most places. I can also see that this is a very winding little river, one of those streams with two miles of bend for every mile ahead.

I look closer to see where the contours cross the valley. I mark these in on the map and pick out the section with the greatest gradient, in the middle section of the float. To figure out the ballpark river gradient I add up the miles between contours and divide that into the elevation loss. To make the math easy, say that the middle section, marked by four contour crossings, is twenty miles long (figuring in the bends). To get the gradient

(continued page 36)

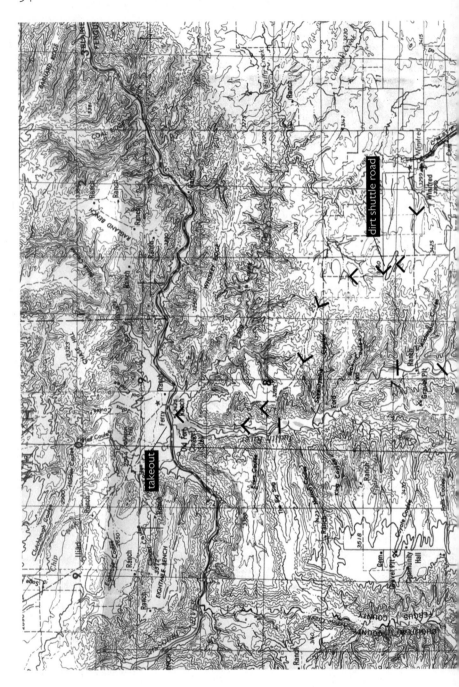

Use **1:250,000 scale topo maps** to flesh out the early details of a trip itinerary (reproduced at 89%).

TRIP INFORMATION
IN 1:250,000 SCALE

(continued from page 33)
(drop per mile) I divide twenty miles into three hundred feet and come up with fifteen feet per mile. That's a steady drop, a fairly vigorous flow, but not likely to be extremely difficult.

Finally, I notice that much of the surrounding country is ranch land. It even says so on the map. With all those ranches, one of my biggest concerns would be fences across the river. The Judith is small enough that ranchers would have to worry about livestock crossing at low water, so I wouldn't be surprised to find a handful of fences that could be troublesome if you aren't on the lookout.

From the looks of it, the Judith would make a pleasant, scenic trip, best taken in spring or early summer. I'd give about three days to the float. It may be only thirty or thirty-five miles in a straight line, but counting bends I'm guessing it's closer to sixty.

PART TWO

ON THE WATER

FIVE

The Partnership Tango: Two Vignettes

DIVORCE VESSEL

Carol and John seem nice enough. They're friends of friends, part of a gaggle of us getting ready to put in for a day on the upper Gallatin River in Montana. Like everyone else they're bustling around their boat, cinching up life vests, coiling their bow line, rolling up the dry bag full of extra jackets and lunch.

Before launching, we gather to discuss the run. The Gallatin is one of those rivers you can scout from the road as you drive upriver to the put-in. Scouting water while driving sixty miles an hour on a curvy road, in fact, is the most dangerous part of this outing. It's a relief to have that hazard behind us.

"The water looks pretty low," John says.

"It's going to be more rock dodging than usual," Marypat agrees. "Two weeks ago there would have been a lot more flow. Now there are some pretty long rock gardens. But it'll be fun!"

Carol looks dubious. "I'll bet it's been five years since we paddled anything you'd really call whitewater," she says. "It looked pretty rocky to me."

"We'll be fine," John says. But in the glance they exchange I notice that subtle, ambivalent aura of distrust and insecurity that some couples give off just before they step into a canoe together.

"Okay, let's go!" somebody shouts, and we all migrate toward the fleet of waiting boats lined up along the riverbank.

Right off the bat the channel is a maze of rocks and narrow chutes, no time to warm up and practice technique. As soon as we push off we're fully occupied, but I hear John and Carol's boat bang a boulder. John says, "What are you doing?" in that tone parents use with misbehaving children.

"I'm trying to miss the rock you aimed us for," Carol says.

"I was going to miss it anyway. You just lined us up to hit the one next to it!"

I wince, but we're soon out of earshot and busy with our own negotiations.

The Gallatin, at this level, is more technical than we bargained for. At higher water it's a rollicking ride through class II water with lots of fun maneuvering and minor consequences for mistakes. At low water the run is like playing pinball, and your canoe is the ball. When your technique is on, the stretch is great fun and good practice.

If, on the other hand, your skills aren't up to the mark and your teamwork is rusty, fun is not the word that pops to mind.

A quarter mile downstream we eddy out to let John and Carol catch up. Their canoe looks exactly like a pinball coming toward us. It careens from boulder to boulder, listing alarmingly from side to side. Their paddle strokes aren't synchronized—more like flailing than teamwork. When they come closer we get the audio component over the sound of the river.

"What are you doing?" is the most common phrase, coming alternately from the bow and stern. "Didn't you see that rock?" is a close second, along with "Where did you think you were going?" and "Why didn't you go around that one?" There's quite a batch of colorful description mixed in at the same time, none of which sounds much like two people who supposedly love each other.

"Should we offer to split up and paddle with them?" Marypat suggests.

"Nah," I say. "They'll figure it out." Truth is, I'm too selfish to give up the good time we're having.

John and Carol stop insulting each other as they come near, but they're grim-faced and tense. "Is this what the river's like all the way down?" Carol asks.

Unfortunately it mostly is, and by the time we stop for lunch the two of them have had more near capsizes than most boaters have in a career. They stomp up the bank from their boat and sit at opposite ends of the group. John eats his sandwich like he's attacking it with every bite. Carol ignores her food and lies back with an exhausted sigh. There's an uncomfortable tension among the rest of us as we all try to pretend everything is fine while we know full well that John and Carol are about to murder each other.

The day doesn't get any better for the two of them. The river stays pretty challenging, and whatever harmony they had as a paddling team slipped away in the first minutes on the water and only recedes further as time goes on. The rest of us make a point of staying out of earshot, which isn't much of a struggle since their canoe spends more time hung up on rocks than moving ahead. By the day's end they aren't even saying much. By that point any attempt to paddle as a team has long evaporated, and they horse the canoe this way and that like two teenage siblings on a tandem bicycle.

The only reason they don't capsize half a dozen times is that the river is too shallow. At the end of the day Carol opts to ride home in another car. John doesn't say a thing; he just gets in his truck and drives away.

Two years later I run into Carol at a meeting in town. "You know," she says, "that damn canoe has been in the yard ever since that day on the Gallatin. If you know anyone who wants a beat-up boat, I think it's for sale. Neither one of us has ever suggested going paddling again. I don't think our marriage can stand it!"

SWEET HARMONY

Same river, different year. Marypat and I unload the canoe from the rack in the shadow of the Yellowstone National Park boundary sign. It's late spring; the river is high and silty with snowmelt sluicing down from the snowy peaks, chattering and vigorous.

The kids are playing with cousins for the day, and we get to paddle the way we used to in that prechild era when whitewater was something we embraced instead of avoided. Even so, it's the first run of the year together, and we aren't exactly honed and toned. I notice my life vest seems tighter than the last time I wore it, and when I step into the canoe it seems less stable than I remembered.

We pivot away from shore and immediately scrape over a barely submerged rock, tipping heavily, leaning wrong. "Okay, okay," I mutter to myself. "Get it together." Then we scrape across a gravel bar we should have gone around. I see Marypat breathe deep and settle her shoulders.

Three bends downstream the river braids through some swamp and we take a narrow channel through a grassy meadow. The canoe barely fits around the corners. We stop talking. I watch for Marypat's moves and then counter with mine.

At the head of the first sharp bend she draws hard. I pry in the stern and the canoe pivots smoothly into the next stretch. The water is fast and churning. There are a quick series of bends, a tiny, constricted channel.

The canoe slides around more corners, bumps the bank a few times. Moments of grace alternating with clumsiness.

There's a midriver boulder coming up, with a large eddy behind it. "Let's catch it," Marypat shouts, and I angle the canoe for the top of the eddy just behind the rock. Marypat leans out and plants her paddle squarely behind the rock. I pry in the stern, then brace, and the boat pivots hard, as if it's been brought up short by a rope. We're in tight, bumping against the rock.

For the first time I hear Marypat's irrepressible giggle, that outburst of joy on water that I fell in love with on the first trip we took together. "We're getting it," I shout, and we spin out of the eddy, headed downstream for more.

For a while we discuss strategy along the way. "Let's go on the outside of this bend," I say. "See that sleeper in the middle of the channel?" Marypat asks.

A mile or two and dozens of maneuvers downstream, I realize we aren't saying a thing, that we're simply dancing down the flow, knowing each other's moves, anticipating, communicating in our leans and strokes and body English. The canoe is connecting us, and it's a good connection, something bigger than just the two of us.

Marypat reaches for a cross-bow draw, one of her sweetest strokes, and I counter with a draw. The boat sideslips left of a ledge and plunges down a chute into standing waves. Marypat leans back, paddling to slow us through the waves, and we coast right over them without shipping a drop. A tree sticks out over the river downstream; I set up a ferry angle just as Marypat starts to backpaddle, and the boat angles across current and away from the obstacle.

The water is cold, our knees are wet, our hands are rigid as claws, but we don't stop. This is too good to stop. For hours it goes on, dodging and spinning down the spring-high mountain river, in and out of eddies, surfing waves, sweeping around corners, plummeting down tongues of water, hardly talking at all. Just Marypat's laugh and the occasional whoop of exhilaration.

At the take-out we stand next to the canoe, the river loud and hurrying, and hold each other for a long time. My teeth chatter with cold, but I don't feel the least bit chilled inside. I even feel a tad thinner when I zip out of my life jacket.

PARTNERSHIP ADVICE

There are few expressions of teamwork more fraught with danger to a relationship than canoeing. This is especially true for couples linked romantically. Paddling tandem is pure teamwork, like dancing, and when it goes wrong it is seductively easy to blame the other guy. When things go really wrong, the consequences tend to be wet, scary, or both. Here's some advice.

1. Keep talking. Not arguing, but talking. At least in the first stages of paddling together, it's best to keep up a constant dialogue to work out strategy and think out loud. Even if you don't accomplish in practice what you plan in theory, at least your intentions are in synch. Wordless dancing in a canoe comes later, when you've been at it a long time and know your partner's moves as well as you know your own. The conversation might sound something like this:

    "See that tongue downstream, right of center? Let's aim for that."
    "Okay, but watch the sleeper on the right."
    "Got it. I'm staying left, then we can sideslip right to line up."
    "Maybe we should ferry right instead. It seems kind of tight, but let's see."
    "Oops. Sorry. Didn't even see that little bugger. This sunlight on the water makes it hard to make out the rocks."
    And so on ...

2. Switch bow and stern positions. I've noticed that it's a guy thing to want to paddle stern. If you switch, you get an immediate appreciation for what the other paddler is dealing with. The bow and stern positions offer unique experiences and vantage points, and the only way to truly understand that is to try both. Also, the bow paddler is the one who identifies hazards on the fly and reacts with strokes that the stern paddler needs to follow. Finally, it's often best to have the stronger paddler in the bow providing power for speed and emphatic moves. Keep yourselves honest by agreeing to switch each day, or at some prearranged point en route, like after lunch.

(continued next page)

PARTNERSHIP ADVICE

(continued from previous page)

3. Look far ahead as well as close up. Usually the stern paddler reads downriver, identifies the general line to follow, then steers toward it. The bow paddler concentrates close up, reacting to the little obstacles and problems that aren't obvious from a distance. Follow each other's lead and respect each other's judgment.

4. Weight the canoe so the bow is somewhat lighter than the stern. Waves are less apt to break over the bow, and the stern paddler has more control this way. If the bow paddler outweighs the stern person, shift gear or slide the adjustable seat (if you have one) to compensate. The only time you want the boat trim, or even slightly bow heavy, is when paddling against the current or in a wind.

5. If you simply aren't getting along, for whatever reason, see if you can switch partners with another paddling team and take a break.

6. Admit it when you blow it, even if it's tempting to blame the other guy, and graciously accept such admissions from your partner.

7. If paddling harmony is an experience you simply can't achieve, it probably isn't worth risking your relationship. Could mean some counseling wouldn't be a bad idea.

8. When everything fails but you still hanker to paddle, there are always solo boats.

SIX

Negotiating Current

E arly in my paddling career, when I got into moving water
that was at the frontier of my limited ability, my first impulse
was to paddle harder, as if speed and power were the antidote to the
absence of skill and control. It was the "ramming speed" phase of
my evolution, which I count myself lucky to have survived, when
paddling through rapids had more in common with driving bumper
cars at the amusement park than with navigating current with any
semblance of grace.

It happens that greater speed is called for about 10 percent of
the time. The other 90 percent, more speed just makes bad things
happen sooner and more emphatically.

Most of the time it pays to be going about the same speed as
the river, or slower. Coasting along at the speed of the current, the
canoe will glide over small standing waves without slapping and
taking on water, and paddlers can "sideslip" past obstacles (see
page 46). When you're going slower than the current, backpaddling
gently, the challenges of the river unfold in slow motion and paddlers can control the action by "ferrying" (see pages 46–47) across
the current and picking the best course.

About the only time more speed is called for is when the canoe
is going through large standing waves, or when paddlers identify
a general line to follow from well above and can afford to simply
paddle forward into position.

On trips, when the canoe is loaded down with gear and a capsize is inconvenient at best and life threatening at worst, whitewater is a challenge to take cautiously. Save the rodeo moves for outings with empty boats and a road nearby.

COMMON RIVER SCENARIOS AND RESPONSES

Sideslipping through a Rock Garden

In moving water with moderate current and well-spaced obstacles, sideslip left and right of obstacles by coordinating draw strokes and pry strokes. The stern paddler needs to time strokes in synch with the bow person to get a smooth slide across the current and to avoid a rocking motion. When the bow person does a cross-bow draw, the stern paddler draws on the same side. When the bow paddler draws, the stern paddler pries on the opposite side. The result is a simple slide left or right. The bow paddler is the one calling the shots, since he or she is in the best position to see the next obstacle.

Ferrying

Ferrying allows you to move sideways in current by paddling against the flow while angling the canoe to expose the hull to the force of the river, which pushes the boat left or right. It's exactly the way a river ferry motors across current without losing ground. The stern person is responsible for maintaining the boat's angle in the current (the slower the flow, the greater the angle you can get away with). Occasionally the angle will be too great and the river will push you broadside, and then the bow person can help regain the angle. Once the angle is achieved, the bow paddler strokes backward, against the current. The canoe will migrate across the river in the

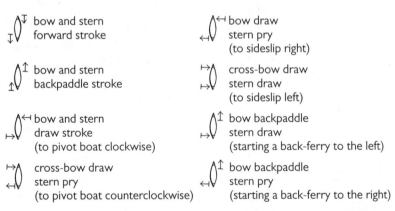

The **key** to the following canoe stroke scenario diagrams; bow generally faces in direction of current (top here).

direction the stern is pointing. In really strong current, it's sometimes best to pivot the canoe upstream, establish an angle, and then forward paddle, in which case the canoe will move across current in the direction the bow points. The forward ferry is a more powerful maneuver than the back ferry. Ferrying is an ideal way to run big water, since it slows the action and allows paddlers to pick their way down through ledges and tight obstacles.

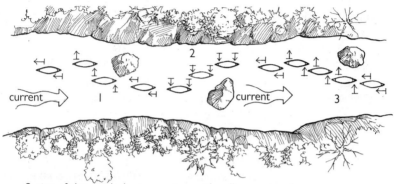

Series of three sideslip moves to avoid well-spaced rocks.
1. Bow draw–stern pry. 2. Cross-bow draw–stern draw.
3. Bow draw–stern pry.

Sideslipping *works best in moderate current with well-spaced obstacles.*

Canoeists back-ferry to skirt two ledges.
Bow backpaddles while stern adjusts the boat angle and
backpaddles when possible. Bow helps adjust boat
angle at the end of the ferry.

The **back-ferry** *may be the most important technique in a paddler's repertoire.*

Cornering

On sharp corners (those approaching a right angle) the strongest current flows forcefully into the bank on the outside of the bend, sometimes even undercutting that bank or cliff. The outsides of bends are almost never where paddlers want to be. The flow becomes more moderate toward the inside of the curve, and at the very inside the river is often eddying back on itself, sometimes powerfully. The trick is to ride that line between the eddy current and the downstream flow, avoiding both the outside bank and the clutches of the eddy. In very strong current that runs hard into a wall, an upstream or forward ferry may be the best way to avoid the wall and slip around the bend (see page 49). In these cases paddlers may want to tuck right into the eddy to avoid the wall and then paddle out the bottom of the eddy. Generally speaking it's prudent to approach bends on the inside of the curve until you can see around and assess the best strategy.

Waves

A healthy percentage of capsizes are, more accurately, "swamps." They happen when a canoe goes crashing through a set of standing waves, taking on dollops of river with each one and filling to the gunwales. They happen pretty regularly during the ramming-speed phase of a canoeist's life. In a loaded canoe, big waves are best appreciated from a distance, preferably as you sneak past in more moderate flow. Spray decks (see pages 175–76) are good protection from swamping in waves. Smaller waves (under two feet) are easy to negotiate by slowing the boat's speed to that of the river. A gentle backpaddle allows you to coast over waves at the river's pace without taking on any water. If you feel the boat starting to wallow and turn sideways, you've slowed too much. If you can't avoid large standing waves, it's best to paddle forward through them, maintaining headway, while bracing for stability (see page 49). Usually the bow paddler strokes forward while the stern person leans out on a brace to stabilize the canoe. Without a spray deck, it's almost impossible not to ship some water in large waves.

The Fine Art of Sneaking

Any expedition paddler worth his gorp is practiced in the art of sneaking down big water. Many rapids, especially on larger rivers, are famous for huge waves, rocks, and ledges in the main flow, obstacles most tripping paddlers want nothing to do with. More often than not, however, you can get past those pitfalls simply by hugging the shoreline and working carefully through the shallower, slower current (see page 50). I've worked down miles of big water by leapfrogging along, stopping to scout, paddling ahead, stopping again, slipping blithely past all the big stuff, and avoiding the work of a portage.

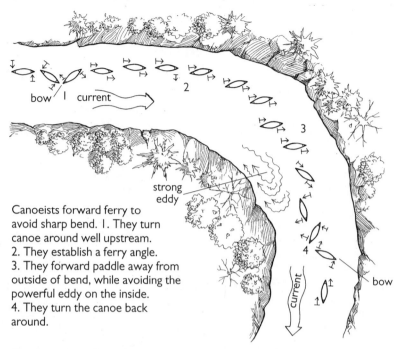

Canoeists forward ferry to avoid sharp bend. 1. They turn canoe around well upstream. 2. They establish a ferry angle. 3. They forward paddle away from outside of bend, while avoiding the powerful eddy on the inside. 4. They turn the canoe back around.

bow   current

strong eddy

current

bow

Sharp corners on rivers always warrant a cautious approach.

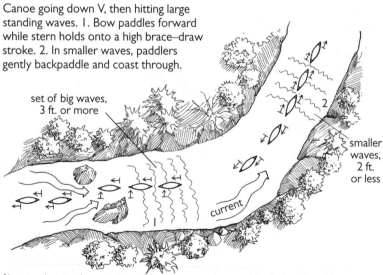

Canoe going down V, then hitting large standing waves. 1. Bow paddles forward while stern holds onto a high brace—draw stroke. 2. In smaller waves, paddlers gently backpaddle and coast through.

set of big waves, 3 ft. or more

smaller waves, 2 ft. or less

current

Slow to the river's pace in moderate waves, but paddle forward and brace through really large ones.

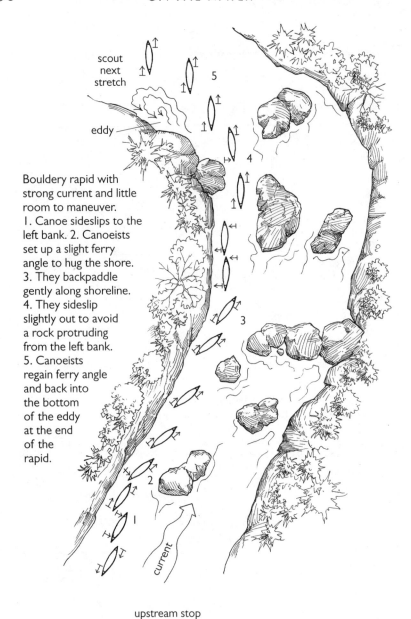

scout
next
stretch

5

eddy

4

Bouldery rapid with strong current and little room to maneuver. 1. Canoe sideslips to the left bank. 2. Canoeists set up a slight ferry angle to hug the shore. 3. They backpaddle gently along shoreline. 4. They sideslip slightly out to avoid a rock protruding from the left bank. 5. Canoeists regain ferry angle and back into the bottom of the eddy at the end of the rapid.

3

2

current

1

upstream stop
to scout first

*A good **sneak** has its own exhilaration, one made up of mastering technique.*

THE EDDY TURN

On expeditions, I rarely do much in the way of eddy turns unless I'm playing around in a safe stretch of water or coming to shore into a big swirl. Eddy turns are more appropriate for whitewater days with empty boats. When turning abruptly into a powerful eddy the boat is inherently unstable. With a loaded boat I much prefer backing into eddies stern first (see the "sneaking" illustration). By doing so, you avoid the moment when you cross out of the main river current into the upstream flow of an eddy.

Still, eddy turns are fun, kind of like playing crack the whip on ice skates. You sweep around as if the bow rope has caught in a tree, the stern making that dizzying turn, and suddenly you're stopped in the middle of the river, current rushing past, and looking upstream. So an eddy turn is a heady moment, when done right, and it's worth practicing for the times you really need one.

Eddies are the places in river current where the flow circles back upstream, sometimes with almost as much force as the main current. Usually eddies occur behind boulders or on the insides of sharp corners. Here's how to catch one.

Identify the target from as far upstream as possible, and start angling the bow slightly toward the upstream end of the swirl (just past the boulder in the illustration on page 52). As you come closer, broaden the angle of the canoe and paddle forward to have some momentum as the boat enters the eddy. At the top of the eddy, the bow paddler reaches into the swirl (with a cross-bow draw in the illustration) while the stern paddler helps pivot the stern (using a pry in the illustration). As the canoe enters the eddy, lean into the turn. This ensures that you'll be leaning away from the upstream eddy current as the boat gets captured. (Always lean away from the force of current on a turn.) In the illustration, the bow paddler hangs on to the cross-bow draw, making it a high brace as well as a draw, while the stern paddler finishes off the pry with a low brace for stability. If you've done it right, you won't even need to paddle forward to the top of the eddy. Usually it takes a forward stroke or two to finish off the move. *(continued next page)*

THE EDDY TURN

(continued from previous page)

Coming out of the eddy is called "peeling out." In strong river current, nose the bow back into the main flow at a narrow angle (too wide and you'll be broadside and vulnerable). Again, the bow paddler crossbow draws and braces while the stern paddler pries. Both paddlers lean into the turn, or downstream to the main current.

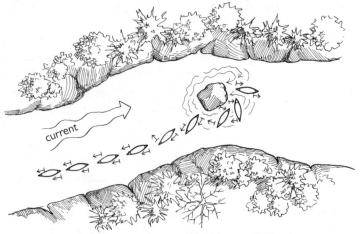

current

Catching an Eddy

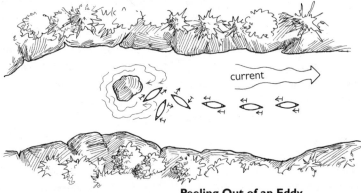

current

Peeling Out of an Eddy

Eddy turns are an essential skill to master, though they're also inherently unstable.

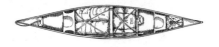

SEVEN

Rating Whitewater and Rivers

P art of preparing for a trip, especially a trip to a new area, involves assessing the challenges en route, then making a realistic appraisal of group skills and abilities. Whitewater is one of the constant themes of a paddling career, whether or not you're a boater who seeks out the exhilaration of rapids, and much of the discussion before a new trip centers on the level of whitewater challenge along the way.

A good deal of information about the character of a river can be gleaned from a close reading of topographic maps (see pages 33–36). Scrounging up old trip reports or following up word-of-mouth leads is also productive. In any event, once we start discussing the level of whitewater challenge, we need some sort of scale to measure against.

The traditional whitewater rating scale is based on a I to VI classification system, where class I is the easiest and class VI the most difficult. Not just specific rapids, but entire sections of rivers can be described as having a class II or IV character. Descriptions for each category go something like this:

Class I: Easy. River speed less than hard backpaddling speed. Route finding simple. Occasional small rapids, or riffles, with regular low waves. On narrow class I rivers some care may be required to avoid gravel bars, fallen trees, and overhanging brush.

Class II: Moderate. River speed sometimes exceeds hard backpaddling speed. Current generally easy to read. Rapids more frequent but unobstructed, with regular waves and easy eddies. Scouting often not necessary.

Class III: Difficult. River speed often exceeds hard backpaddling speed. Maneuvering in rapids required. Numerous rapids that require scouting, with large standing waves, ledges, strong eddies, and other obstacles. Main river current pushy and challenging.

Class IV: Very difficult. Long, obstructed rapids with unavoidable turbulence, very large and choppy waves, powerful eddies and boils, abrupt river bends and strong crosscurrents. Scouting always necessary and route finding complicated. Difficult and infrequent landings increase the dangers of long and hazardous swims in case of capsize.

Class V: Exceedingly difficult. Wild turbulence. Very powerful and conflicted current. Scouting often problematic. Life-threatening consequences in the event of mishap.

Class VI: Limit of navigability. All whitewater dangers taken to the upper limit. Negotiable only by experts at favorable water levels. Even then, cannot be attempted without risk of life.

This framework for discussing a river's difficulty, and particularly its whitewater challenges, provides a general foundation. Most conversations about a river go beyond these generalities to cover such things as the changes wrought by different water levels and the specific character of whitewater.

Class III rapids can be "big wave rapids" or "technical rock gardens." A river may be class II overall, with one class IV ledge drop that is an obvious portage at most water levels. Other rivers will have discrete sections of very different character. The Green River in Wyoming and Utah, for instance, has big rapid runs through Split Mountain and parts of Gray's and Desolation Canyons, but it's quite benign and placid through Stillwater and Labyrinth Canyons. Rivers may also alternate between flatwater stretches and canyon sections with more difficult water. The Rio Grande in Big Bend National Park, Texas, is a good example—meandering current across open country interrupted by sheer-walled limestone canyons with some formidable water. Finally, when you travel a long section, or the entire length, of a river, there's almost always one particular stretch that is most notable for turbulence, where gradient or topography conspires to create the most significant whitewater.

In the world of serious whitewater boating, the old classifications have become outmoded and inadequate. In terms of canoe tripping and general discussion, the old I to VI guidelines are still workable, but in the realm of cutting-edge paddling, the old guidelines cried out for revision.

American Whitewater (AW) has developed a new set of whitewater rating guidelines devoted to addressing problems with the old system, and they are useful additions for all paddlers. The former categories are too general, for starters. Class IV rapids can run the gamut from rollicking rides down a big wave train to really gnarly runs through boulder fields that require repeated and very difficult maneuvers. Also, whitewater boating has evolved to the point that the skills of paddlers and evolution of equipment have rendered rapids previously thought unrunnable accessible to a significant number of boaters.

The new system retains the I to VI categories but adds pluses and minuses to levels I to IV. Class V has been radically altered, much like the revised rating system for rock climbing that came into use years ago, when the limits of that sport were being pushed. Class V now begins with 5.1, goes to 5.2, and so on, without an upper limit. Each point jump is equivalent to a leap in class. In other words, going from 5.3 to 5.4 is similar to moving from class II to class III.

Class VI has been turned into an exploratory category until a rapid can be placed in the new class V hierarchy. There is no established cubbyhole for unrunnable water, largely because so much water once deemed unnavigable is now run routinely. Each rapid is assessed from the perspective of how it feels to a boater making a first run down it. Furthermore, the ratings are pegged to specific water flows.

More than a hundred well-known rapids have been used to set "benchmarks" for categories of difficulty. For example, Diamond Splitter Rapid on the Ocoee River, at 1,200 to 1,600 cubic feet per second (cfs), is a standard class III. Hermit Rapid in the Grand Canyon, when the Colorado River is flowing at 15,000 to 22,000 cfs, is the epitome of a class IV.

Of course all this is just the corral we construct to contain the discussion of whitewater. There's still lots of wiggle room. Consider water flow, the ability to sneak along the edge of a rapid, the particular challenges of turbulence and how they match against a boater's skills and the design of the canoe. How remote the river is, whether the boat is full or empty, whether it's a sunny, warm day or a sleety, gray day. Whether there's a nice pool at the bottom of the rapid where you can collect yourself (and possibly your gear). How skilled, fatigued, appropriately dressed, and mentally prepared other members of the group are at a particular moment.

In the end, these may be the more important calculations that each boater looking at every new rapid has to reckon with before coming to a sensible decision.

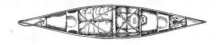

EIGHT

Why Wood and Water Don't Mix

Dave is one of those paddling friends with hours of hilarious canoeing stories, none of which, when you think about them, are the least bit funny. Most of them involve snags, log-jams, deadfall, or other incarnations of wood in moving water. They're hilarious because Dave's enthusiasm outstrips his paddling technique by a wide margin. They aren't funny because I much prefer Dave as a living friend rather than as a character in a comic, but tragic, story.

One of his best tales takes place on a small Wisconsin river, early in the summer. Dave is paddling stern. Lee, his friend and frequent partner on ill-fated outings, is in the bow. The water is high with spring runoff. Dave has paddled here before, but never this early in the year. The water is a good deal pushier than he remembers, and there seems to be a substantial increase in the number of obstacles in the river channel.

Things go well for a time, until they sweep around a corner and confront a boulder-strewn rapid with several deadfall logs protruding from the banks. They're too close to pull over and scout, but Dave spots a stout overhanging limb leaning about five feet above the river.

His overwhelming preoccupation is with the need to stop and have a look at the rapid, so without thinking he stands up and takes hold of the branch. Of course Dave is the only thing that stops. Lee and the canoe continue downstream unchecked, and unaware of the developing drama.

Dave doesn't stop for long, however, because his pant leg gets caught on a screw under the stern plate and he's stripped from the tree, dragged downriver by the ankle like a cowboy who's been thrown from his horse but has his boot stuck fast in the stirrup.

About this time Lee turns around to start discussing strategy, only to find his partner's foot kicking energetically near the stern seat. In the ensuing desperate moments, Dave finds the strength to rip his pants free of the canoe, while Lee occupies himself with the new challenge of paddling solo. Still underwater, Dave somehow gets ahead of the canoe.

He struggles to the surface, but just as he gets his first lungful of air, he's draped like a rag doll over a barely submerged log. The force of current doubles him at the waist and pins him there like a large bit of river flotsam. In fact, river flotsam is exactly what Dave is at this juncture. Half a second later the bow of the canoe slams into the same log like the blade of an ax biting into wood, about six inches river left of Dave's kidney.

Pretty comical, you have to admit, but also not funny. I laughed hard the first time I heard the tale, mostly out of relief that it wasn't me bent over that log with a pushy, cold river holding me fast.

Like most good paddling stories, there are some morals to glean. In this one there are at least three pivotal lessons about wood in moving water.

The first has to do with the time of year. Early in the paddling season rivers are typically flowing at their greatest volume and have been busy landscaping the channel with flood wreckage and forest detritus. Even a river you know well may be significantly reconfigured by high water, especially in flood years. Logjams, snags hung up in shallows, and trees lurking on the outside of sharp bends are among the most dangerous of river hazards.

I have a few harrowing springtime stories of my own. I paddled a notable stretch of the Swan River in northwestern Montana early one summer. We had been able to scout most of our route from the road, but there was a loop about five miles long out of sight of the highway.

That bit of river was very nearly our undoing. The water was high and full of wood. At one point a raft of logs blocked the entire flow. We had to half swim, half drag the canoe through the surrounding forest. Time and again we came around corners to find gnarled stumps hung up in shallows, whole trees toppled into the fastest current, and sections of river cluttered with snags. It was one of those trips where you get all religious and thankful at the take-out bridge.

The second lesson embedded in Dave's story is that wood may be stationary, but the river keeps going. What makes wood so much more dangerous than rocks and boulders is that the current flows right through the branches of a tree or the logs in a jam, whereas rocks force the current around them.

PRINCIPLES OF WOOD AND WATER 101

BEWARE OF SPRING FLOWS

Even familiar rivers can be transformed by high water. Research unknown stretches of river through guidebooks, local paddlers, or by road before setting off. Any spring flooding is cause for heightened caution. On the first run of the year (or first time down a river), be extra careful at blind corners, bridge abutments, and shallows.

BE CAUTIOUS ABOUT BRAIDED SECTIONS

Rivers full of gravel bars, islands, and small, braided channels are particularly prone to logjams and snags.

WEAR A KNIFE

Get in the habit of wearing a knife on your life vest or belt. It may be the only way to cut yourself free of an entanglement. (Knives designed for paddlers are available at paddle sports retailers.)

FAVOR THE INSIDES OF CORNERS

The pushiest current, and the most dangerous snags, tend to combine on the outside of river bends. As a general practice, sneak around the inside of a curve, where the current is moderate and you can quickly get to shore.

SLOW UP AND PRACTICE YOUR FERRY

Backpaddling and ferrying are the safest ways to navigate water mined with wood. Proceed slowly, ready to sideslip or ferry to avoid snags.

LEAP TO SAFETY

If you find yourself at one of those moment-of-no-return crossroads with wood in moving water, do your darndest to stay on top. Leap onto the tree trunk, climb up branches, scramble on top of a logjam, anything to remain above the flow. You may lose your boat or some gear, but at least you'll be breathing. The last place you want to go is into an underwater embrace with wood.

(continued page 60)

In a boat, or swimming, you tend to go where the water goes. In most cases the current will wash you over or around a rock, but it will push you into a tree like one more piece of debris. Believe me, pinned in the embrace of a submerged tree is not a place you ever want to be.

The third lesson is really a corollary of the second: that woody objects are renowned for their ability to entrap and entangle. It's bad enough to get folded in half over a log the way Dave was. There's nothing like it for rekindling respect for the strength of current. But Dave was lucky. His head was above water, and the log was a smooth one.

Much deadfall bristles with tangled roots, the sharp ends of broken branches, and thickets of limbs. Stories of perishing in the woody grasp of a tree are legion in the paddling world, and many of the victims have been experienced paddlers. Once in that awful clutch, it doesn't make a bit of difference whether you're an Olympic competitor or a neophyte.

I can't come up with a single situation where wood in the water is a good thing. It is, on the other hand, featured in a healthy percentage of the accident reports compiled by river rescue teams. With the possible exception of lowhead dams, wood is the most prominent and consistent danger for paddlers on moving water.

Wood plays a positive role in only one of Dave's stories. In that one Dave and Lee are out paddling so early in the season that ice still lingers on the banks. They're near the bottom of a small rapid that has taxed their skills to the limit and has filled the canoe to the verge of swamping. They make for shore as fast as they can. When they get there, the boat coasts right up onto a sheet of ice and then continues to skate along at a good clip on its metal keel. Into the forest they go, where Lee embraces the first poplar he comes to for all he's worth.

PRINCIPLES OF WOOD AND WATER 101

(continued from page 58)

1. Paddlers approach first bend by adjusting ferry angle.
2. They gently backpaddle around the inside curve until they can see downstream.
3. They switch ferry angles for the next corner and backpaddle into it, but then see a rock river right.
4. They paddle forward to midriver to avoid it, but a big deadfall confronts them just downstream.
5. Canoeists backpaddle hard in order to back into the eddy below the rock. 6. From there they can sneak past the deadfall river right.

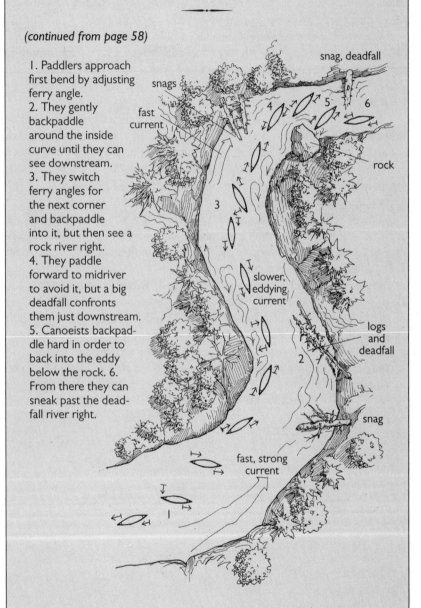

snag, deadfall

snags

fast current

rock

slower, eddying current

logs and deadfall

snag

fast, strong current

Coast around on the inside of a bend until you can see downstream and identify problems.

NINE

Open Water Hazards

Kamilikuak Lake, Northwest Territories: an out-of-the-way place in an out-of-the-way quadrant of the globe, where we have been windbound for a day and a half. Our canoes lie like colorful beached whales at the margin between rock shore and tundra moss. A dazzling chunk of shorefast ice is visible on a distant island, even at the end of July. Waves have been crashing in, hour after hour, a maddening percussion section played by the wind.

We go to the tents vowing to get up very early to check conditions. No one has a watch, and the sun is above the horizon twenty hours a day, so early is a relative thing.

A short night later the wind has died, the sun is astride the horizon again, and we are poised for escape. Silence is so complete it's eerie. Our strokes puncture the stillness. We've lost the wind, but now fog lies against the frigid water in a quilt so thick we can only dimly make out the shoreline a few canoe lengths away. Relatively warm air condensing against cold water produces the ground-hugging cloud conditions, and we're paddling through the pea soup variety.

Around a point we have one of those "one mile across or six miles around" decisions to make. Through the fog, a mile away, lies the far side of a deep bay. To cut across saves us two hours of travel time. It's calm, but we might as well be blindfolded. If we wander off course, we could paddle blithely into the middle of this big, cold lake.

We succumb to temptation and huddle with map and compass. Declination is a major correction. If we add when we should subtract, we'll be wrong by thirty-five degrees. When we're confident of the bearing (see pages 106–7), we lay the compass at the feet of one bow paddler, get the arrows lined up, and strike off. The shore disappears in twenty strokes. We're encased in a gauzy bubble. It's the paddler's version of vertigo, as if we're balanced at the edge of the world.

We say nothing. Two boats slapping through small waves on a sub-arctic morning, blind as bats. The bow paddler points left or right when we slip off course. The canoes stay close. Everything is contained in this muffled, embracing, disorienting room. The crossing seems to go on for a long time, long enough that our minds start to play tricks and we doubt the flickering compass needle.

When land finally comes looming up out of the mist, we laugh out loud, babble with relief. Tension escapes like a breath held too long. But in another mile the fog has burned off and the wind starts to build again. Before lunch we're surfing down wavefronts and have to make for land.

Another bit of cobble beach, another patch of tundra. We unpack only enough to boil up some coffee and soup, find books and journals, and pull out wind jackets. To while away time we take naps with our heads pillowed on life jackets, make short exploratory jaunts inland, eat snacks, talk.

It isn't until after dinner that the wind dies again. It takes five minutes to pack and get on the water. Then we paddle for miles in the lambent light to a camp at the beginning of a short portage that will take us into the next large lake.

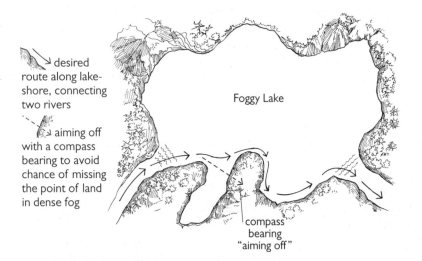

desired route along lake-shore, connecting two rivers

aiming off with a compass bearing to avoid chance of missing the point of land in dense fog

Foggy Lake

compass bearing "aiming off"

*Take a **bearing** on a crossing to ensure landfall, even if it adds a little distance.*

At first light the wind is gusty and cold. The portage has no trail, simply a marshy slog between lakes. Wind torques the canoes like weather vanes, grinds them against our neck vertebrae. We skitter across, stumbling over hummocks. On the far side the next lake is lathered like meringue. We hunker down in a hollow, wearing gloves and wool hats, and play euchre using a flat, lichen-encrusted rock for a table. The wind doesn't quit until evening. We unbend, settle into boats, and paddle a dozen miles through a twilight that lingers half the night.

Where we stop there are tent rings left from an old Inuit summer camp. We lie on the same lumpy ground as they did. Our dreams hum with air tugging across the barren miles, but by morning it's quiet as a cave, sun washed.

So it goes, day after day.

Weather is a compelling factor on any outdoor journey. In paddling boats across open water, weather is arguably the only significant factor. In thousands of paddling miles it has invariably been the stretches of open water that have proved my greatest obstacles and have served up the most vivid moments of danger. Moving water has its own set of challenges, some of them daunting enough, but when things go awry on a big watery expanse, it opens up the pores of fear like nothing else.

WIND

Wind is the breathing of the earth, and the bane of paddlers. It is caused by the interplay of cold and warm temperatures. On a global scale, for example, warm air rising at the equator produces a vacuum that pulls in cooler air from the north and south to create prevailing winds. On a local level the differences in heat between land and water, peaks and valleys, forest and rock produce smaller wind patterns. Onshore and offshore breezes. Upslope and downslope winds. Chinooks. All are the result of air flowing from cold to warm.

Large bodies of water are often significantly colder than the surrounding land, especially during the heat of the day. They are also flat, exposed topographic plains where winds gather over unimpeded miles, building waves as they come. Although there is no strict formula for safe travel in windy conditions, some guidelines are worth considering.

- Take advantage of the calm times of day—most likely early in the morning and again in the evening. Make miles early and then enjoy lazy afternoons in camp.
- Plan trips to capitalize on the least windy blocks of summer weather. In the Canadian subarctic, and on long trips on Lake Superior, July has invariably been the quietest month, while spring and fall trips are almost always plagued with wind.

- Given the choice, pick a convoluted shoreline dotted with islands and points over a straight, exposed coast. You can often use topographic windbreaks to your advantage and make headway when you'd be pinned down along an unprotected shore.
- If possible, situate camps in sheltered bays or behind a point of land. Sometimes just getting off the beach with waves breaking in is the trickiest move of the day.
- Stick close to land in breezy conditions. The waves are always bigger once you get out in the open, and a few extra miles won't kill you, whereas a capsize very well might.
- When paddling in waves, play around to find the best angle for your bow. Many experts suggest "quartering" waves, but that depends on the shape and size of your hull and the load you're carrying. Hitting waves straight on can be as safe as angling into them and avoids the risk of broaching sideways.
- Shift your load toward the stern to ride bow light and minimize the tendency to ship water.

Islands and points offer cover from wind and often allow for travel on gusty days.

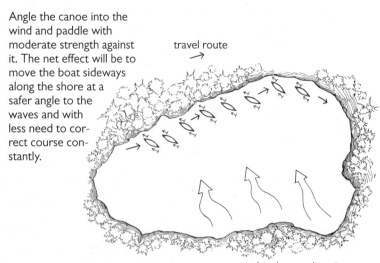

Angle the canoe into the wind and paddle with moderate strength against it. The net effect will be to move the boat sideways along the shore at a safer angle to the waves and with less need to correct course constantly.

travel route

wind and wave direction

Angling a canoe into a wind to move sideways down a shore.

- In the case of a side or quartering wind, you can sometimes angle a canoe crabwise and ferry, using wind against the boat hull to push you in a desired direction, the same way you'd use current on a ferry maneuver on moving water.
- It's best to keep boats moving in choppy water. Momentum is a stabilizing influence, and paddles in the water have some of the effect of outriggers. As soon as you stop, the boat will start to wallow.
- In rough weather the temptation is to cling right against shore. In some cases breaking surf or waves rebounding off of a coastline can create difficult wave patterns. Experiment to find the best compromise between exposure and tricky water.
- Just as in whitewater, paddlers should kneel to lower the center of gravity.
- Fabric decks, or spray covers, add a tremendous margin of safety (see pages 175–76). Waves won't swamp you in a decked boat, and if you get ambushed by a sudden blow, you'll be much more capable of reaching shore without mishap.
- Finally, any trip with lots of open water on the itinerary should be planned with extra time for windbound delays. An average of twenty to thirty miles a day might be feasible on moving water, but on big lakes I figure on ten to fifteen miles a day. It won't

always come that hard, but there have been trips where I've been windbound five days straight and had to struggle to manage a ten-mile average. Bring cards, miniature Scrabble, books, and other diversions to fill those enforced layovers.

SUDDEN SQUALLS

If thunderheads are building around you and the air grows gusty and turbulent, it's not a good time to strike off into the open. When a storm cell pounces, it can hit in seconds and pummel you with the force of a mini-hurricane. In regions that are serviced by twenty-four-hour weather reports, it can be worth packing a weather cube radio, but don't treat the predictions as gospel. There's nothing as accurate or immediate as your own commonsense reading of conditions.

Stay close to land in this kind of weather, or find a sheltered place to wait it out. Unfortunately, land can sometimes be as dangerous as water if trees and branches start to break off. The most protected spot I've ever waited out a fierce squall was in a shallow bed of marsh grass along shore. The vegetation damped down the waves, and I was clear of falling debris. I cowered under the onslaught in my raingear, feeling damn puny but relatively safe.

If you are caught in the open, hang on for the ride and summon all your reserves. The only good news is that the episode probably won't last more than twenty minutes. The bad news is that twenty minutes will be an eternity.

Face bow into the wind and paddle just enough to maintain your position. Lower your profile as much as possible and be ready with a high or low brace to counteract sudden gusts or breaking waves.

FOG

As we discovered on Kamilikuak Lake, cold water and relatively warm air often conspire to produce a smothering blanket of fog. On large, cold lakes fogs are common, and they can be as disorienting as a howling blizzard in Nebraska. We've all heard of farmers who perished between the barn and the house in a snowstorm. Exactly the same fate can befall paddlers.

Early morning is the most common time to encounter fogs. They'll usually burn off before noon, but any time a front moves in to change air temperature, fog can quickly develop. You can generally keep paddling as long as you navigate cautiously and keep land in sight.

The most foolproof preparation for fog is to have a compass always handy and to know how to orient it off a topographic map (see pages 106–8). Once you have your bearing set, stick with it. A global positioning system would help in fog too, but a compass is a lot cheaper and more satisfying to master.

LIGHTNING

Paddling an exposed stretch of water when a lightning storm comes up is like being the high point in a flat grassland, only more so. Getting to shore is the most prudent course of action. Once on land, pitch a shelter away from summits of rock and clear of the tallest trees.

The theory that aluminum canoes are somehow more dangerous in a lightning storm is the stuff of myth. If you get zapped, you're fried, no matter whether the boat hull is Royalex, wood, or Kevlar.

If you must keep paddling despite the threat of lightning, the safest corridor is right against shore. There's a "shadow zone" of protection that generally extends at about a forty-five-degree angle from the top of the bank or forest out over the water. It isn't guaranteed protection, but it's safer than out in the open.

TIDES

On oceans and estuary waters, tides are an important factor to reckon with. Some places are noted for huge tidal swings of thirty or forty feet, enough to dramatically change the character of river rapids dozens of miles upstream. Other coasts are so flat that even a minor tidal shift can send the water miles offshore. Much of the Hudson Bay coastline, for example, is prone to significant tidal effects.

Canoeists stranded by low tide in Hudson Bay, near Churchill, Manitoba.

It pays to have a tidal chart for these areas and to adjust your daily regimen accordingly. It sometimes makes sense to paddle only at high tide. If you go far out with a low tide and the weather changes, you might be in big trouble when the water comes back in.

Tides can also set up strong currents through tight channels. The Inland Passage along the western coast of Canada and Alaska is full of necks and channels where if the tide is shoving you back you might as well give up. By the same token, intelligent use of tides can make paddling like riding an escalator.

In tidal zones, pitch camp and stow boats well above the high tide and storm line, which will be marked by wave wash and lines of debris. Tie boats to rocks or vegetation for good measure. Nothing induces that empty feeling in the pit of your stomach like waking up one morning to find your boat has floated off.

CROSSINGS

Extended crossings on lake and coastal trips are an inevitable temptation, and arguably the greatest paddling danger bar none. Time and again on these journeys the topography will tease you with shortcuts across bays and inlets. The temptation is tremendous, especially when the distance saved is significant.

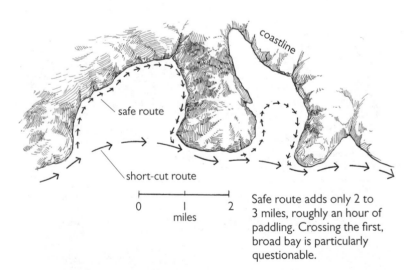

coastline

safe route

short-cut route

0   1   2
         miles

Safe route adds only 2 to 3 miles, roughly an hour of paddling. Crossing the first, broad bay is particularly questionable.

Don't assume distances are necessarily much longer along shore. Measure first to judge whether a crossing is really worth it.

Any crossing, even a mile or less, is potentially dangerous and deserves careful assessment. The shortcuts are often not as efficient as they first appear. Measure the actual map distances of a crossing against sticking near shore to see if the risk is worth it. If it seems to be but the wind is up, opt for the more rigorous, but safer, trip along shore. Even if the waves don't seem bad near land, they are invariably larger and more dangerous out in the open.

Maximize the use of calm early morning and evening hours for larger crossings. I've made many a successful dash at first light that wouldn't have been feasible two hours later.

ICE

In the Far North, and at the edges of summer, paddlers may encounter ice on large lakes. Before traveling to ice-prone country:

- Research conditions by studying weather and climate charts to pinpoint the most ice-free windows for travel. July and August are usually safe months even at high latitudes, but don't make rash assumptions. Stories of expeditions stymied by ice in any month of the year are common above sixty degrees north.
- Contact guides, outfitters, aviation companies, and the like to find out about local conditions for a given year.
- Look at maps to search out alternative routes around larger lakes, in case you encounter ice there.

If, despite pretrip planning, you find yourself blocked by ice:

- Wait a day or two to see if a change in wind direction will drive the ice pack away, at least temporarily.
- Remember that travel around an icy lake is usually best along the shore, because the rocks and land will hold heat and melt the ice margins.
- Sometimes paddlers have to haul boats across the obstruction, if the ice is firm enough to bear weight, or skate boats along with one foot inside the hull and the other pushing off the ice.
- Confronted by impassable ice, pore over those maps to see if a portage over a neck of land, or into a parallel waterway, might bypass the icebound area.
- Keep in mind that the horizon from inside a boat is only two or three miles long. What appears like a heart-rending world of frozen pack may actually be pretty localized.
- As a last resort, include a radio or emergency beacon in your outfit in case the ice is so bad you can't complete the trip.

COLD WATER

If you've seen the movie *Titanic*, you've been vividly reminded of just how lethal cold water is. That scene with hundreds of lifeless bodies bobbing around in the North Atlantic was literally chilling. Paddlers often dwell on the more exhilarating dangers posed by raging whitewater, but simple cold water is an equal, if not greater, threat.

HYPOTHERMIA SYMPTOMS AND TREATMENT

Mild to Moderate Hypothermia

(core temperature between 90° and 97°F)

Symptoms

- Awkward motor control (lighting a match, zipping zippers)
- Shivering
- Minor mental confusion
- Severe shivering
- More severe confusion, incoordination

Backcountry Treatment

- Adjust clothing layers (wind or rain gear, fleece)
- Eat some quick-energy food
- Exercise harder to produce heat
- Drink plenty of fluids
- Stop to build fire, boil water for hot drinks, change clothing, find shelter

Severe Hypothermia

(core temperature drops below 90°F)

Symptoms

- Mental status severely limited, loss of consciousness
- Shivering stops
- Pulse and blood pressure decreases

Backcountry Treatment

- Apply external sources of heat
- Get out of wet clothes
- Get in sleeping bags together to warm
- Rewarm slowly, then provide warm food and shelter, monitor for at least one day following
- Evacuate if possible

Even southern waters are colder than you'd expect. Unless the water is body temperature, lengthy immersion will inevitably sap heat from the body core, leading to hypothermia. Cold northern waters can be deadly in half an hour or less.

Practice self-rescue and group rescue techniques to avoid long immersions. If you can't rescue yourself and have to wait for help, haul your body as far out of the water as possible on the hull of your boat and kick in toward the nearest landfall.

If a companion boat goes over, concentrate on rescuing people before gear, even if it means throwing some of your own outfit overboard. Canoe over canoe rescues seem neat on a calm pond but are often impractical, if not impossible, in big waves. Tie off packs and loose gear to bow and stern lines if necessary, but save people first and worry about gear later. The likelihood is that gear will eventually be driven up on shore.

Make sure everyone on a trip knows the basics for treating hypothermia. The most important thing to remember is that victims of hypothermia are not able to generate their own heat. External sources of warmth are critical. Far and away the best heat source is another warm body inside a sleeping bag. Other options include warm drinks (without caffeine) and food, fire, and warm sun. Keep close watch on victims of hypothermia for several days, since relapses can occur even after people appear fully recovered.

Well. By now you're spooked enough that you won't even venture out on the neighborhood pond. What I've neglected in all this fear-and-loathing diatribe is that open water travel is very rewarding, full of tranquil moments of beauty and exhilarating challenges. Prepare well, use good judgment, stay patient, and the benefits of paddling toward open horizons will overwhelm the risks.

TEN

Against the Flow

The Peel River doesn't feel particularly speedy. It winds in lugubrious coils through the delta it shares with the Macken-zie River, above the Arctic Circle in northwestern Canada. But where we turn our boats off, at the mouth of the Rat River, and start the seventy-five-mile ascent toward McDougall Pass, it feels as if someone just ratcheted up the treadmill. Getting ahead suddenly feels like hard work, though the current is hardly perceptible.

It leans against us, a quiet, insistent force that we have to pad-dle hard to resist. When we stop, even momentarily, the canoes slip back, losing precious ground. The Rat twists slowly through the delta flatlands, but this slow current is only the prelude to an uphill climb of one thousand feet. At the top, if we meet the challenge, we will sit astride the Canadian Rockies and straddle the watershed that separates the Mackenzie drainage from the Yukon. This is the easy part.

We settle into the grind, dropping to our knees for better pad-dling leverage. The lazy conversation between boats dies out. Within three short bends we stop to strip layers of clothing. I pad-dle, much of the time, with my head down. The slow progress to the next corner is too hard to watch.

I pay closer attention to the current, start adapting to the flow. Near the bank the river has less velocity. We hug shore, noticing beaver slides and the stick-toed prints of sandpipers in the mud. My expectations start to adjust. We can do this. On the insides of sharp bends, the current eddies back on itself. From time to time it helps us along; occasionally we even slide upriver without

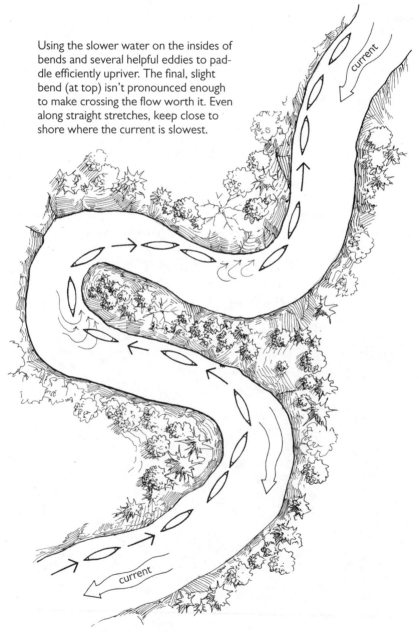

Using the slower water on the insides of bends and several helpful eddies to paddle efficiently upriver. The final, slight bend (at top) isn't pronounced enough to make crossing the flow worth it. Even along straight stretches, keep close to shore where the current is slowest.

Efficient use of river channel to paddle upstream.

needing to paddle at all. Soon we're ferrying back and forth across the narrow channel to take advantage of eddies, hopping on these little escalators of current, then slogging up against another straight channel.

Very slowly the miles drop away in our wake. It's work, but we get the rhythm, learn the subtleties of the bends. It becomes a game, playing the current to our advantage, working out the riddle of the Rat.

It takes two days to reach the first really fast water. The view opens up, the river gradient cants visibly uphill. There's a disheartening vista of gravel bars and chattering current. In the far distance, the foothills of the Richardson Mountains rise into the Arctic sky. The trip we so confidently planned for suddenly looms ahead like a long and expensive lesson in masochism.

It seems only fair to reward ourselves with a day off. We busy ourselves cutting poles, slender shafts of dead standing spruce about twelve feet long. The poles are only an inch or two in diameter, and we spend much of the day stripping off the bark and twigs with the hatchet, then rubbing them smooth with rocks from the gravel bar.

In the late afternoon we practice. I have never poled a canoe before. Marypat and I take turns standing in the space between the stern seat and the center thwart, feet spread for balance, knees bent. We plant the pole against

Simple poles harvested from the boreal forest.

Poling *is an ancient technique and often the best way to travel against moderate current.*

the bottom of the river, then push ourselves upstream, climbing the pole hand over hand as we go. At the top of each stroke we slide the pole quickly back through our hands, plant again, and repeat.

It sounds perfectly reasonable in theory, but we spend a good bit of our time saving ourselves from near capsizes, flailing with the pole, missing the bottom of the river altogether, stumbling around in the boat, getting the angle wrong so the canoe gets broadside in the river, and otherwise looking about as graceful as four-year-olds learning to ride bikes. There's a fair amount of giggling at each other's expense.

It turns out there are several tricks to this poling business. First, you have to get the angle of the canoe right, so you don't drive the bow into the shore on one side or get pushed back downstream by the current on the other. Second, the transition between strokes needs to be a smooth and fluid retrieval. Too slow and whatever momentum you've managed to build up is lost and you start back into that inevitable embrace of gravity. When we stop practicing a couple of hours later, the gap between theory and practice is still considerable.

The next morning our upstream work begins in earnest. In this faster water, the paddles are forgotten bits of equipment. For that entire exhausting day we either flail away with the poles or wade up against the fast river, hauling the canoes along like recalcitrant mules. At the end we've climbed a paltry three miles. The next day we make four, but when I hike to the top of a nearby knoll, I can clearly see our previous campsite, a few short bends downstream. The mountains look no closer.

There are fleeting interludes when the poling seems rhythmical, when the cadence of climbing hand over hand, whipping the smooth pole back up, planting against the bottom, and climbing again has a lovely sweet grace combined with actual forward momentum. They never last long.

I have read of people who pole up and down rivers with nonchalant dispatch, who make their way up rapids, dodging from eddy to eddy and muscling up little chutes, holding the canoe's angle just so, mapping the route as they go. They "snub" their way down rapids just as confidently, picking and choosing between rocks, slipping down Vs of current, holding themselves poised as they assess the next move, then shifting deftly across the current to another slot.

I am never even close to that level of poling technique. In fact I never rise far above the tenderfoot merit badge. My few moments of grace are inevitably capped with rapid descents into ignobility.

Over the course of days, we settle into a pattern of several upriver techniques, depending on the character of the river and the topography of the banks.

Occasionally the current is slow enough, or winding enough, that we can paddle, using the water on the insides of bends to our advantage. More often the river is too strong to paddle against, and we resort to poling in our clumsy way from bend to bend.

When the riverbank consists of low gravel bars, we take to "tracking" the canoes upstream on foot. At first we work with bow and stern lines, keeping the bow angled just enough into the current to keep from bumping into shore, but not so much that the current grabs the hull and whips it back downstream or, worse, broaches the canoe into the current. Once or twice one of the bow people lets the boat too far out, where the flow grabs at the hull and starts to tip the canoe. At that point it's disastrous to try and pull back in, and the bow person has to let go, hoping the stern rope holder is paying enough attention to hang on while the canoe swings around downstream.

Later on, we adopt the technique of hauling the canoes upriver by the bow line while our partner holds the hull away from shore with the spruce pole. This technique turns out to be much more efficient, since no time is spent fussing with the angle of the bow in the current and we can simply walk upstream.

Long stretches of the lower Rat run through braided gravel bars, and we track along for good distances, ferrying across the channel from gravel bank to gravel bank. Again, I've read about people who are accomplished at tracking boats and who even master the solo technique of tying the bow and stern lines together with a well-placed knot and hiking off upstream, making subtle adjustments on the rope to shift the canoe's angle as they go. I've never seen any such expert in action, and until I do I prefer to believe

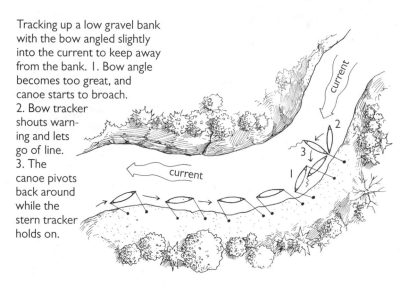

Tracking up a low gravel bank with the bow angled slightly into the current to keep away from the bank. 1. Bow angle becomes too great, and canoe starts to broach. 2. Bow tracker shouts warning and lets go of line. 3. The canoe pivots back around while the stern tracker holds on.

When the canoe turns sideways in the current and begins to tip, the only alternative is to let go of the bow line and let your partner hang on while the boat pivots.

*Less elegant, but faster, **tracking technique**.*

*In fast current where the river banks don't allow for tracking, **wading uphill** is the only option.*

it's another paddling fabrication designed to make the rest of us feel clumsy and imperfect.

The most brutal form of upriver travel is the wading technique. Frequently, either sections of the Rat are too fast to negotiate any other way or the river flows past banks that are too steep or too choked with underbrush to track along. Here we gird ourselves, step into the numbing current, and start walking uphill, hanging onto the canoes.

The bow person angles for the shallow sections of current, aims for little rests in the eddies behind boulders, maps out the route through rapids. The stern person is left to anticipate the next move, sometimes timing a step in perfect harmony, more often ending up chest deep in a hole or left teetering on a slippery rock. All the way we feel blindly along the cobblestone river bottom, getting our feet wedged painfully between rocks, slamming our knees into unexpected boulders, leaning against the rush of glacial melt that is doing its damnedest to flush us out to the ocean.

Our wading clothing consists of quick-drying wind pants. It's too cold and buggy to consider shorts, and the wind pants offer some slight protection against abrasion. At first we wear neoprene booties, which are nice in terms of warmth but offer scant protection against the bruising of river cobbles. When possible we lean some of our weight over the canoe hull to relieve the constant punishment on our feet. Eventually most of us fall back on some version of tennis shoes and socks, opting for the protection of soles over warmth. Within days those shoes are tattered and holey, held together with layers of duct tape.

So it goes, day after Arctic day, beetling our way into the loom of mountains, climbing over topographic contours. Three miles. Five miles. Four miles. Bit by bit, uphill all the way.

The one smart thing we did was to allot ourselves plenty of time. Every third day we reward ourselves with a rest day, a reprieve from the toil. We fish. We bake bread. We hike off across the tundra and up to rocky summits. We bathe and drink pots of coffee and read books and write in journals. We try hard not to dwell on the next day's activity.

Twelve days after first turning onto the Rat River, we pole our way up the final, twisting, beaver-dammed channel. It's twilight, that velvet time in the Arctic summer night when the tundra world hums with the quiet, intense flourishing of season. Our poles plunk into the still water, our wakes ripple behind us.

Just then, ghosting along in the misty, wild evening, our accomplishment, at least briefly, is enough to defeat the throbbing pain in my feet. Just for a second, I stop thinking that our ascent of the Rat has been an exercise in self-flagellation and feel an upwelling of pride that almost outweighs the half-crazed, grueling climb we've subjected ourselves to in the name of adventure.

ELEVEN

To Run, to Line, to Portage

The four canoes are pulled up on shore, still loaded, a colorful little fleet awaiting our next move at the upstream end of the wide portage trail that bypasses Clarno Rapid on the John Day River in eastern Oregon. The whitewater, at this river level, is a long and tricky class III+ run with major consequences for mistakes. We already know we aren't going to paddle it. This is a family trip. We're piloting undecked boats full of toddler-sized chairs, coolers, and little backpacks stuffed with beach toys.

Tim and I stroll downstream for a look. It's the unvarying ritual at rapids to go have a preview, talk over strategy, pump up adrenaline. This is one of those rapids that is agonizingly tempting. Much of it is quite runnable. We point out the obvious lines to follow through the upper end. There to there to there. Lower down it gets problematic. The hydraulics are bigger, the obstacles more fearsome, the moves more technical and daunting. Still . . . doable, given the right boats and circumstances and skills.

But we aren't running it, I remind myself. This is an abstract exercise, a "what-if" scenario.

These rapid-side strolls are notorious for their seductive power. There is no other paddling situation, save perhaps open water shortcuts on lakes, where desire is so likely to worm its way in and sway good judgment. Partly it's a matter of simple laziness. Who wants to portage when you could paddle? Partly, too, it's a competitive challenge. You stand there, the din of pounding water surrounding you, mist in the air, and you imagine the moves you'll make, the lines to follow, the exhilaration of a ledge drop, the triumph at the bottom. Adventurous seduction, pure and simple.

More than once I've sat down to eat lunch next to a rapid that we have firmly decided to portage around, only to find myself getting into the boat to sneak down it by way of some route we've talked ourselves into over crackers and cheese. I've lured myself into lining, or sneaking, or running, or portaging gear and running empty boats scores of times by virtue of these innocent little exploratory jaunts. Once or twice I've talked myself into runs I had no business on and have been extraordinarily lucky to make it down whole, body and boat.

I should know better. If it's a portage, carry around first, then come back to admire the sight. A simple lesson I doubt I'll ever absorb. It's too scintillating and delicious to go look first.

These scouting forays inevitably have a constricting effect on the bladder. Tim and I both go behind rocks to pee, then start back upstream.

"What do you think about lining?" Tim calls out from behind.

"I think I'm going to portage," I answer. The portage trail is as wide as a road and only a hundred yards long. This time, at least, I'm not tempted.

"It doesn't look too bad along shore here, in the shallows," Tim goes on. "We could portage gear and line the boats empty."

"We could," I agree, "but I'm going to carry." I can tell that Tim has talked himself into the lining option.

Back at the boats, the rest of the crew has already unloaded. The gear is piled around in chaotic heaps, the boats lie empty. I start consolidating equipment. On this short carry, where we plan to camp at the end anyway, I don't get compulsive about compacting the loads for efficiency. What's one more trip?

I content myself with strapping extra paddles and life jackets onto packs, combining several day packs into one, forcing the boys to carry their sleeping bags, and cinching a dry bag under the lid of the equipment pack. On longer, tougher carries I go to some trouble to streamline the load to the point that two of us can get everything across in two loads. Only occasionally have I subjected myself to three trips, usually at the beginning of a really long expedition when the mound of food was too great to pack down. Even then it's hardly ever necessary for both partners to make three full trips.

I do take the extra time to rig a portage system for the canoe. Years of portaging have worn my neck vertebrae sensitive. That grinding of the thwart has gotten intolerable, even over a short distance. Some canoes come outfitted with center-thwart carrying yokes that are pretty comfortable, especially if you loop a life jacket around your neck for padding. Uncustomized thwarts, and some others that pretend to be customized for portaging but are actually cruel delusions, warrant taking the time to rig a portaging system out of paddles.

You need two straight-shaft paddles and about twenty feet of bow line. Lay the blades of the paddles on the center thwart, leaving a gap in the center just wide enough to get your head through. The grip ends of the paddles will lie across the bow seat. Using the bow line, lash the grip ends tightly to the bow seat, then go back and tie the blade ends to the center thwart. (See illustration at right.) Loop a life jacket around your neck for extra cushioning, and off you go. The shafts of the paddles offer good grips to hang on to and help adjust the boat's balance over rough terrain, and the flat blade surfaces sit firmly on your shoulders.

You can get more efficient about this by attaching permanent bungee-cord lashings to the center thwart, just the right width for your paddle blades, but lashing with the bow line goes pretty quickly once you've done it a few times. You can also add homemade portage pads made of foam layers glued to squares of plywood and bolted through the center thwart. Portage pads are particularly appropriate if you opt for bent-shaft paddles (which won't be coaxed into a good yoke system no matter which way you turn them).

Since I'm feeling a tad wimpy about portaging rather than lining, I hoist the canoe overhead with the one-person hip-snap (see page 85) rather than asking Marypat to hold the stern up while I duck under-

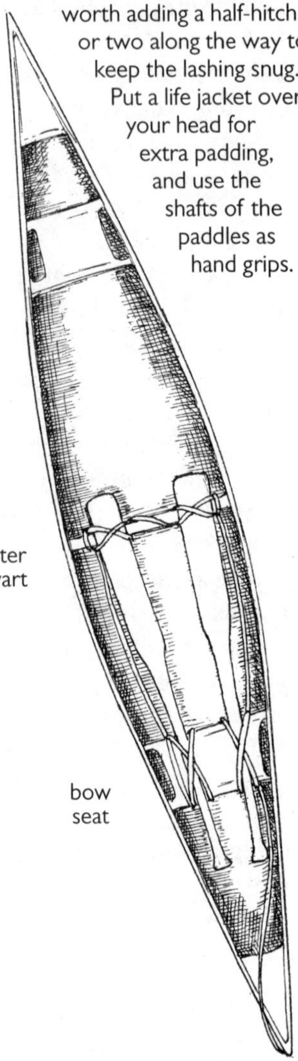

Paddle blades head-width apart on center thwart. Use bow line to lash paddle to bow seat, then blades to center thwart, then back to second paddle on bow seat. Sometimes it's worth adding a half-hitch or two along the way to keep the lashing snug. Put a life jacket over your head for extra padding, and use the shafts of the paddles as hand grips.

center thwart

bow seat

Simple **portage yoke system** using two paddles.

neath. It's an impressive move, done right, and I only scrape one ear on the edge of a paddle blade as the boat settles heavily onto my shoulders. Nobody notices—if, in fact, anyone is watching in the first place.

By the time I get back for the next load, Tim is ready to start lining. His technique is suited to going down shallow and not overly forceful current. He noses his canoe out into the river while he hangs on to the stern plate to guide the boat's direction. In his left hand he holds a coil of stern rope in case he loses his grip.

As he walks slowly downstream, he leans on the canoe for support and balance while angling it between rocks along the shore. Here and there the best course is farther out, in deeper water; Tim lines the boat up there, then lets it down with the stern line to a point where he can wade again. Little by little he makes it downstream, looking pretty controlled, letting his canoe down ahead, until he rounds the bend near the bottom.

I guess I could have done that, I think, but my portage is already over, and I award myself maturity points for not being seduced into risk. Heading back for my next carry, I mutter the saying I once heard attributed to a Cree elder from northern Québec: "Nobody ever drowned on a portage."

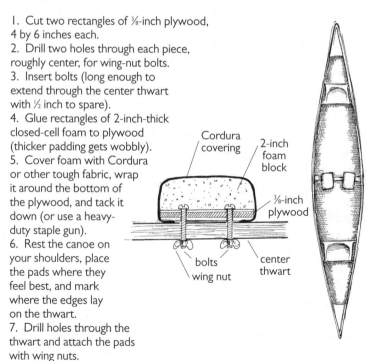

1. Cut two rectangles of ⅜-inch plywood, 4 by 6 inches each.
2. Drill two holes through each piece, roughly center, for wing-nut bolts.
3. Insert bolts (long enough to extend through the center thwart with ½ inch to spare).
4. Glue rectangles of 2-inch-thick closed-cell foam to plywood (thicker padding gets wobbly).
5. Cover foam with Cordura or other tough fabric, wrap it around the bottom of the plywood, and tack it down (or use a heavy-duty staple gun).
6. Rest the canoe on your shoulders, place the pads where they feel best, and mark where the edges lay on the thwart.
7. Drill holes through the thwart and attach the pads with wing nuts.

Cordura covering

2-inch foam block

⅜-inch plywood

bolts

wing nut

center thwart

*Homemade **portage pads** that can be left in place on the center thwart.*

SCOUTING TECHNIQUE

I have never regretted stopping to scout. But I have several vivid memories, filled with regret, about deciding not to stop and have a look. Scouting can be a hassle, a disruption, a bother, but it's never a matter of regret. Even when you stop, lose time, and find that you could have shot right through with no problem, you're filled with the satisfaction that comes from making competent, safe, sensible choices.

The times I regret fall into two categories. First, overconfidence based on "knowing" a rapid. I've run this before, I tell myself. I know how to do it. Usually I'm right, but once in a while there will be a surprise lurking— new deadfall in the channel, different water level . . . Then I'm facing that "no going back" bind. It's too late now, and I'm winging it through stuff I have no business attempting. If I'm lucky I dodge through, heart in my throat. If I'm not, it's a moment to regret.

Second, and worse, I overwhelm my cautious side with bravado and laziness. I convince myself that I can handle whatever the river has to throw at me. Maybe I stand up in the boat and see what looks like a line to follow—a silly risk, and one I've paid for with dented boats, cold and scary swims, lost gear.

Better to scout, every time.

- Stop well upstream of the rapid. You may need to cross to the opposite side of the channel, so leave enough room to ferry over. The safest way to come to shore is to back in using a ferry angle rather than making an eddy turn. Sometimes, in strong current, you're better off turning the boat around well upstream, then forward ferrying into shore.
- Tie off the canoe securely. You'll feel pretty silly if the empty boat comes cruising past while you're still standing on the bank scouting.
- Walk down alongside the rapid, reading potential routes as you go but not making any firm decisions before you look the whole thing over.
- If you can find a high point from which to survey most or all of the run that's ideal, but looking from river level is important too.
- Walk all the way to the bottom and then back up. You see different things going upstream, and you can start defining your route as you come back. Also, it's important to see what's below a rapid. If there's a nice tranquil pool, you'll be able to collect yourself even if things

go wrong. If you start right into another rapid or have a tricky move to make just downstream, consequences start to accumulate.

- Pick out markers along the way to use as you descend. From river level, in the canoe, many of the obvious points of reference you can see from above disappear. Pick out a couple of big rocks, a tree on the bank, the main tongue through a ledge, and use them to identify the moves you need to make as you go.
- Remember that you don't have to run the rapid. There are options, even if they might be time consuming, laborious, and less fun. If things go wrong in the middle of whitewater wilderness, none of those hassles are going to seem like much.

HIP SNAP MOVE

OK, you want to impress your trip mates with this spiffy move? Here's the drill:

1. Stand at the middle of the canoe, facing the hull, with the center thwart directly in front of you and the bow to your left.
2. Bend across the hull, taking hold of the center thwart with your left hand gripping the far side and your right hand on the near end. (If your hands are wrong, you'll end up facing the stern at the end of the move, feeling foolish.)
3. Pick the canoe up and rest the hull against your thighs, with your knees slightly bent.
4. Rock the canoe once or twice, then in one smooth motion, bounce the boat up off your thighs and swing it over your head while you swivel underneath it, facing the bow.
5. Lower the hull onto your shoulders and move your hands up along the gunwales to balance the weight.
6. Walk off on the portage trail as if you do this all the time, no big deal.

LINING TECHNIQUE

Walking Your Boat

This is the most controlled lining method, since you're literally holding on to the stern of the canoe while guiding it down through obstacles. It's suited to shallow channels where the current isn't forceful enough to make balance a problem. Be sure to hold the stern line with your non-controlling hand as a backup. There may be short stretches that you can't conveniently wade, where you may be able to lower the canoe at the end of the stern line. Even in the best circumstances there are likely to be places where you have to lift the canoe over a ledge or rock or past a fast chute of water, and it will be handy to have a partner along.

Rope Lining

The traditional method of lining down fast water uses the stern and bow lines. In deep water, fast current, or along banks that don't allow easy access to the streambed (low cliffs, for instance), rope lining is your only option. Twenty-five feet of rope on the bow and stern is usually adequate. More than that gets clumsy, and lining from a distance of more than twenty-five feet is a pretty dicey operation.

Traditional lining *utilizes bow and stern lines to maintain the canoe's angle while it's being lowered down rapids.*

Lining solo is a bit more challenging than with a partner, but certainly doable. The ropes are the reins by which you guide the canoe. The trick is to coordinate the effort so the stern gets far enough out into the current to keep moving downstream without getting the canoe hull broadside and broaching.

If the stern gets too far out and starts to tip, don't try to horse it back to shore. The boat will flip in a heartbeat. Instead, let go of the stern line at the same time you warn your partner to hang on to the bow line. As long as there isn't an unfortunately placed midstream rock in the path, the canoe will flip gracefully end for end without capsizing and you can carry on.

For long or difficult lining stretches, rig rope harnesses around the bow and stern seats to line from. These are much more stable points of control than the actual bow and stern points and will lessen the threat of broaching in fast current.

TWELVE

Going Solo

I t took me years to discover the charm of paddling off into the wilderness all alone. It took so long because conventional wisdom holds that there's safety in numbers. Two boats at least, preferably three. Then if you get into trouble, the theory goes, your partners, and their boats, will be there to rescue you or to go for help. True enough. Keeping that in mind, solo paddlers need to ratchet up their safety awareness. Every decision—running whitewater, risking waves on an open lake, pushing the weather, should be assessed not simply on your skills and experience but also on the fact that you are absolutely alone to deal with the consequences. Self-sufficient by definition.

Enough said. The solo choice offers the compelling experience of gliding off all alone in a single sleek boat, deeper and deeper into the wilds. I have never met anyone who regretted taking a solo journey, but I've heard some gruesome group dynamics testimonies from multiple-boat trips. (I have a few to share myself.)

My solitary revelation came on a one-week jaunt in the wilds of Ontario when I'd had my fill of work, had to escape or I'd explode, and couldn't convince any of my usual accomplices to pack up and head off on short notice. Hell, I'll go alone, I thought. Yeah, I'll just do that!

Three days in, this is what the experience was like.

Dawn. That gray seam between night and day when birds rouse themselves and mist lies like a quilt on the water. I emerged from the tent shivering. Mosquitoes announced themselves almost immediately, so I opted for a quick cup of coffee and cold cereal. In twenty minutes I was packed up and had the canoe loaded. I stood for a moment next to the boat, listening through the layers of silence, until another mosquito lined up for a run at exposed flesh.

The boat slid smoothly down the ramp of polished bedrock and into the black lake water. My strokes barely whispered. The canoe rippled through the mist, towing a V-shaped wake through the velvet morning. A whitetail doe lifted her head from the water, muzzle dripping. A young beaver slapped water nearby. Loons called from out of sight, down in a bay.

Sunlight slowly burned off the fog, warming the air. I stopped to shed a layer, then regained my rhythm. I started to find my all-morning pace. Hours later, almost lunchtime, I realized I hadn't uttered a sound since dawn. It felt as if I'd been holding my breath.

Now. Imagine that same morning scenario in the company of four or five paddling buddies. First off, the dawn start would be fraught with problems. Someone has to agree to wake the group. Despite the best of intentions, at least one slacker will burrow into the warm cocoon of sleeping bag and ignore the alarm call. But let's say the wake-up arrangement works and the entire group is now assembled in the predawn chill. A discussion about breakfast ensues—hot or cold, coffee or tea, and so on. Packing the boats proceeds at various paces, with the slowest team dictating the moment of departure. Chances are the mist on the water will be long gone by the time you glide away from shore.

Suppose you manage to overcome all that and get off at that misty, magical hour. Two or three canoes are more than two or three times as noisy as a solo boat. Inevitably, someone will want to discuss the itinerary or the lunch menu or a comical event from the night before. The whitetail doe wouldn't be there. You might not even hear the loons. The spell of rippling water, wildlife greeting the day, and sun melting the morning off would be a pretty quiet background to the general group chatter.

This is not to say you wouldn't remember the morning fondly. You'd almost certainly recall it as peaceful and cool and quiet. But not like paddling alone. Think of it as a quality-of-life choice. Sometimes the group scene is exactly what you want. Once in a while, though, a solo trip is the only prescription for what ails.

I like solo jaunts. I think of them as pilgrimage, spiritual renewal, battery recharge, life affirmation. Solo trips are my way of going to church. But my favorite traveling style is with Marypat. She was my paddling partner long before she was my partner in life, and I prefer to see our relationship in that order. It sort of maintains my perspective.

We've paddled many thousands of miles together now. Enough so that hours and big hunks of landscape tend to go past between words. Our thoughts wander off into whatever interior landscape we're exploring. The

The draw-forward combination stroke is my most common technique, especially on a winding river. I paddle on the side of the canoe on the inside of a river bend and use the stroke to keep sideslipping away from the strong current on the outside, and at the same time I maintain downstream momentum.

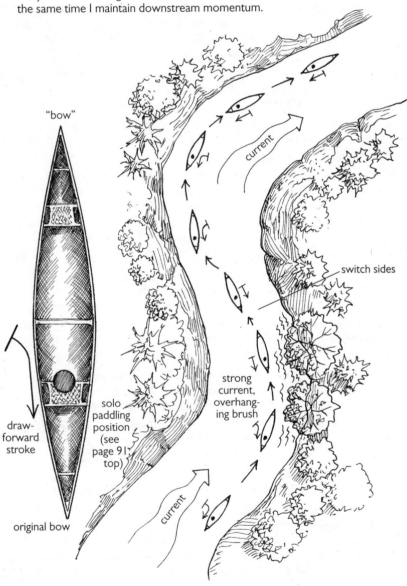

"bow"

draw-forward stroke

original bow

solo paddling position (see page 91, top)

current

current

switch sides

strong current, overhanging brush

Solo paddling makes use of several combination strokes. The draw-forward stroke may be the most common.

TURNING A TANDEM CANOE SOLO

That you haven't bought your solo canoe yet isn't any excuse not to go paddling off alone. It's as simple as turning the canoe around. Really.

When you swap ends and make the stern the bow, you end up sitting backward in the bow seat. That puts you almost midway in the canoe hull, the point from which most solo canoes are paddled. Load your gear well toward the front (formerly the stern) to counterbalance your weight, tie everything in, and you're off. I'm not kidding, it's as simple as that. I've done more solo paddling in tandem boats than I have in solo boats. Partly it's because I'm too cheap to go buy another boat for the occasions I paddle alone. Mostly it's because turning the tandem canoe backward works just fine.

paddle strokes become a kind of mantra for the imagination. We can cruise on autopilot, reacting to wind and current, breaking loose only when a rapid comes along or the weather kicks up. Sometimes we just float downstream wordlessly, sneaking up on wildlife, feeling the cadence of current beneath the hull, the afternoon sun warming our backs.

I'll admit I've been lonely paddling solo, and even occasionally with Marypat. Two-day rainstorms come to mind, or moments of danger and tension, tricky maneuvers I'd try with a partner but not on my own. There have been times in camp when I longed for someone to share my thoughts with.

But then, think how infrequently we are really and truly alone. When was the last time you didn't say a word for an entire day? Have you ever gone two days without seeing another person? Have you ever just sat while the sun flamed over the trees, with water caressing the beach, with your canoe turned over nearby and the sounds of the forest at twilight behind you?

Going solo is the difference between becoming part of the environment, letting it enfold you, and imposing your presence on a place. We humans impose ourselves on our surroundings as a matter of course. A little humility and quiet is a relief to the soul.

When all the safety arguments are stripped away, when all the yammering about weather and food and road access and judgment calls recedes, when the chatter finally quiets down . . . it's dawn again. You wake with the birds and peer through the tent door. Mist hangs over the dark lake. The water is still as glass. On impulse, you dress, clamber out of the tent, and start the stove for a quick cup of coffee. It isn't long before you're on the water, the damp air wreathing your face, the canoe wake rippling behind you across the reflecting surface, the quiet that surrounds you a welcoming immensity.

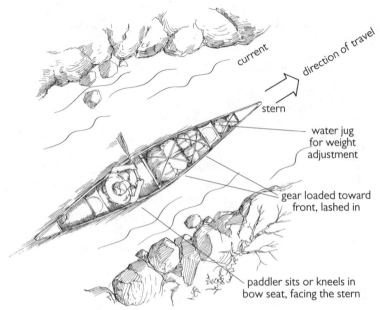

current

direction of travel

stern

water jug
for weight
adjustment

gear loaded toward
front, lashed in

paddler sits or kneels in
bow seat, facing the stern

A tandem canoe rigged for solo travel.

MAKING A REMOVABLE SADDLE
FOR SOLO PADDLING

Solo paddlers who do nothing but go alone, and who prefer big water, will trick a boat out with a permanent saddle, thigh straps, thick knee pads, flotation, and all the rest. For tripping, a solo saddle is nice when the conditions turn demanding in whitewater or wind, but it's also nice to sit more comfortably in the bow seat facing backward when the paddling is easy. It's also convenient to pull the saddle out when you need the room for gear or want to go tandem.

You can run down to the paddling retailer, get advice on installing a saddle, and spend lots of money on a spiffy kit, or you can create your own.

The saddle I use in my 16-foot canoe was designed by a friend, Tim, who coached me through the installation process just as I'm about to coach you. For the most part I just leave it in the canoe, although it's been great to be able to take it out when necessary. The dimensions work for me and my boat (Marypat uses it too), but your situation may differ in terms of body size, hull depth, how low you like to kneel, and so on. Adapt as you see fit.

Remember, too, that directions like these always sound more complicated and difficult than they really are.

MATERIALS AND TOOL LIST

- closed-cell foam pedestal (saddle)
- barge cement (for laminating layers of foam together if necessary)
- 1-inch webbing (about 15 feet)
- one 4-foot-long raft strap with cam-lock tightener
- four 1-inch Fastex buckles
- six 1-inch Fastex Triglide gizmos to cinch webbing ends together
- 2-inch webbing for thigh straps (about 12 feet)
- two 2-inch Fastex buckles for thigh straps
- two 2-inch D-ring kits mounted on rigid plastic plates (for thigh straps)
- three 1-inch D-ring kits mounted on rigid plastic plates (for saddle)
- one 1-inch D-ring kit on circular, flexible mounting (to go behind saddle, on floor)
- one 2-inch D-ring kit on circular, flexible mounting (to go ahead of saddle, where thigh straps attach to floor)
- two knee pads (I like half-inch closed-cell foam rectangles about 8 by 12 inches)
- tube of appropriate contact cement for gluing stuff to the hull (Vynabond, Mondobond, whatever is recommended for your hull—follow directions on tube for application)
- handsaw
- rasp (one side flat, the other half-round)
- propane torch
- fine-grit sandpaper (to rough up hull before applying glue)
- damp rag (to clean hull)
- weights to hold down D-rings while glue dries (sandbags, shot bags, or sacks of flour work well)

MAKING THE SADDLE

You may find a good deal on a premade, preshaped pedestal, or saddle, that you like. In that case you can skip the foam-shaping section of the directions. If not, here we go.

1. Get a block of closed-cell foam roughly 12 by 17 by 6 inches. Mine is made of three pieces of 2-inch-thick foam glued together with barge cement. (continued next page)

MAKING A REMOVABLE SADDLE
FOR SOLO PADDLING

(continued from previous page)

2. Shape the saddle to your liking, making the first rough cut with a handsaw, then honing it with the rasp. Mine is U-shaped, but you can play with what seems to work well for you. At the same time, use the rasp to shave the upper edges of the saddle so it won't chafe your thighs. On a narrow pedestal like this one, you may not need much. One warning: be careful about cutting too low a saddle at first. There's no going back, so begin with a fairly high cut and rasp it down after you try it out if necessary. It's a delicate balance between lowering your center of gravity and getting so low that it's uncomfortable to kneel. The low spot in my U is 9 inches high, and I shaved the edges just a hair. (See illustration.)

3. Once you get the saddle just right, seal the rough foam by touching up the worked area lightly with a propane torch. Be careful, because direct flame will crater the foam. Just brush the area with heat until it smooths a bit.

4. Now rig the saddle for installation by wrapping 1-inch webbing around the base (about 2 inches up), securing the ends with a Fastex triglide, and adding a Fastex buckle at the back so you can cinch the whole thing nice and tight when you're done. Then add a band of webbing over the low spot of the seat and around the base webbing, securing the loose end with another Fastex triglide. This will keep the base webbing band from sagging.

5. Almost done. At the front and rear of the base webbing band, weave extra lengths of webbing through triglides on both sides so the loose ends extend out from the ends of the saddle. At the rear, add a Fastex buckle piece at each side (this will loop through a D-ring attached to the hull). At the front, add the male end of a Fastex buckle to each free end of webbing (these will clip to two female buckle ends permanently attached to the hull). (See illustration.)

INSTALLATION

1. Again, make sure the canoe is turned backward.

2. Take a 1-inch D-ring kit with a rigid base and make a loop of 1-inch webbing to go through it that has the two female ends of Fastex buckles strung through (the ones left over from those you put on the webbing at the front of the saddle). Sew the loop closed with a box stitch, so you have a single unit made up of the D-ring, the buckle ends, and the webbing. (See illustration.)

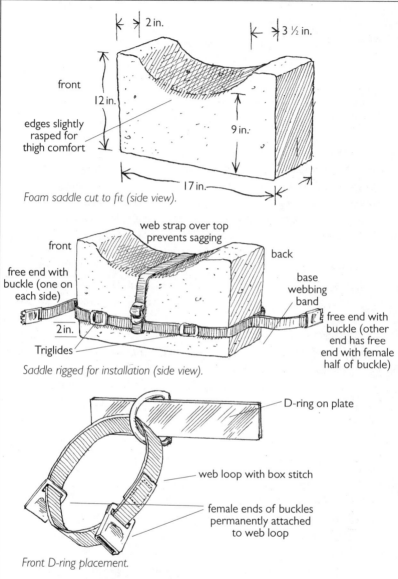

Foam saddle cut to fit (side view).

Saddle rigged for installation (side view).

Front D-ring placement.

3. Mark the center of the canoe hull, about an inch back from the center thwart (remember, when I say *back*, I mean measuring back toward the bow seat), and glue down the D-ring with buckle ends there.

4. Take the 2-inch D-ring kit on the circular, flexible mount and cut about a third of the circle off so one side has a flat edge. Glue this down

(continued next page)

MAKING A REMOVABLE SADDLE
FOR SOLO PADDLING

(continued from previous page)
right behind the 1-inch D-ring you just finished, with the flat edge butting up against the rigid plastic plate. (See illustration.)

5. Set the saddle pedestal in place right behind the circular D-ring you just installed and mark the center of the hull about 2 inches behind the back of the saddle. That's where you glue the 1-inch D-ring kit with the flexible, circular mount. On my boat it's 23 inches from the center of the front 2-inch D-ring to the center of the rear 1-inch D-ring.

6. While you've got the saddle in place, mark the spots just to the side of the saddle and even with the low spot of the U (see illustration). Glue in two of the 1-inch D-ring kits on rigid plastic plates, one on each side of the saddle.

7. Nearly there now. The 2-inch D-rings on rigid plates are for the thigh straps. They get glued to the inside of the hull up near the gunwales. Mine are 17 inches behind the center thwart and five inches below the gunwale. (You'll probably want to do these after you weight down the bottom hardware and let the glue dry. That way you can put the canoe on its edge, one side at a time, and make sure the contact is solid and completely dry.)

8. Once the hardware is in place, set the pedestal in, clip the buckles together in front and back, and cinch the front ones tight. Loop the 4-foot raft strap through the side D-rings and over the low spot on the seat, then cinch it down. String the 2-inch thigh straps through the big D-ring in front, then up to the D-rings on the inside of the hull, and thread the 2-inch Fastex buckles so you can adjust tightness.

9. Finally! Only the knee pads are left. Kneel in the boat and mark the comfortable location for the pads, then glue those babies in.

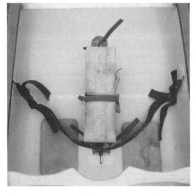

You're done! I know, you probably killed half a million brain cells with all the concentration, but now that you're through it wasn't as bad as all that, was it? And imagine how impressed your buddies will be at the next put-in.

The installed saddle

PART THREE

NOMAD SKILLS

THIRTEEN

Finding a Way: Navigating

I know I drive Marypat absolutely bonkers, but I can't help myself.

It's my day in the stern, which means that Marypat is in charge of map reading in the bow. That's our system. We figure that the stern paddler is busy enough sighting off a point, or reading current, staying on course, and that the bow person is better able to keep track of our progress on the map.

If the spray deck is fastened on, the map is in a Ziploc bag taped to the deck just ahead of the bow skirt. If the boat is open, the map is in a waterproof bag, folded to expose the day's route, and kept somewhere handy for frequent checks. Sometimes we lay it on the ammo box that contains the camera and other odds and ends, resting between our feet. I like to tuck the bag under my thigh on the seat. That way I can glance down and keep track of landmarks or just grab it quickly for a closer look.

In any case the map is never more than three feet from the bow person's eyes, and the only time we stow it away is when we're running a piece of demanding whitewater, after which it comes right back out.

Marypat tends to be a bit cavalier about keeping track of our position, if you ask me. If you ask her, I'm on the obsessive side. Generally speaking, we get where we're going without a hitch and with only occasional lapses into geographic confusion. Not exactly lost, mind you, just momentarily unsure. The main problem with the system is that it makes me crazy not to be able to see the map for hours at a time.

MAP TREATMENT

Map care is like trip hats. Very personal. Some folks, and I admire them, are fastidious as sin about their maps. Maps are THE WAY, after all. They laminate their quadrangles, encase them in clear plastic, bring special markers to write on the topo sheets, have cunning zippered bags to carry them in. Their maps will last pretty well forever. The whole deal is so tidy it makes your mouth water.

Not me. I throw my maps, unprotected, into a plastic bag inside my ammo can and head off. I write on the quadrangles, usually in pencil, to note campsites and portages or remind myself how I ran a rapid. Sometimes I'll even draw in my route with a dashed line. Maps, in my book, are meant to be used, directly. They aren't like museum specimens behind glass or fine jewelry that never gets worn. They're like clothes, to be worn, used up, worked into shape.

Every day I fold the map du jour to expose the country we'll paddle across. By the end of a long trip, quadrangles tend to be creased in many places, sometimes worn on the folds to the point of illegibility. They're stained with cocoa and mosquitoes and water spots. They're not pretty. About the most protective I've ever gotten is a Ziploc bag, and that's rare.

I like to have the bare naked map to look at, not even a layer of clear plastic between us. I like to be able to open it out large or fold it up small. By the end of a trip, if I've been on a quadrangle very long, the map will be worn and tattered. If I go somewhere often, I'll need a new one every few trips.

It's a little embarrassing when I'm out with one of those tidy map types. Makes me feel as if I haven't brushed my hair in the morning, but the intimacy with landscape on paper is worth it.

So it's midmorning. A calm day on a big lake. The paddling is peaceful and quiet, a tad monotonous, and the route finding is challenging. The lakeshore is a chaos of points and bays and channels. The open lake is choked with islands of various sizes, and the map must have been drawn when the water was at a different level, because many of the islands seem too large or small or aren't even on the map. Wrong choices will lead us down dead-end bays or on convoluted detours. The map reading takes terrific concentration. For the one in the stern, it requires absolute trust and an ability to blindly follow directions.

Given the circumstances, Marypat doesn't seem to be looking at the map nearly enough. A long peninsula I think I recognize from my map study the evening before looms in the foreground. I remember there's a break near the tip that we might be able to squeak through and save a mile or more. Marypat seems to be aiming us for the far tip. I keep my suggestion to myself for a very long time, probably five minutes at least.

"Is that the big peninsula about eight miles along?" I ask. I use that "just checking in" tone.

"What peninsula?" Marypat's voice has an edge of exasperation right off the bat.

"The really big, obvious one, kind of hook-shaped at the end."

"I don't know, I'm going off the three islands to the right."

"Well, when I was looking at the map I noticed a break in the peninsula that might save some distance." I'm sounding helpful now.

Marypat stops, lays her paddle down, picks up the map. "There are peninsulas all along here," she says. "The islands are a lot more reliable landmarks."

"It's the biggest one, by far. Look for a break just before it makes the hook."

"Now you've got me all screwed up. I knew exactly where we were by the islands."

"Can I look at the map?"

I can hear her muttering, looking hard at her landmarks, her concentration ruined. Finally she leans back and flings the map bag toward me.

I'm like an addict with my fix in hand. It's been hours since I got a glimpse of the map. Now I can try to imprint our progress in my mind, get a position. I'll be good till lunch if I study it well.

"Okay," I say, after a minute, "I think I have us. That peninsula is actually blocking our view of the really big one. It should be coming into sight soon. Let's look for the shortcut when we get close."

"Are you happy now?" Marypat grabs the map back, bends to study it, tries to regain some semblance of her navigational rhythm.

"I just don't want to go down some dead-end alley," I say, but I'm not fooling anyone. Marypat's on to me.

From my point of view, maps are everything. To begin with, they're incredibly evocative and stimulating. There it is, all this wild country laid out on a sheet, full of potential for exploration or shortcuts or new wrinkles in an old route or danger or canyon stretches or long beaches. Just country, full of mystery, all around. The maps are a preview of what's around the corner and a satisfying record of what lies in our wake. No matter how many times I've unfolded a quadrangle and studied a piece of it, there are inevitably new surprises hiding in the contours.

"Look at this," I'll say. "Check out this river bend. It must be nine miles around. And look at that tight spot. I wonder what the current will be like through there."

By the time I get to looking at a map in camp, I've already studied that same stretch dozens of times. First on a really large-scale, route-planning overview map, then on the smaller-scale trip maps to check the general itinerary (see pages 33–36 for getting the most out of maps), then each day as we travel on. Still, nothing compares with actually being there, on site, for revving up the level of meticulous attention. Suddenly I'll notice the potential campsites on gravel bars or clearings; I'll be looking for springs and small tributaries for water sources; I'll be peering at sharp corners or constrictions for tricky current; I'll be reckoning the shortest route through a

LAKE NAVIGATION

In the illustration, you're on a remote trip down the Kamilikuak River in northern Canada and you encounter the island-filled, unnamed lake. Each square on the map represents ten miles, so the lake navigation between sections of river comes to almost thirty miles that will require terrific focus, with a pretty good chance for confusion and testiness.

This is one lake where taking a map bearing or two along the way, just for peace of mind, might be prudent. Fortunately, the route is relatively straight, but there are still numerous possibilities for going off down dead-end bays or missing landmarks. About halfway along, at the northeast end of Casimir Island, for example, there's that tricky little jog that, if missed, will send you off on a frustrating detour.

My experience has been that the little islands are very confusing, and changes in water level may make them look quite different than they appear on the map. I'd hunt for major, unique landforms like the squat, T-shaped peninsula near the southern end of the lake, or Casimir Island. Once past the tricky jog, I'd cling to the mainland coast for my reference points and ignore the islands altogether.

This is one of those stretches where the map will always be in view and you hope you have a patient, relaxed partner. On the cheerful side, there's a good chance that many of the islands will be beautiful places to explore and camp.

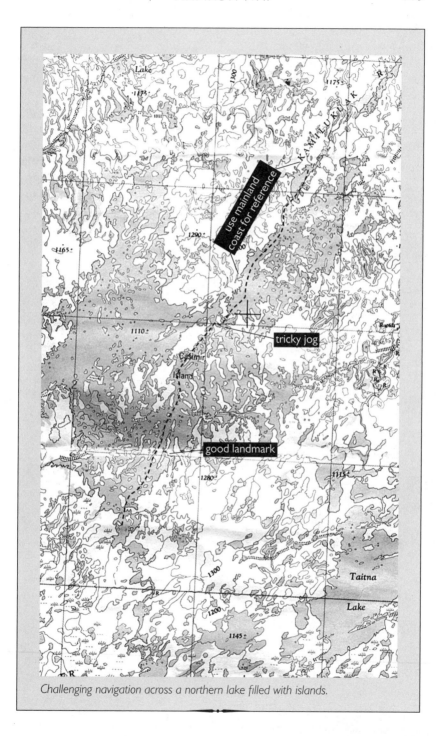

Challenging navigation across a northern lake filled with islands.

maze of islands; or I'll be planning strategy for the course most protected from a pestering side wind.

I study maps at lunch breaks, when we stop to scout a rapid, around the fire in the evening, in the tent before I drop off to sleep, again in the morning over coffee. By the end of a trip I have that map in my head.

And when it's my day in the bow with the map, I'm on it like a beagle on a scent. All the while an internal dialogue is unspooling, like this: "Right turn, long straight stretch, left turn past a tributary." Or, "Three little islands, deep bay on the left, cliffs coming up around the headland." Little by little the landscape falls away. In my next life I'm going to be a global positioning system. This life is the apprenticeship. (See pages 203–4 for the limitations of GPS.)

RIVER NAVIGATION

The challenge is to get from Ameto Lake to Kinga Lake, following the Padlei River to its confluence with the Maguse River. Again, each map square is ten miles across. A rough estimate puts the travel distance at about fifty miles, give or take a few. Contour intervals are twenty meters, or roughly sixty feet, with most of the elevation loss apparently coming in the last third of the trip. If you look closely at the last ten miles of river for where the contours cross the channel, you'll see where the biggest drop in gradient lies.

I like the looks of the long esker ridge (those caterpillar markings on the map) after the rapid that's marked at the outlet of Ameto Lake. It might be a pretty place to explore and a good candidate for a campsite. The most iffy section of the route lies just north of the 185 elevation marker near the esker. The connection between lakes is by way of some very small squiggles, which may or may not be navigable pieces of current. If they aren't, you could be in for some longish portages through swamp and muskeg.

The second half of the journey is dominated by river current full of the hash marks that denote rapids. They may be easy riffles or roaring cataracts. In any case, you're certain to be doing a lot of scouting and perhaps some lining or portaging.

Along the way there are several prominent hills that might be worth a climb for the view, and the tall, strange-shaped peninsula sticking into Kinga Lake near the river confluence. My guess is that with luck you might make the stretch in two long days. If the questionable spots all turn out to be rigorous, it'll be more like three or four days.

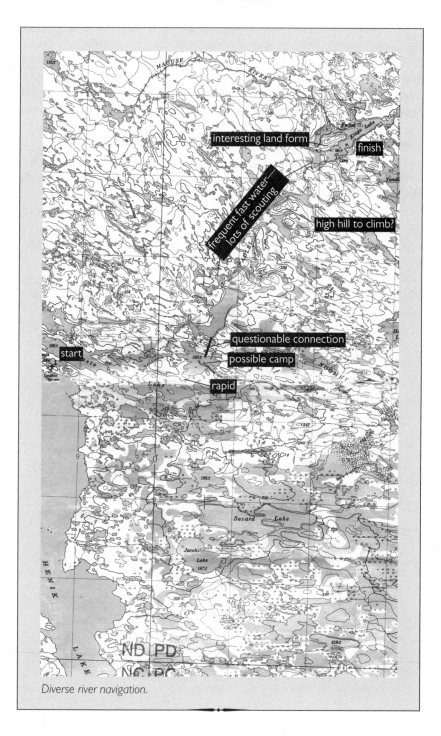

interesting land form

finish

frequent fast water—lots of scouting

high hill to climb?

questionable connection

possible camp

start

rapid

ND PD
NC PC

Diverse river navigation.

Once in a while I can relax my vigilance. There might be an unmistakable island two-thirds of the way down a lakeshore, for example, or a major bridge crossing the river, or a can't-miss river confluence halfway through the day. Then I relax and wait for the big landmark. But even then I enjoy testing myself against the map, knowing just what bend I cruised around, or how deep that bay is, or the exact location of a pretty campsite, or how far over the ridge the next drainage is.

OK, so I'm addicted to maps. There are worse things.

And to be honest, the compass almost never comes out of its case. It's absolutely critical that I have a compass along. When I need one, nothing else will do. And it's important that I know how to take a bearing, correct for declination, or triangulate a position. But I admit I've actually been in need of a compass bearing about three times in the past twenty-five years.

Really. Once when I crossed a bay by compass bearing through impenetrable fog (see pages 61–62). Once when I needed to decide which of two side-by-side river outlets to aim for from across a lake. Once when I followed a compass bearing across a trailless portage between two pothole lakes in black spruce bog country. That's it.

Trust me. Maps are where it's at. On trips, it's best to succumb to the obsession, wallow in it, get good at it. And hope your partner is an understanding sort.

THREE STEPS TO A COMPASS BEARING

Orienteering is fun. Mastering the combination of map and compass so that you can travel through untracked country and come out bang on a point is one of the more satisfying of outdoor skills. Right up there with being able to make a fire after a two-day rainstorm.

On trips, though, the need to orienteer arises pretty rarely. Mostly you can get from point to point by paying attention to the map and getting used to interpreting landforms: river tributaries, major bends, islands, large hills. If you keep on it, it's pretty tough to blow it. Besides, in most cases you're just going downstream or following a shoreline, and when you come to the end, there you are.

Still, there are times. Times when it isn't good enough to just generally know where you're going. Times when you admit that you're temporarily confused and really need some help getting clear again. Times when the woods are deep and thick and the objective is not on a path. Times when you need a compass bearing.

Advanced orienteering includes all sorts of Eagle Scout techniques like taking cross-bearings, triangulating a position, aiming off a point, and so on. But 90 percent of the time what you need is a simple bearing, a reassuring line to follow that will take you from where you stand to where you want to be. Almost always, you'll want to get a bearing off the map to use in the field. Here's how to get one, in three easy steps:

1. Line up the edge of your compass along the route of travel, from where you are to where you want to go. (It isn't necessary to orient the map quadrangle first, but it helps to have it generally lined up.)

2. Holding the compass in place, turn the dial of the compass housing, with the permanent north–south lines drawn in, until those lines are parallel with the north–south lines on the map (make sure the north end of the compass housing points north on the map).

(continued next page)

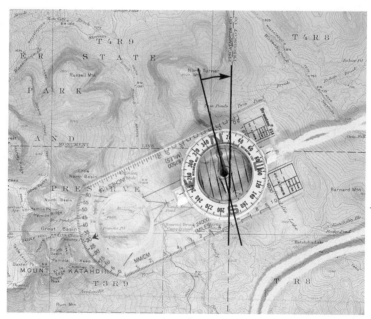

With edge of compass on line of travel, turn dial to align north–south lines.

THREE STEPS TO A COMPASS BEARING

(continued from previous page)

3. Lift the compass off the map, then correct for declination. Declination will be shown at the bottom of the map quadrangle. Going from the map to the field, if declination is east of magnetic north, you need to subtract that amount from the compass reading to get your precise bearing. If declination is west of magnetic north, add that amount. (Use the old east-is-least [subtract]..., west-is-best [add]..., adage if it works for you.)

4. Turn the compass until the magnetic needle lines up with the permanent one drawn in the compass housing, and you should have the correct bearing to your destination. Lift the compass to about the height of your chin, making sure the floating needle is swinging freely, and sight along that bearing. Pick a prominent point on course (large tree, point of land, etc.) and aim for that. When you get there, sight again, find a point, and travel to it. And remember the old orienteering truism, "Always trust the compass." Your mind is capable of playing beguiling tricks on you, and a compass is almost never devious.

FOURTEEN

No Grit:
Life in Sandy Camps

I will admit I'm jaundiced when it comes to sand. I've arrived at a point in my paddling career where the only things I think it's good for are pretty pictures and kids with plastic buckets. Even on a beautiful stretch of beach on a warm, calm day, I'm jumpy. Any minute the wind is sure to come up, or a tent zipper will fail, or someone will scuff sand into the dinner pot. Bad things are bound to happen.

I wasn't always this way. On my first boating trips I sought out beach campsites. Nothing better than a smooth crescent of warm sand at the back of a calm bay. Just like a postcard. But postcards are one-dimensional, superficial, and shot from a distance. Up close, inside the panorama, the true grit reveals itself.

All right, I'll give sand its due. Sand beaches are pleasant places to spend time as long as conditions behave. Kids love to play there. The swimming is nice. You can manicure a tent site to your heart's content. Beaches are the ultimate no-trace camper's friend. Just sweep up and it's as if you were never there. The next breeze (and there'll be one soon) will erase every last footprint. Tent sites, kitchen areas, a place to read . . . pretty well unlimited choices. With the notable exception of sand flies, insects tend to be less fierce in open, sandy areas than in the forest.

What else? Beaches are good for evening strolls with your sweetie. Sunsets and moonrises and cloudscapes are impressive. You can go barefoot. OK, that about covers the good side. At first blush, sand seems to offer a lot.

Until you have to live there regularly. And paddling is clearly the outdoor activity that subjects its practitioners to the highest incidence of sandy living conditions. Riverbanks and lakeshores and seashores are sandy by definition. Often the campsite alternatives are limited to cobbles, bare rock, or impenetrable brush. Given the options, sand is routinely the home of choice.

It doesn't take long for the drawbacks to start popping up. At the beautifully manicured tent site, the stakes won't hold against the barest puff of wind. Soon you'll be trudging off after rocks to hold the corners down. An hour or two after you arrive, with the sun beating down, you'll realize that the shadow thrown by your tent is the only shade in sight. No matter how careful you are in putting gear away, there will quickly be little gritty drifts on the tent floor, inside your sleeping bag, and in the clothes bag. After a few days everything, including your skin, takes on the texture of fine-grade sandpaper.

At the kitchen site the cook will be cursing anyone who comes within three yards of the dinner pot. When you try to set up the kitchen fly, there's nothing to tie off to, and it ends up taking an hour to rig up a canopy contraption that looks like a Frank Lloyd Wright construction with dementia, guyed to paddles, driftwood logs, and errant boulders.

When the wind comes up—and sooner or later it will—the camp scene immediately unravels into something like a stage set for a disaster movie. The paddling version will be titled *Sand!* and will feature scenes cast in clouds of swirling dust, with shadowy figures running by in pursuit of tents

Sandy camps are the norm on paddling trips.

cartwheeling into the distance. When the wind blows, sandy campsites are largely uninhabitable.

Looming over this seething cauldron lurks the granddaddy of sand campsite disasters: tent zipper failure. Before dinner one night, someone will traipse over to get a book and not come back. You hear muttering, then see a body kneeling at the front of the tent in prayerful position, hands fumbling with the zipper slider as if it were a set of rosary beads.

This is not an "if" proposition, it's a "when" proposition. Camp on sand, and your tent zipper will eventually fail. When it does it's like having your car doors fall off as you zip along the interstate. Can you spell *e-x-p-o-s-e-d*?

The first time it happened to me we were five days into an expedition above the Arctic Circle. The zipper on one of the tent doors started to separate on one side. For a few days we got by using the other zipper slider, until that one failed too. After that we closed the solid door panel and sweltered through the nights in the land of the midnight sun. Before long the outer door started to go as well, and the insects found the breach in our defenses. By the end of the trip we were reduced to jamming everyone into the remaining tents to avoid slow death by hemorrhage.

I know enough now to go prepared (see sidebar, pages 112–14), but zipper failure remains one of my most dreaded outdoor catastrophes. Another land mine on the sandy battlefield.

The worst thing is that there really is no escape. Sand is a fact of paddling life. Learn to cope or give it up. And there aren't really any foolproof coping strategies. The best you can hope for is a draw; you succumb to the gritty reality but get smart enough to avoid an absolute rout.

There are several body mannerisms it's critical to perfect. The first is the "hand swipe," which should become so ingrained as to be almost unconscious. Every time you pass something into the tent, you swipe your hand underneath it to knock off the sand. Every time you go to dip your cup into the hot water pot, you swipe the bottom. Before you put a dry bag in the boat, you brush away . . . and so on. The swipe becomes a kind of universal body tic within paddling groups.

Then there's the "sand shuffle." You master this after the first three times you kick sand into the stew pot and have to eat food spiced with quartz grains. It's a variation of the Frankenstein walk and requires that you never lift your feet more than an inch off the ground or attempt any fancy moves. Tiny, shuffling, baby steps.

In the kitchen the best coping strategy is to elevate yourself above the fray. The real flying-sand zone is a layer about a foot off the ground. Once you get higher, you'll rise above the worst of it. Find a big flat rock, a wide tree stump, or a big driftwood log to cook on. Turn a canoe over to use as a table for food bags and utensils. If you've got the cargo space and aren't portaging, consider one of those roll-up camp tables (see page 146). Some stoves are designed to hang from a tree branch or be fitted to a telescoping stand. Finally, site the kitchen near available trees for shade and tie points for pitching a tarp.

Scrutinize camps for no-sand tent zones, and always assume that a windstorm will spring up sometime during your stay. If you're outfitted with good sleeping pads, you can sleep comfortably on gravel or smooth bedrock and do away with tent grit. Even if the main living area is sandy, you can often find small openings in the forest to pitch tents and avoid most beach pitfalls.

If you simply can't avoid sandy tent sites, search out the firmest surfaces, face the door away from prevailing winds, and look for topographic aid—small hollows near the forest margin or behind a protective boulder.

In the end, dealing with sand is one of those Zen things, much like coping with bugs. "This too will pass," is a phrase worth chanting under duress. You have to rise above it mentally or you're doomed. Do what you can to mitigate the grainy onslaught, prepare yourself intelligently, bring an extra tent zipper, and then aim for that higher plane of consciousness, hovering above the gritty cloud.

TENT ZIPPER MAINTENANCE

PREVENTION

1. On a tent door, any zipper smaller than #7 is suspect. Some manufacturers skimp on weight by using small-gauge zippers, but it isn't worth it in sand country.
2. Zipper sliders made of nickel are far superior to those made of steel or nylon in terms of durability and susceptibility to grit.
3. Shake tents out frequently on trips, avoid sandy tent sites when possible, and be meticulous about minimizing sand inside.
4. Alternate using the sliders on both ends of zippers to equalize wear.
5. Never open a zipper by pulling apart the fabric; always use the sliders.
6. Even after a zipper starts to go, you can prolong its life by being gentle with it and using the slider on the opposite end.

Repairs

Slider crimping. When a zipper starts separating, the first line of defense is to take a pair of pliers and crimp down the back end of the slider so it has a tighter grip on the zipper track. That simple step can prolong zipper life by weeks.

Slider replacement. A new slider will be your next move. It's far easier than replacing the entire zipper, and it won't damage the tent.

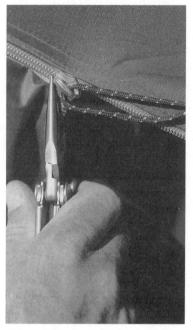

1. Remove old sliders by ripping out the stitching at the ends of the zipper tape and pulling them off. Notice how they are oriented and how the material matches up so you can put the replacements on the same way.

2. Rip out the stitching along both sides of the zipper track two to three inches above the ends to give you some "zipper tail" to work with.

3. Feed both sides of the zipper tape through the new sliders, keeping the two *Crimp the back end of a zipper slider with pliers to extend its life.*

sides even. As you work the slider on, the zipper should close behind it. Be patient—getting the slider started is the trickiest part.

4. Restitch the zipper track by hand and sew a line across both ends to keep the sliders on.

Zipper replacement. If new sliders don't do it, the problem is with the zipper itself, and you may have to sew in an entire new one. In the field, this is done by hand. *(continued next page)*

TENT ZIPPER MAINTENANCE

(continued from previous page)

1. If your spare zipper doesn't already have sliders, install them from each end first.
2. Do not remove your old zipper! If you do, the job becomes almost impossible.
3. Hand stitch the new zipper tape right on top of the old one. This way you don't harm the tent fabric or mosquito netting, and the old zipper maintains the correct door shape and tension. It's easiest to do this while sitting inside the tent, with the old zipper closed as well as possible. Don't make the new zipper too tight.
4. Once the zipper is installed, snip off the excess ends and sew a line at the bottom of each side to keep the sliders on.

   Zipper repair supplies:
   - one or two sets of #7 zipper sliders with two-sided pull tabs
   - spare #7 nylon zipper (measure it against your tent door; you'll be surprised at its length)
   - seam ripper or pair of small, sharp scissors
   - needle and thread

FIFTEEN

Rigging for the Day

About halfway through the first round of morning coffee, I notice Marypat scanning the sky. Dark, roiling clouds are sliding in upstream, clouds with bruise-colored underbellies and beards of rain. She looks at me.

"Think we can beat it?" she asks.

"Worth a try. Do you want to finish making breakfast or break down the tent?"

"I'll cook," she says, "but you better hurry."

I keep glancing at the dark front rolling in as I strip the fly off the tent and stuff it into its bag. Then I burrow in the door and start jamming sleeping bags into the stuff sacks lined with plastic bags. I roll up the sleeping pads, gather the books, flashlights, journals, and ditty bags strewn around, and throw everything into the waterproof clothing bags.

When I emerge the weather is almost overhead. In fast motion I flatten the tent, fold up the poles, wad it into its storage bag. Then I ferry everything to the packs, stuff in clothing bags, food bags, loose equipment, and strap on pads and tent and poles. Then one at a time down to the boat, where I slide everything under the hull of the overturned canoe.

By now Marypat has oatmeal ready. We stand together, facing upstream, and watch the impending storm while we shovel food down the hatch. The wind is gusting through the trees, burring the surface of the broad river, catching at the hoods of our wind jackets. The dishes get a cursory rinse before we gather up stove and pot and other utensils. They go into the top of the equipment pack and get cinched under the lid.

Quickly we turn the canoe over and slide it into the shallow water. I hop in while Marypat hands me our two personal packs, loaded with clothing, sleeping bags, tent, and whatever food can be stuffed into empty crannies. I lay these two packs next to each other the long way, in the space between the center thwart and the bow seat. As I shift back, Marypat wrestles the equipment and food pack toward me. It's the biggest load by far, and I help her get it over the gunwale and flop it down across the hull just behind the center thwart. On most trips three packs will do us, but on longer jaunts we pack the spillover food and gear into a smaller pack or duffel and lay that in next to the gear pack.

GEAR FOR THE DAY

A surprising medley of stuff seems to come out regularly during a day's travel, especially when the weather is fickle. Unsnapping the deck, untying packs, rummaging inside for snacks or rain gear or compass or whatever other item has suddenly become essential is a drill no paddler wants to repeat. By the same token, it's really bad form to leave all the riffraff of equipment you might need between campsites exposed and disorganized.

I use three types of containers for day gear. First, the ammo box, usually one per paddler, filled with the clutter of bug dope, maps, journal, camera, film, compass, and such (see page 188 for an ammo box list). Some people prefer a more modern and expensive dry box, along the lines of those advertised in rafting catalogs. Be my guest.

Second, the hip sack, with a waist strap that fastens either around a thwart as a tie-in precaution or around your waist for day hikes and portages. The hip sack carries lunch and snacks for the day. At those hungry moments, pull out the small pack, open it up, and dine. I sometimes keep a few lunch-type condiments like mustard or salsa inside too. The hip sack can also be where you accumulate the little odds-and-ends baggies of leftover food that you might dip into for another meal.

Third, the coat bag. Sometimes I simply use the stuff sack from the spray cover for this, but more often I'll bring along a medium-sized dry bag. Either way, I load up a set of rain gear and wind gear for each paddler and secure the bag behind the stern seat, where I can grab a rain jacket or wind shirt as soon as the weather shifts.

The only things left relatively loose are the spare paddle, which I usually wedge up alongside the hull, and the maps for the day, which I can throw into an ammo can for protection.

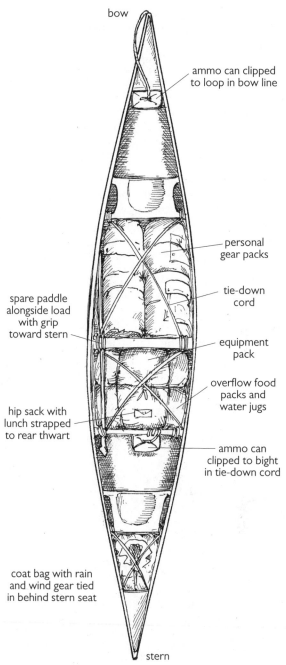

bow

ammo can clipped
to loop in bow line

personal
gear packs

spare paddle
alongside load
with grip
toward stern

tie-down
cord

equipment
pack

overflow food
packs and
water jugs

hip sack with
lunch strapped
to rear thwart

ammo can
clipped to bight
in tie-down cord

coat bag with rain
and wind gear tied
in behind stern seat

stern

Tandem canoe packed for an expedition.

I start lashing in the load, using a cord left permanently tied at the bow seat, looping it through a sturdy strap on each pack, winding it under the center thwart, and finally tying off at the rear thwart, leaving a long bight, or loop, in the end.

Marypat is busy with odds and ends. She's in the bow today, so she arranges her ammo box—full of camera, binoculars, maps, bug dope, journal—in the bow ahead of her feet and clips the carabiner attached to the box handle to a loop in the bow line. She gets her paddle and shrugs into her life jacket. In the stern I set my ammo box behind the gear and clip its carabiner into the bight of cord. Behind the stern seat I stow the dry bag full of rain gear and tie it off to the stern line.

Finally, the hip sack with our lunch clips around the rear thwart, and I slide the spare paddle up along the inside edge of the hull, held in place by the pressure of the packs. All of this has taken less than five minutes, but when we finish the first drops are hitting, big as marbles.

We stop long enough to shrug into rain gear and then shake out the fabric spray cover (see pages 175–76). On nice days we just snap the deck over the canoe's midsection, covering gear, but this morning we go full length, quickly working up each side until the boat is fully decked.

Now the raindrops are whacking into the river, cratering the surface like a huge school of fish rising. Marypat climbs in first, stepping into the cockpit skirt, drawing the elastic tight around her, then fixing her rain jacket to lie outside the skirt so rain will drain off instead of funneling inside.

When I do the same and we push off, we're snug as ducks on the water. The canoe seems to be listing slightly to the left, so I slide my ammo box a foot right to compensate. Within ten strokes of shore, the rain starts in

Spray deck rigged for good-weather paddling.

earnest, beating on the boat, pummeling the hood of my rain jacket, throwing up spray with every impact on the river surface.

Our tent is dry, our gear is dry, everything is lashed down, we're buttoned into rain gear. Unless the wind gets scary or lightning starts up, unless the cold seeps in past layers of clothing as the day goes on, we're as secure in the canoe as we would be in the tent, and nothing will be getting wet even in a downpour. I can't think of a more delicious smugness than the one that comes right after winning a race with the elements.

ADJUSTING TRIM

A canoe is trim when the hull is balanced in the water, both front to back and side to side. For most paddling situations it's best to be trim, or slightly bow light. When the bow is a bit high, small waves don't tend to splash in, and the stern paddler has better control of the canoe. About the only exception is when you travel upstream. Then you like to be slightly bow heavy for control.

Side-to-side trim, unless it's really off kilter, is easy to adjust by making slight shifts in the gear load. Sometimes just pushing your camera box six inches one way or the other is enough. On trips where you have to carry large water containers, the water jugs are good ballast to move around.

Front-to-back trim can be more of a problem, especially if the two paddlers aren't matched in weight. Some canoes come outfitted with a sliding bow seat that can be moved to adjust for weight discrepancy. If not, shift the packs to compensate. On days when Marypat paddles stern, we load the heaviest pack and water jugs toward the stern to compensate for the seventy-pound difference in our weights.

Canoe trim adjusted to be slightly bow light.

SIXTEEN

Finding a Home

Luckily the day has stayed warm. In every other way the weather has been dismal and dreary. Driving rain, drizzle, gray, lowering sky, gusty winds. We've managed fifteen miles, but mostly because we've had a bit of river current to help us on our way and no portages to contend with. The feeling of triumph at dawn, when we got off before the rain hit, has long since dissipated. Now we're looking for a home.

The rain has stopped, but it looks like a brief reprieve rather than a real change. There's an oppressive quality in the air, as if the next storm is about to pounce. We've been looking for a camp for two miles. The gravel bars have been too barren and exposed, openings in the forest that looked promising from a distance turn out to be choked with vegetation, a clearing that had campsite written all over it ended up being impossibly lumpy.

We're getting testy with each other, chemistry produced by a day spent in marginal conditions with no relief on the horizon. Nothing personal, but who else are we going to take it out on?

"Let's check that little island coming up," I suggest.

"Fine," Marypat says. "Whatever."

We paddle in silence. I'm sweating inside my rain gear in the brooding, close air. A great blue heron rises out of some shallows, slate gray, prehistoric looking. The air is absolutely still, but not comfortably so.

The bow scrapes up against shore. Marypat stands, disengages from the cockpit skirt, and steps out to investigate. I lean back against the stern plate when she disappears up the slope. She isn't gone long, but by the time she returns I'm fully informed on mosquito density. They seem to rev up to a frenzy in this sort of heavy, prestorm air.

"Looks doable," she says, "but the bugs are intense."

"I think it's going to rain any minute. With our luck today finding sites, we might want to make do."

Both of us open our ammo boxes and apply bug dope to hands and faces, then I start unsnapping the deck. When the deck is peeled back past the center, Marypat takes over and I unlash the load as quickly as I can. One by one I heave the packs and loose gear forward as I free them up. Marypat

---

CAMPSITE PRIORITIES

Pitching camp under benign conditions is no big deal. You can do things in whatever order you feel like, take a walk before you set up the tent, go fishing. But eventually there will come a day when the weather slams you, or bugs are intense, or the wind is roaring, and you're faced with the final exam of campsite erection. These are my priorities, in order:

1. Scout the site with two essential ingredients in mind—a place for the kitchen tarp and a spot for the tent(s).

2. Unlash and unpack the boat, working as a team, and pile the packs nearby. Don't go off on trips with gear until the canoe is unloaded.

3. Get the boat onshore, in a secure spot, and turn it over. Tie the bow line to a stout anchor—tree, solid root, clump of willows, big rock. Stow the paddles and odds and ends under the hull.

4. Take some packs to the tarp site, pull out the tarp (which should have been packed on top that morning), and start pitching the fly. If one person can handle the tarp, the other can keep ferrying gear.

5. With the tarp rigged, at least at the corners, get the packs and gear under shelter.

6. If you're in the middle of a hard shower that looks like it will taper off soon, wait for a break to set up the tent. Otherwise, get the tent up and rain fly on as efficiently as you can and stow the sleeping gear inside.

At this point you've managed the basics. If you're building a fire, you may want to get in some dry wood, but you've kept your gear as dry as possible, you've erected the cooking and sleeping shelter, and you've gotten the canoe stowed for the night. Maybe it's time, right about then, to uncork that merlot!

wrestles them ashore and leans them into a pile. When the canoe is empty we drag it upslope into a sheltered alley behind shrubbery, turn it over, and tie off the bow line to a stout clump of willows. Under the hull we store our paddles, life jackets, the deck, and other bits we won't need in camp.

At one point I look down at the back of my hand and count eleven mosquitoes all pumping away like greedy oil rigs. Light rain starts as we heft the first packs and stumble uphill toward the campsite.

"I figured the tarp can go over there," Marypat points to a small clearing between low trees. "The only tent site is here in the woods. It's marginal, but protected."

"Let's get the tarp up first," I say, and pull the ten-by-ten square of coated nylon from the top of the equipment pack. I tie off the front corners as high as I can reach in the trees, high enough so we can easily stand under the eave of the tarp. Marypat attaches the back end about waist high in some vegetation, so the fly slopes down to about the height of the packs. As soon as we have the corners rigged, we hustle the packs underneath. Everything is still pretty dry.

Marypat unstraps the tent and poles from the gear pack, and we traipse over to the small opening between shrubs, barely large enough for the tent floor. Being of the old school when it comes to ground sheets, I lay out our plastic ground cover first, then roll the tent out on top of it. I understand the rationale of the ground sheet inside the tent school of thought. In my

tarp with eave strung over a line
between two trees

high end pitched so canoeists can stand under, away from wind

low end about waist high, with packs stowed along back

Tarp rigged for shelter and cooking area.

heart I even admit that it probably keeps you drier in a hard rain. But I don't like sleeping on my ground sheet, and it's one of those new, improved practices I refuse to adopt. Must be getting old and irascible.

I do, however, make sure there's no corner of ground sheet peeking out under the eave of the rain fly. Too many times I've been ambushed by a

TAUT-LINE HITCH

That I love this knot so much has nothing to do with the fact that I learned it from a young woman I was infatuated with in college. Anyway, that was twenty-five years ago and I have no idea where she is now, but the knot has withstood the test of time and faithfulness.

The great attribute of the taut-line hitch is that it's fast and easy and that it tightens up without slipping back. Those qualities make it the perfect knot for pitching tarps and guying out tent lines.

Take the line around the tree trunk, branch, or rock you want to tie off to and bring it back against itself in a bight. Make two wraps on the inside of the bight, then take the free end over those wraps and cinch down a final half-hitch (see illustration). Cinch the knot tight, then slide it taut. The tension of the wraps keeps the knot from slipping back while still allowing you to tighten the line. If the cord is slippery nylon or doesn't seem to be holding as well as it should, add one or two more wraps to the first part of the knot. Often, simply tightening the knot on itself is enough to stop slippage.

Trust me, once you get it, you'll use it so much you'll never forget it.

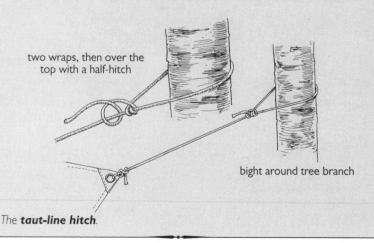

two wraps, then over the top with a half-hitch

bight around tree branch

The **taut-line hitch**.

little rivulet of water dripping onto the ground sheet, wriggling its way under the tent, and pooling where it shouldn't. I tuck the ground sheet a good six inches under the sides of the tent to compensate for any sagging of fabric or shifting of the winds.

Tent up, we quick-march the sleeping pads and bags, along with the clothes bags, over to the door and throw them in fast before the bugs invade. Marypat crawls in to set up the bedroom, and I head back for the kitchen tarp to think about dinner.

First I finish the tarp rigging. I tighten up the corner lines and tie off a couple of side cords to convenient shrubbery. There's no good tie point at the middle of the back of the tarp, so I go to the canoe and retrieve a paddle. A snug clove hitch around the paddle shaft keeps the cord from slipping, and I angle the line down to a small stump of wood to tie it off taut. Now the kitchen tarp is tightly in place. Rain drains off the back. Our packs stand at the rear of the shelter, leaving us room to stand or sit while we cook.

Rain is falling harder now, beating down the bugs. We've managed to make it through a day of pretty awful weather, from morning to night, without any gear getting appreciably wet. I start up the stove under a pot of water. A first course of hot soup seems only fair. Marypat comes over from the tent, and we both strip out of our clammy rain gear. I pull over the ammo box, get out the journal, then sit on top of the lid to write while the water comes to a boil.

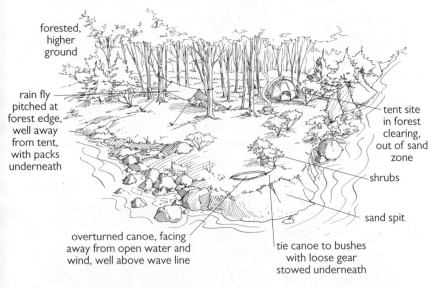

forested, higher ground

rain fly pitched at forest edge, well away from tent, with packs underneath

tent site in forest clearing, out of sand zone

shrubs

sand spit

overturned canoe, facing away from open water and wind, well above wave line

tie canoe to bushes with loose gear stowed underneath

Camp setup, with everything in its place.

SEVENTEEN

The Fiery Debate: Stoves versus Campfires

At the risk of indulging in some literary hyperbole, not to mention losing my membership in the leave no trace club, I think that fire defines us as a life form. Our ability to harness fire ranks with opposable thumbs, tool use, and complex language in setting humans apart. Fire is how we get away with not having fur. It's how we express culinary eloquence, drive back the night, and thrive in climates that force other species into hibernation or migration.

Over the millennia we've tended the flame, carried sparks from camp to camp in folded leaves and skin pouches, sat on our haunches to collect the warmth and smell the meal cooking, let our thoughts wander in the dancing light. Every new spark fanned into flame is another link in a continuum of heat and brightness and security that stretches back somewhere primal.

Without a fire in camp, something at the core of being outdoors goes out of the experience. When I pull on my trip coat and smell wood smoke, it's a sensory event that evokes a gush of outdoor memories. In the field, I enjoy the routine of gathering wood and finding a good fire site. I'm proud of being able to coax a flame from wet wood after two days of rain. I want my children to know how to collect tinder and arrange twigs and encourage a fire into life from the flare of a match. On the other hand, that they learn the care and maintenance of a lightweight stove is about as passionate a fatherly yearning as their mastery of the art of spitting.

There's something about firelight and wood smoke that makes a group of humans draw close in a circle, break into song, share stories, and stay up until the stars are out. Fire is warm. Fire is mesmerizing. The ragged orange circle of light is a beckoning corral of comfort. When was the last time you gathered around a gas stove and basked in the camaraderie?

Campfires suffer from an anachronistic reputation. They hark back, in many people's minds, to the days when camping meant hacking down ridgepoles, trenching a tent site, and soaping up in the nearest pond.

The antifire crowd makes do with candle lanterns, a cup of tea, and the inner glow of doing good. Stove advocates declare that they leave no trace of their passage, or at least of their cooking. They argue that stoves are clean and efficient, that their pots won't be black and sooty, and that they find other ways to achieve evening intimacy with their surroundings.

All well and good, but they don't usually confront the fact that stoves require fuel—fuel that is extracted from somewhere, refined somewhere, packaged and shipped and dispensed somewhere. Stoves are made from metal and plastics. What's a campfire ring compared with a smelter, an open-pit mine, or a manufacturing plant?

Packing a featherweight stove doesn't guarantee that you're a no-impact camper any more than building campfires in the wilderness automatically defines you as a throwback to the tree-hacking prehistory of environmental ethics. Like most things, the fire or stove question hinges on making appropriate choices, based on common sense and a responsible environmental assessment.

In many backcountry areas campfires are forbidden, and rightly so. Where large numbers of people travel, where wood is scarce and its regeneration slow, where fire scars are difficult to clean up and may endure for decades, and when fire danger is acute, building a fire is almost always an irresponsible act.

That said, waterways tend to offer campers some of the best, and most defensible, opportunities to indulge in campfires and cook fires. River corridors and shorelines often have quantities of driftwood available that is regularly replenished. Sand and gravel bars are easy to clean up, and if fires are made below the high-water line, floods will eventually scour the kitchen site. Finally, canoes have enough volume to include a fire pan in the gear and avoid the issue of scarring the ground altogether. Using cook fires, water trips can be extended without the need of a fuel resupply and without the significant additional weight and bulk of weeks' worth of fuel.

These are the criteria I use to judge whether fires are justifiable:

- There's plenty of available fuel. By fuel, I mean downed and dead wood, or driftwood in amounts that ensure you won't strip the area. Dead wood still attached to trees doesn't count.

Small cook fires are possible more often than you'd expect.

- Fire scars can be either avoided or thoroughly cleaned. Some sites are outfitted with fire rings and grates. Others may have a fire ring made by a previous camper that you might use and clean up afterward. In wilderness areas that don't see much travel, it's sometimes reasonable to build a fire below the high-water mark where any traces will be scoured by later flooding.
- Conditions are safe. High winds, drought, and fire danger warnings all argue against lighting a fire.
- You can make a fire with minimal use of rocks and only minor disturbance of soil and vegetation.
- The wood available is small enough to burn completely to ash. Small fires are more efficient than large blazes for cooking in any case, and they're easier to clean up after.

Over a quarter-century of paddling, I've probably built fires to cook on about 50 percent of the time. Dutch ovens, grills, and griddles have accompanied me across thousands of watery miles. Much of that time, however, has been concentrated in remote wilderness areas where wood is plentiful and people are scarce. Even on those trips I carried a lightweight stove and enough fuel to fill in the gaps when situations precluded fires.

I cook on stoves more these days, mostly because I'm camping with kids and quick meal preparation is usually a priority, and partly because

STOVE CARE

Even if you plan to cook on fires, you'll probably carry a stove along for backup. These days the array of backcountry cook stoves is varied enough to preclude a simple, all-inclusive course in care and maintenance.

Some, like the canister stoves, have almost no removable parts to maintain. They almost never break, but if they do, you're out of luck unless you've brought a spare. Even the liquid gas stoves have evolved to become pretty simple systems without many parts to mess with.

For stove tools I carry a small wrench (sometimes stoves come with a lightweight wrench to fit), a light pair of pliers, and the flat screwdriver blade on my pocketknife. When I buy a stove with parts that may fail, I order a repair kit from the manufacturer. Many stoves now come with a little parts bag of O-rings, gaskets, fuel-jet cleaners, and spare generators. If yours doesn't, consult the store or call the manufacturer to create your own.

Stoves are most vulnerable in the pack, where they can get squashed in the load, bent out of shape, and broken. In the interest of creating very lightweight backpacking stoves, many are pretty flimsy when it comes to trip abuse, especially if they get packed in a stuff sack. Weight isn't as important on a canoe trip, so I opt for a more rugged stove design that won't fall apart the first time it gets knelt on by someone climbing across the loaded boat, and I shop for a metal or plastic packing container that will protect it.

If a stove isn't working the way it should, just taking the obvious connections apart and cleaning the parts in a little cup of white gas is often enough to fix the problem. If not, go to the spare parts bag and start troubleshooting.

*Stove **paraphernalia** and **storage box**.*

much of my paddling now is on water that's more civilized. Still, I remain an unabashed lover of open flame. Even if I can't indulge what I consider the luxury of cooking over a fire, I go to great lengths to at least get in that evening blaze with water murmuring in the background. (See page 189 for gear lists for fires versus stoves.)

fire pan made from oil pan

fire built on mineral soil platform

fire tarp under soil

Fires don't have to be an environmental blight. Several strategies can be used to minimize scarring.

FIRE BUILDING 101

Remember that scouting merit badge you got for fire building? The one where you had to make log-cabin fires, build teepee fires, and shave little curlicues of kindling and got one match to work with? It was probably one of the most valuable scout lessons in the book. Even if it got a tad anal about construction techniques, the principles were right on.

A fire needs dry tinder, open spaces for air flow, and increasing thicknesses of wood to build flames with. Those scout techniques have all that.

My own tried-and-true style is a good deal messier than the Boy Scout ones I learned, but it remains true to the same fundamentals. Remember: dry tinder, plenty of air, building the flames—in that order.

(continued next page)

FIRE BUILDING 101

(continued from previous page)

I prefer to start a fire with "twiggies," those tiny branch ends and bits of dry forest litter. The best place to find a good dry supply is at the base of a conifer, right against the trunk, where bunches of dead, protected twigs poke out. I collect a big messy handful, the more twisted the better, and lay them in a crude pile with plenty of air space. Sometimes I'll angle the pile against a larger stick to increase the air pocket and give me a place to insert the match when I get to that stage. Then I start collecting dry twigs about the thickness of my little finger, along with a few slightly larger ones, and place a stash of them to one side.

Time for the single match, which I strike on my pants zipper or a rock. I let the flame take hold, then push it gently into the center of the twiggy pile. Once the twigs start crackling, I feed in the slightly larger pieces I've collected, crisscrossing them on the fire in a sort of flat-teepee rendition of the old scouting routine. When those start burning, the fire is pretty well ensured. I toss on some larger branches and sit back, backcountry merit badge reconfirmed.

Now, it isn't always that easy. Sometimes it's been raining hard for two days, or the river you've picked is in a rain forest where all the wood is saturated and covered with moss. That's when you get a crack at the master's degree in flame study. Some tips:

- Birch bark. If you have access to birch bark, you almost feel like a cheater. Collect a big curly mass of bark and the flammable resins will coax flame from a wet sponge.
- Go to the big conifers, if there are any, and push in past the thick skirts of lower branches, into the protected alcove at the tree's base. That's the most likely place to find the last dry tinder in an otherwise waterlogged landscape.
- If dry wood on the ground is impossible to come by and you're in dire need of a fire, you might still manage a blaze by sawing down a couple of standing dead saplings. Pick trees only an inch or two in diameter that are clearly dead, cut them into lengths, then split them with a hatchet until you get to the splinters of very dry wood at the center.
- You can also get to dry inner wood by shaving away the wet outer layers of bark and wood with a pocketknife and then whittling the stick so curls of wood remain attached.

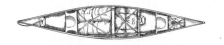

EIGHTEEN

Bears, Bugs, and Boonies: The Bad Bs of Wilderness Paddling

Right here is where you get the paddler's version of the secret handshake. Commit this to memory: *The bugs were unbelievable. It was crawling with bears. The wilderness was a big, scary wasteland.* Practice saying it until you sound charged with conviction and passion. A little shakiness in the voice helps. Try it out on family and friends until it seems good and righteous.

Fact is, bugs are only rarely intense, bear confrontations happen about as often as you get mugged in your neighborhood, and your house—crammed with electrical outlets, slippery tubs, and steep stairs—is objectively more dangerous than the wilderness. But that's our secret.

Public perception is everything. As long as people are duped into believing that commuting at high speed, living in the midst of toxic pollution, and merging with millions of strangers in crowded cities is the sane way to live, the wilderness experience will survive. Hollywood is in on this. Why else would they be churning out movies featuring meteorological catastrophes, slavering bears the size of allosauruses, and puny, hysterical, hairless humans stranded in the howling wilderness? Just keep it up.

Meantime, for those few moments in the wilderness when things do turn a tad sour, some rational advice.

BUGS

We tend to remember the truly horrible episodes—the portage so dense with black flies that your face looked as if you'd gone a few rounds with Mike Tyson; the lunch stop in a fog of mosquitoes so thick it provoked a frantic stampede to the canoes; the swampy camp so intolerable that the only recourse was a retreat to the tents.

Memorable indeed, but exceptional. On the water the bugs are rarely bothersome. They seem to get nervous away from land and won't follow you far. A breeze will keep all but the most stalwart fliers grounded. Most insects have a distinct window of activity—right at dusk, on sunny, still afternoons, after dark—when they're most active. The rest of the time they're pretty dormant. Cool, blustery weather slows up insects remarkably.

I've gone for weeks in country renowned for its bug intensity and never once unscrewed the top on the bottle of insect dope. Admittedly there have been a couple of bad moments when some glitch in the life cycle of an insect denizen, or some conspiracy of temperature, humidity, and season, has provoked a horror-movie bug frenzy that I happened to be there for. Comfort yourself with the knowledge that it's just those occasional outbreaks that keep the myth of the three Bs alive and well in the consciousness of the masses.

- Dress to cope. Pants cuffs and jacket sleeves should have bug-proof closures (elastic, drawstrings, etc.). Socks should be thick enough to thwart stingers and tall enough to pull up over pants cuffs. Wind jackets and pants (light, breathable material) are ideal for bug protection. Dark clothing (navy blue, black) seems to attract insects more than light-colored clothes, so keep that in mind when choosing the trip ensemble.
- Take a headnet if bugs are a real threat. My experience is that you almost never use it, but when you need it, you really need it.
- In true insect territory, consider a bug jacket. They're sold under several brand names, but all of them are loosely woven mesh with long sleeves and hoods. You treat them with bug dope and then put them on. They often avoid the need to apply insect repellent directly on your skin, and you can wear light, cool clothing underneath. One treatment generally lasts several weeks. Ankle gaiters are also available, but they seem like overkill. Bug jackets are sold in outdoor catalogs and in many stores throughout the North.
- Take some repellent. DEET (n-diethyl-metatoluamide) is the active ingredient in the most effective repellents. Bug dope with a high concentration of DEET (90 to 100 percent) really works. Often it's enough to put a dot on the tip of your nose and your cheekbones. It's prudent to use it sparingly, because DEET is strong stuff with a penchant for corroding plastics like camera bodies and paddle shafts. Tests on the side effects of DEET have been mostly reassuring, but still . . . Problem is, DEET repellents are far and away the

most effective. In real bug country, I wouldn't trust anything else.

- Listen politely to folk remedies touted by your friends. You'll hear about garlic, skin moisturizers, vitamin B, and various environmentally friendly concoctions. You'll see little battery-operated gizmos that supposedly emit the sound a dragonfly makes hunting mosquitoes. That sound, of course, is outside the range of human hearing, which makes you wonder if the only real sound is your money going down the drain. Try them if you like, but stash at least one little bottle of the real stuff in the pack, just in case.

Bug jackets are invaluable when things get nasty.

- Practice some behavior modification. Plan trips for the times of year least likely to be buggy. Fall and early spring are usually safe. Make local inquiries about the worst bug seasons. In the field, situate camps on breezy elevations or in open clearings. Always face into the wind. Learn to love wood smoke. On bad days, eat lunch in the canoes. Work on achieving Zen indifference.

- If everything else fails, retreat to your tent and hope the mosquito netting on that cheap dome you bought is fine enough to keep out the hordes.

BEARS (AND OTHER CRITTERS)

Bears are the great white sharks of the land, one of the few animals before which humans turn into quaking, meek puddles of flesh. Lord knows it's good for us to experience a dose of abject powerlessness once in a while. But once again, the perceived threat is a lot more potent than the real one. It's much more likely that you'll be laid low by a microscopic parasite, or that you'll choke on a bite of bratwurst at your take-out picnic than that you'll ever have to deal with a bear attack.

In hundreds of nights camping in bear country, I can think of only three times when a bear made me uncomfortable, and only once where I felt I had to protect myself. In true wilderness bears tend to be very shy. Most sightings you'll make will be of the hind end of a bruin moving off at a remarkable rate. Well-used areas are more questionable, but confrontations are still rare. Prevention is the name of the bear-proofing game.

- Avoid surprising bears: make noise on portages and walks. Warning bears of your presence is simple and prudent. On the other hand, making noise to scare a bear that has already invaded your camp is, in my experience, not very effective. I've stood and banged pots and shouted like a madman at bears that just looked back at me with bland curiosity.
- Check campsites in bear country for signs—footprints, scat, claw-marks in tree bark—and try to skip sites with fresh evidence of bear activity.
- When possible, avoid the well-established campsites in favor of more remote, less-traveled ones, even if they aren't as attractive.
- Follow instructions in established sites with known bear presence.
- Pack food in double thicknesses of plastic to minimize odor. Fold-down dry bags are also effective scent-masking food containers. Screw-top plastic barrels are available through river outfitting catalogs and are a very good way to cut food odors.
- If possible, don't camp in the same site in bear country for days on end. Over an extended period, resident bears eventually tend to come around and investigate.
- Pitch your tent well away from your cooking area, although I like to be able to see where my packs are at night. I try to pile my gear away from both the kitchen and sleeping zones and cover the pile with a tarp for protection.
- Some people mask food smells by putting containers of mothballs or vials of ammonia around the pack stash. I don't know. Seems marginal to me.
- Hanging food is still widely advocated, but in my opinion it's only somewhat useful. Some designated campsites have hanging poles in place or provide "bear boxes" for food storage. All well and good, but the rest of the time it's pretty hard to find a tree adequate for the job, and you can waste the better part of an evening struggling with the hanging system. Even then, black bears are incredibly adroit, athletic, and powerful climbers, especially when they're motivated and frustrated. Hanging your food doesn't do anything to stop the smells from wafting around and attracting wildlife,

which will then keep you awake and cowering in the dark while the family of black bears plays food bag piñata.

- The most important practice is to maintain a clean, odor-free camp and kitchen area and keep food away from your tent.

Critters other than bears are far more likely to inflict mayhem on your camp. Raccoons, skunks, ring-tailed cats, pack rats, mice, and other nighttime invaders are all far more real threats. For the most part, the same measures you take against bears will work for other animals. In some established sites, particularly ones with sleeping shelters in place, mice can be a real problem. I'll sleep in a tent over a shelter any time. In mouse country, try hanging the food bag from a rafter or branch, with a can lid placed halfway down the cord (see page 136).

Beyond preventive measures, we move into the murky realm of self-defense. Deep in the wilderness, protecting your food stash is almost as important as protecting yourself. After all, starvation is only a slower incursion against your health and well-being than an actual attack!

Attach a weight (carabiner, rock) to the end of about 40 feet of ¼-inch line. Throw it over a branch 15–20 feet off the ground. Attach the food bag and haul it up about 10 feet, then tie off the free end of the rope.

If you decide to hang food, at least do it effectively.

coffee can lid with hole punched through, resting on a knot in the cord

food bag

Mouse-proof the food bag with a can lid on the cord.

Firearms are certainly the most dramatic and, some would say, reliable form of self-defense, but they're also extremely dangerous, prone to lethal accidents, and often prohibited in wilderness areas. Although I went through a phase of wilderness travel when I carted along a shotgun and slugs, and though I once felt compelled to use that gun in self-defense against a bear, I'm reluctant to advocate the use of guns.

I've settled on taking pepper spray in canisters specifically developed to thwart bear attacks. Pepper spray has several compelling advantages over guns. First, it isn't lethal to humans or animals. Second, it's compact and lightweight, and it comes with a holster so you can carry it on your belt and keep it as available as you like. One of the drawbacks of guns is that they're often packed away or inaccessible when you need them most.

People argue over the stopping power of pepper spray. There are always what-if scenarios to haggle over. What if the wind is blowing? What if you miss with a shot of spray and don't get a second chance? My conclusion, having used both, is that the canisters are more convenient and less problematic than guns. I suspect they're most effective as a "me or the bear" last-minute defense, when the bear is pretty well in your face.

The bottom line: we take our chances when we travel in bear

country, just as we take our chances on a subway late at night. The odds are overwhelmingly in our favor and worth the risk. If things go badly wrong, I'll just have to trust my wits, call for courage, and hope for the best.

BOONIES

The middle of nowhere is almost always a cathartic, renewing, awe-inspiring, life-affirming place. Finding those large empty spaces between people is one of the compelling motivations for going off in canoes. More than anything else, it's the reason we go and the powerful draw that keeps pulling us back.

Remember I said "almost always." Wilderness regions are bereft of humanity for a reason. They tend to be areas that are expensive to get to, difficult to penetrate, prone to environmental rigors, and infrequently patrolled. Once in a very long while, the same wilderness qualities we embrace turn inhospitable, forbidding, and frighteningly impartial. Those fleeting moments of danger and vulnerability are the ones to prepare for. Hopefully that preparation will be for naught, but that doesn't make it any less critical.

- Consider an emergency locator transmitter (ELT), also sometimes known as EPIRB, for the most remote expeditions. They cost roughly $200 and are available through marine equipment suppliers. ELTs weigh about a pound and are the size of a transistor radio (see page 138). When you turn one on, it emits a constant distress signal on a frequency monitored by satellites and aircraft. Local authorities will presumably be notified and a search begun. Turning on an ELT should be a response to life-and-death problems like acute appendicitis or the loss of your boat. Searches are expensive and risky, and if it turns out that you didn't really and truly need rescuing, you may very well end up paying the bill. I've also known people to take shortwave radios or satellite phones, but I've never been convinced that the security even comes close to justifying their bulk and weight. Cell phone range is iffy, and I have a visceral aversion to packing a telephone.
- Wilderness first aid training is critical for people who wander off into blank spots on maps. Carry a complete, well-stocked first-aid kit (see pages 155–57) and get appropriate first-aid instruction. Inquire at outdoor stores or paddling clubs about local first-aid and safety courses. There are a number of instructional programs that specialize in wilderness applications and go well beyond the standard urban first-aid shtick. Along with your first-aid supplies, include a manual oriented to wilderness settings. There are several good ones available (see appendix 2).

- Put together a basic survival kit in an easy-to-carry container like a small hip sack or Tupperware box (see list on page 139). If you lose your boat or other gear, these supplies will help you get by until you get out on your own or are rescued.
- Be physically and mentally prepared. The assumption of wilderness travel is that you are both self-contained and self-sufficient. Make sure your paddling, navigation, and backcountry skills are up to the challenges of your route and that your supplies are adequate. Once on the water, factor the level of remoteness into your decision making. There are rapids I'll run without hesitation when a road is handy but that I'd portage or sneak when I'm deep in the wilderness with a boat full of gear.

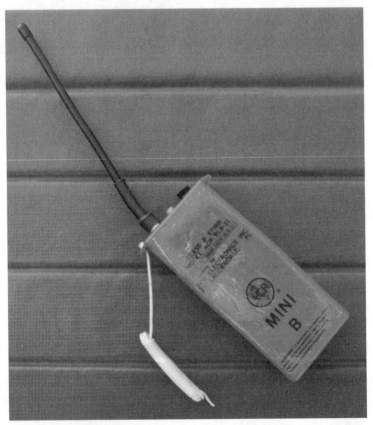

Emergency transmitters are reassuring but should only be used in life-and-death situations.

SURVIVAL KIT CONTENTS

The survival kit is just that, some minimal gear that will allow you to subsist until you can get to help or help comes to you. It should be compact enough that you can wear it as you travel. A light hip sack works well, or a plastic box that you can slip into a shirt or coat pocket. You may have some things to add (personal medications, for example), but the basics should include

- needle and thread
- waterproof match safe
- small compass
- mirror (signal)
- lightweight space blanket (shelter, warmth, signal)
- stub of pencil and little pad of paper
- fishing line and lure
- lip balm
- bug dope (optional)
- small pocketknife
- small roll of adhesive tape

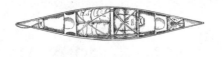

NINETEEN

Kitchens on the Go

Give me a flat table-sized, belly-high boulder and I'm happy. There's nothing like a ready-made camp table to take the strain off creaky knees and a kinked lower back. Used to be I didn't mind hunkering over the flames or stove, stirring the pot, but I used to be younger. I used to be less cranky, too, and I could touch my toes without stretching my hamstrings for ninety seconds first.

A *five-star* **kitchen rock.**

There's something about operating the kitchen off a central flat surface, well above the kicked-sand zone, that makes me feel as if I'm conducting the meal, a culinary maestro rather than a riverside vendor doling out another rendition of one-pot glop. On top of the time-hardened table I dispense hot drinks, soup courses, the entrée, and dessert with the commanding flourish warranted by a couple of billion years' worth of metamorphic seniority.

Even one or two knee-high side table boulders or a broad driftwood log go a long way toward making a camp kitchen more serviceable. Anything to keep food and utensils out of the moss or sand or gravel and out from underfoot.

A table boulder, in my book, rivals a good tent site in the triage of camp selection. I've pitched my tent on bare bedrock (as long as I have an inflatable sleeping pad) because a nice granite table rock caught my eye.

Big flat rocks aside, the kitchen is arguably the most important, and certainly the most central, part of camp. It's where you'll spend most of your waking time and where a good part of trip social life takes place, around meals and snacks.

FIRESIDE KITCHENS

If flames and wood smoke are the kitchen ambiance, try to find a site below the high-water mark or storm line in sand or gravel. Fire scars will be erased by the next flood or storm. Locate near some convenient driftwood or river rock that will provide handy prep surfaces and some protection from wind gusts. The kitchen site should also be well away from the tents and gear (see page 134).

Gather enough dead and down wood to keep your fire going through the meal and haul over the kitchen gear, the dinner stuff sack, your ammo box, and things to do while the meal simmers (maps, journal, the pants that need patching). Kindle a small blaze and settle the grill into the sand so it's stable, level, and several inches above the flames.

I like to sit on my ammo box while I cook. I move around and need to tend the pot too much to want to keep hauling myself up off the ground. The backrest chair comes into use after the meal is ready. Before I sit, though, I open the lid and get out my journal, a pen, and the set of maps.

Everything I need is within arm's reach. The dinner food bag sits to my left, the pot and utensil bag rests on my right, the grill and fire are front and center with wood to the side. Whenever I get a break while dinner simmers or dehydrated ingredients hydrate or the fire burns down to coals, I study maps or scribble in my journal or drop into that current-induced trance next to the river.

Waterside cook fire *built below high-water mark.*

STOVE MEALS

Site selection isn't as critical with camp stoves, since fire scars aren't an issue. Far more important is finding a stable and level surface for the stove, preferably a slightly elevated one. The depression that sets in after a nearly cooked dinner tips into the reindeer lichen has to rank as one of camping's top three bummers. It's also nice to reduce the grit factor by locating the kitchen out of the sand, or at least on a rock or stump. Sand has an insidious, evil way of working into the innards of stoves and spicing food with silica grains.

At the end of each stove meal prep, check the fuel level. There's nothing like getting five minutes into the next day's rice dish and running out of gas.

Unless you have the luxury of a two-burner stove, meal prep has to be carefully choreographed so that everything comes together in the right sequence. On a fire you can have one pot keeping warm while another comes to a boil or have several courses in progress at the same time. On a stove it pays to simplify meal preparation with one-pot concoctions or think through the sequence of more involved dinners to stay efficient.

WEATHER IN THE KITCHEN

In the rain, under threatening clouds, or exposed to desert sun, the essential factor in the kitchen is having shelter overhead. Find a site with tarp-rigging potential (nearby trees, boulders) and tie up the tarp for protection. (See page 122 for tarp-pitching suggestions.) Angle the shelter to protect gear and the flames from wind while providing adequate headroom for the cooks. If the tarp is needed for shade, anticipate the sun's movement and tie the tarp so it will still be providing shade in an hour or two.

Open fires should be sited just out from under the high end of the tarp, within easy reach but not underneath the tarp itself, where smoke gets trapped and sparks might burn holes in the fabric. Clear out any nonessential gear from under the tarp. Put stuff into tents, under canoes, anywhere but in the dining room.

Wind can make food preparation a hassle even on a sunny, otherwise beautiful day. When the wind moans, avoid sandy kitchens at all costs. Cook on the rocks, in the woods, out on the water, but not on the beach. Rig a windscreen with flat rocks, logs, pieces of gear, or an overturned canoe. Try to remember where you got the rocks or logs so you can return them when you're through cooking. And remember that the windscreen will make flames eddy in toward it. If you use gear or a canoe to block wind, keep an eye on the heat.

Kitchen tarp set for protection and comfort.

KITCHEN CLEANUP

The key to avoiding critter confrontations is keeping a clean kitchen and storing food properly. Make sure any food spills get tidied up and that food scraps and leftovers are either stowed in the garbage bag or thoroughly burned in the fire. Wash dishes with biodegradable soap followed by a rinse, and clean prep surfaces.

Pack up all the food into tightly closed bags to keep down those critter-luring smells. Store food by hanging or in bear boxes in bear country (if those facilities are provided), or pack the groceries away securely in scent-proof containers at some distance from the tents. Cover gear with a tarp or store it under a rain fly.

Even if the weather is clear and beautiful and marauding creatures are not a concern, close up the stove, protect enough firewood to get a blaze started, stow the food, and clean up the kitchen. A messy, exposed kitchen is bad karma, sure to usher in rain and wind before dawn.

Finally, allow the fire to burn down to ashes that can be scattered in the water. When you douse the flames too early, burned wood gets preserved as resistant charcoal.

TWENTY

Luxuries of No-Portage Trips

Nestled right near the heart of this attraction to canoe trip-ping is an essential laziness. Sure, there's the love affair with water. The pace and rhythm and peacefulness of river jour-neys. The skills required to move through watery wilderness. But up there with the rest is the inescapable fact that it's an easy way to travel, most times, and that much of the reason behind opting for a boat is that the craft is your mule. None of that backpacking drudgery. Why labor under a fifty-pound pack and succumb to a spartan backcountry lifestyle in the interest of saving every ounce of extra weight when you can load hundreds of pounds into a canoe and slip off downstream without breaking a sweat? The boat totes and the river floats.

And never more so than on a water trip free of portages of any significance. There are times, reclining in camp on such a journey, when I experience a twinge of guilt, just for a moment, over the way my canoe has been transformed into one of those behemoth recreational vehicles crammed with creature comforts. On trips sprinkled with portages I'm kept in check, but when the water is unbroken by trail or bad rapids I'm free to load up until it hardly feels like camping.

Call it the auxiliary equipment list, or the RV appendix to the main equipment list. Much of it seems to center on kitchen gear.

FLOATER'S RV EQUIPMENT LIST

- A roll-up camp table with threaded legs
- A two-burner camp stove

- A waist-high, lightweight telescoping stand for the two-burner stove
- A cooler packed with fresh food, libations of choice, and ice (see page 211 for fresh food ideas)
- A cutting board (lightweight plastic versions sometimes come along on more rigorous trips, but for these jaunts I just throw in the big wooden one from home)
- A small backpacking stove (it's handy to be able to boil a pot of water quickly without dealing with the bigger stove)
- A folding camp chair or two
- Solar shower (small versions can fit in on portaging trips too)
- Bigger, heavier, more commodious tent

Only one thing threatens the decadent elegance of these luxurious pleasure cruises. At some point the extra gear becomes so lavish and uncontrolled that you find yourself spending all your spare time tinkering with this or that gizmo, fussing endlessly with camp furniture, and even breaking into a sweat toting all that stuff from the boat into camp.

Ever notice those folks in an RV campground who erect plastic picket fences around their site, hang a flag next to their door, and stake out whirligig birds and flamingos around their Winnebago? When you find yourself teetering on the brink of that dangerous abyss of campsite madness, it's time to reassess.

A lavish camp on a no-portage journey.

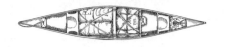

TWENTY-ONE

Water Safety: Getting a Safe Head

The most valuable bits of paddling safety advice I've come across over the years have nothing to do with throw bags or Z-drags or whitewater rating systems or life vest designs. They have to do with mind-set, a philosophy, and a level of paddling maturity when it comes to assessing risk. All the training and spiffy gear and techniques are beside the point if the space above your neck is dangerous.

Jamie McEwan, a world-class boater with decades of experience and a survivor of a Tibetan expedition on which one of his companions died in huge whitewater, used a quotation from Yoga practice to summarize his take on the safety issue. "People get hurt through greed and impatience," he said. Greed and impatience. Not what you'd expect as safety advice, and not nearly so tangible as rope and pulley diagrams, but he gets to the core with those two words. "My mark of a mature and safe paddler is a person who is willing to walk around a rapid when everyone else in the party is set on running it," McEwan added.

Charlie Walbridge, paddling safety guru with the American Whitewater Affiliation, adds another bit of safety pith: "Fear of the water is the beginning of wisdom."

I've talked with a lot of cutting-edge boaters, people who make first descents, who paddle rapids I'd never go near, who drop off waterfalls on purpose. When I ask them about safety, they keep returning to these intangible factors. They talk about paying attention to their intuition, tuning in to the group energy on a given day, looking at the entire picture—how cold it is, how tired people are, what the least skilled member of the group is capable of, how accessible a route is to help, what clothes people are wearing.

This is not to say that the rudiments of safety protocol should be abandoned. It goes without saying that people should be wearing life vests, that a throw bag should be along on a whitewater trip, that provisions for remoteness should be considered (see pages 137–39), that paddlers should think through rescue techniques and practice them. But the important issues and choices are the ones that hinge on these more nebulous safety frontiers, the murky terrain made up of ambition and greed and competitive drive and laziness. When paddlers get to some point of clarity and maturity in that landscape, much of the safety discussion becomes moot.

Easy to say, but as hard to make real as convincing your teenage daughter how dangerous it is to drive a car. My safety judgment has been honed though several decades of decisions and consequences. Along the way I've made a handful of pretty bad choices. I've been lucky enough to live through them, and the fact that I made most of them fairly early in my boating experience gives me hope that I might have learned something from them. Each of those bad moments on the water revealed some truth about paddling judgment. In every instance the danger could have been avoided by being smarter, less greedy, or more patient.

LESSON 1: SCOUT, DON'T POUT

I've written about this event often enough that the account has gained a certain notoriety in small circles. Suffice it to say that Kris and I were out for a fall day on the Rio Grande in New Mexico, along the border of Bandelier National Monument. We had already run the most difficult rapid on the route; we'd stopped for lunch and a quick dip in the river, and we were paddling on downriver without the burden of clothes, feeling pretty free and cocky.

One final riffle faced us before we hit the flatwater. It was a minor rapid that I'd run before in a raft and at different water levels. When we approached I stood up in the stern to have a look. I thought I could see the usual V to shoot for, and when Kris asked "Do you think we should scout?" I overwhelmed her sensible suggestion with the authority of my experience. I didn't want to stop again. We'd just gotten back in the boat after lunch. The rapid was no big deal.

But the rapid was different at that water level. As we came near, I saw that the chute I'd picked was littered with boulders and that the V would funnel us right into a maze of rocks. In that disintegrating interlude of paddling coordination, we tried to ferry away from danger but lost our rhythm,

SAFETY GEAR

Safety is mostly a matter of mental attitude. But a short list of gear, and some practice using it, is not only prudent but may make the difference in a crucial situation down a river somewhere in your expedition future.

Spray cover. I've discussed the importance of a fabric deck on expeditions (see pages 175–76), but it bears mention here as well. Spray decks minimize the threat of swamping in waves, both in rapids and on open water. Spray covers keep your gear dry and safe in stormy weather. And a deck keeps paddlers warm and dry in hypothermia weather. If I had to pick a single safety measure that makes the most all-around difference on wilderness trips, it's the deck, without question.

Throw bag. Carry a throw bag/rescue rope. To begin with, extra rope comes in handy in all sorts of ways, even if it's just to dry clothes on. You may need a long and durable length of rope to retrieve a canoe from a rock or aid in a tricky bit of lining. And you may even need to use the throw bag to rescue a swimming partner. Practice throwing the bag back and forth on land, from various distances, to get used to its heft. Try to slightly overthrow your target. Then practice throwing and catching the rope in moving water. On expeditions, any time you chose to run a rapid at the edge of your ability, station a person with a throw bag at the bottom, ready to go into rescue mode.

(continued next page)

Throw bag downstream of and beyond swimmer, where they'll drift to it. Wrap rope end around your waist in a belay stance and anchor yourself with good footing. Once the swimmer has hold of the throw bag, allow him or her to pendulum into shore, to an eddy, if possible.

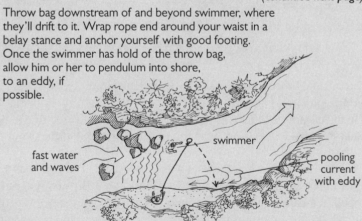

fast water and waves

swimmer

pooling current with eddy

Overthrow the victim and then hang on as they pendulum into shore.

(continued from previous page)

Pulleys. I carry a few carabiners that I can use to construct a pulley system, but you can also buy pulleys for rescue purposes. It's rare that you'll need them, but when you do, nothing else will serve.

Emergency locating transmitter. (See page 137.)

Small survival kit. (See pages 138, 139.)

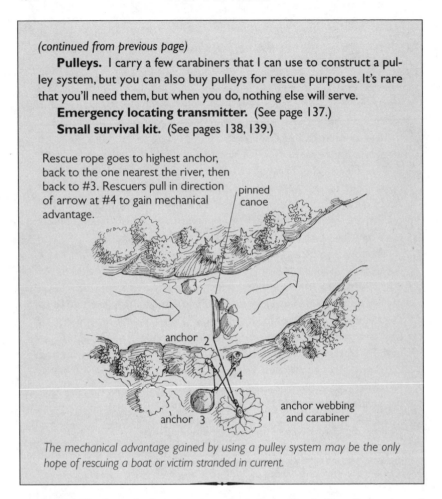

Rescue rope goes to highest anchor, back to the one nearest the river, then back to #3. Rescuers pull in direction of arrow at #4 to gain mechanical advantage.

pinned canoe

anchor 2

4

anchor 3

anchor webbing and carabiner

1

The mechanical advantage gained by using a pulley system may be the only hope of rescuing a boat or victim stranded in current.

got broadside, broached against a rock, and capsized. (See discussion of scouting technique, pages 84–85.)

In the ensuing moments I was able to scramble to the top of one boulder and Kris made her way to the top of another one, but the canoe was stuck fast.

The bad news was that the boat was pinned hard. The good news was that the hull was lodged against two boulders and badly creased, but not wrapped in a hairpin around a single obstacle. The good news was that I could get into the water upstream of the canoe and get solid leverage under the hull. The bad news was that the canoe was full of the river and my most Herculean efforts didn't even budge it. The good news was that when it became clear the boat was pinned irretrievably, we realized that we were near a trail that led to the Visitors' Center at Bandelier National Monument. The bad news was that all our clothes had washed out of the boat and floated downstream and that we'd be walking that trail in tennis shoes and visors.

I'll leave us there, stranded and sunburned, midriver. If you want to know how the story ended, you'll just have to read more of my books. The lesson is that with a brief scout we could have identified the easy run and been on our way without incident. Rest assured that Kris hammered this lesson home repeatedly and vehemently as the day went on.

LESSON 2: NEVER LET DESIRE
OVERWHELM YOUR BETTER JUDGMENT

This lesson applies to mountain climbing, alpine skiing, surfing, and teenage driving as well as to canoeing. It has to do with the very human tendency to color judgment with desire and ambition, and it gets back to McEwan's sage advice about greed and impatience.

Marypat and I were a week into a monthlong expedition in northern Québec. We'd been working our way down a tributary to the main river we would canoe. The water was lower than expected, so working is the right term. Much of our time had been spent dragging the boat down shallow rapids and bumping our way over riffles. It was raining when we approached the next formidable whitewater.

We stopped to scout, having learned that much. The river poured through a narrow cleft in the bedrock, two hundred yards of pretty gnarly water full of sharp rocks. A portage trail led around on river left. We walked down the boggy path, tormented by black flies the entire way, and thought about what fun it would be to make two carries, burdened with heavy gear, to avoid the rapid.

Then we went to look again. The rapid was just as gnarly on second glance, but there did seem to be a fairly straightforward line through it. If we got bumped off course or encountered hidden obstacles, we'd be in big trouble. Northern Québec is remote enough that about the last thing you'd ever want would be to get stranded there without a boat to paddle. We were alone.

Still, the more we looked, the more we thought it could be done. And the more onerous the portage trail loomed in our thoughts. For about five minutes we passed the buck back and forth. "What do you think?" "Geez, I don't know, looks possible but marginal. What do you think?" "Well, we might be able to do it. If we don't, though, it'll be a bummer." "Yeah. So, what do you think?" "Wow, the bugs are bad here aren't they! What do you think we should do?" Like that.

Somewhere one of us said something vaguely decisive and the other one went along and suddenly we were back in the canoe setting up. About ten yards into the fast water I was pleading with the river gods for mercy. Let us get through this one and I'll never do anything this dumb again, I kept thinking. The water was every bit as bad as it looked from the bank, and then some. The rocks, which we encountered regularly and at speed, were every bit as jagged as we'd thought. The clean line was actually a bumpy, frightening ride. The next unforgettable fifteen seconds dragged on for at least three days.

By the grace of the river deities, low water, and our Royalex hull, we banged our way down to the bottom in one shaky piece. "Man, are we lucky!" Marypat breathed.

"Man, were we stupid," I added.

LESSON 3: WHEN IN DOUBT, STICK TO SHORE (ALSO LESSON 2, ENCORE)

My first extended Canadian canoe expedition, many years ago. Two boats, four days in, navigating a series of lakes on our way to the major river we would spend the next few weeks descending.

It was midafternoon when we came out of a small river channel that connected two big lakes and assessed the bay in front of us. It was breezy, but not terribly windy. Straight across the bay, a mile distant, lay the opposite shore, tantalizingly close. The shortcut would save us what looked like considerable time and distance. After a short discussion, we cinched our life jackets tight, dropped to our knees in the canoes, and started paddling across.

The farther from shore we got, the bigger the waves seemed, and the stronger the wind felt. We paddled grimly, angling into the waves, adjusting to the biggest swells, feeling the pulse of the lake through the hull. Halfway across, just as the far shore began to look close and secure, I looked up and saw our companion canoe turtled over, our partners flailing in the frigid water, packs full of gear and food bobbing around them.

By the time we paddled up to them, they had already tried repeatedly to right their boat and bail, but the waves were too big and the canoe kept filling and capsizing. Our partners started towing the packs full of our essential gear and food over to us. One by one we took the waterlogged packs in, getting lower and lower in the water ourselves with every one. It never occurred to me that we wouldn't have the capacity to take people as well, but with the extra load, there was no way to get people aboard.

Hastily we decided to race to shore, dump gear, and come back for our comrades. The two of them stroked back to their foundered boat, draped themselves as much as possible out of the chilling water and held hands.

Barely afloat, desperate for speed, terrified of capsizing ourselves, we paddled for shore. The rest of that day became the most prolonged and gripping flirtation with death in the wilderness I have ever experienced. By the time we returned our partners were nearly dead with the cold. We still had to haul them out of the water and into our canoe in the midst of a welter of three- and four-foot waves. We had to get them to shore, strip them out of their clothes, half carry them into the forest. We had to strip ourselves and climb into sleeping bags, where for hours we hugged our friends' cold blue bodies until they finally revived. (See pages 70–71 for discussion of hypothermia.)

They recovered. We went on, sobered and cautious, to complete the trip. And we learned things we have never forgotten since:

1. We should never have attempted the crossing to begin with. Close scrutiny of the map would have revealed that following shoreline added only a mile to our distance, perhaps half an hour of extra paddling, hardly worth the risk on a windy day.

2. We should have had gear tied into the boats. If we had, we wouldn't have been tempted to take gear before people, and we would have been free of the fear of losing precious equipment and food. (See page 116.)

3. We should have had fabric spray covers (see pages 175–76). If that canoe had been decked, it never would have swamped.

4. Canoe self-rescues and canoe over canoe rescues look pretty slick in diagrams, and they even work pretty well playing around on a calm day, but in big waves and exposed water they're of marginal use.

I'll stop there, but you see what I'm getting at. Every one of those scenarios could have been avoided by above-the-neck paddling maturity. Safety devices (with the exception of a spray cover) had nothing to do with either the problems or the solutions.

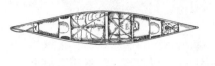

TWENTY-TWO

First Aid

Traditional urban first-aid instruction always ends with the same comforting final step: call for help. Treat for shock. Apply direct pressure to a bleeding wound. Clear the airway. Call for help. Help, it is assumed, is always three minutes and a 911 call away. Even the more advanced, EMT-level training falls prey to the "call for an ambulance" advice once an accident victim has received fairly minimal and immediate assistance.

So what happens when there's no phone to dial 911, and even if there were, help is three days away? I'm not about to pretend to be a wilderness first-aid instructor, but I have some advice for prevention-oriented wilderness travel and some suggestions for supplies that will help get you through the more prolonged response time once you go for help.

PREVENTION

Get some training that goes beyond the usual Red Cross town course. There are a number of Wilderness First Responder courses and backcountry first-aid classes that take the discussion beyond the sidewalk and backyard to settings that are remote and rugged. Courses should cover topics like extended care and treatment, search and rescue, evacuation techniques, and wilderness safety hazards. (See appendix 2.)

Do things to stay healthy in the wilderness. Floss your teeth every day, eat well, drink plenty of water, take vitamin supplements. I've even heard of people who have had their appendixes removed before a long expedition or have had wisdom teeth out to prevent those potentially trip-ending problems. That's probably not necessary for shorter journeys, but if you're off for a year, or going long-term to primitive parts of the world, it's something to consider. Physical and dental exams are certainly prudent before a prolonged journey.

In the field, factor remoteness into every decision. A trip far from help automatically raises the whitewater rating scale a class, for example.

Rather than concentrating on complicated river rescue training featuring things like Z-drag rope systems, work on more basic techniques and experiences that in the end tend to be more useful and instructive. For example, practice swimming in current with your gear on to really get a feel for what the water is doing. Get out the throw bag and practice heaving it to someone in the water, then switch places and see what it's really like to catch the rope and get hauled in.

Everything else aside, a three-canoe trip is the safest scenario. If there's trouble, one canoe can paddle for help while another stays to tend injuries, or two paddlers can duff in the extra boats if a canoe gets lost or irreparably damaged. If you go solo, or even as a two-boat team, that decision has to influence the judgment equation as well.

Be very cautious about open water crossings. They are more dangerous, in my mind, than rapids ever are. Stick to shore if the wind is up, despite the added distance. Capitalize on the times of day that tend to be calm—before dawn and at twilight—to make crossings (see pages 68–69).

On tough stretches of water, keep canoes close enough together to respond to difficulty, and designate lead and sweep canoes with the most experienced paddlers.

Approach water as if every trip were a first descent. Different water levels, new obstacles in the river channel, changed weather, and new group makeup are all ingredients that make even familiar routes surprising and challenging.

Pay attention to the energy of the group. Even if you and your partner are solid and confident, others may be paddling at the edge of their ability, or may be fatigued, or might be shivering with cold, or could be operating more on bravado than skill. If the group energy feels strained or dangerous, take the cautious option.

Listen to your intuition. There are times when everything seems objectively good but there's a niggling voice of doubt whispering in the background. Pay attention. That little whisper is always worth listening to.

WILDERNESS FIRST-AID KIT

Most often it's some maddening little thing that needs treatment. Someone gets whacked in the eye by a tree branch on a portage. A fly bite turns into an infected abscess. Someone on the trip has an allergic reaction to peanut

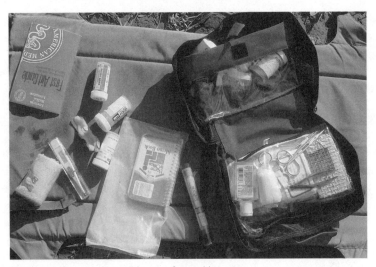

Contents of a complete wilderness first-aid kit.

butter. It's rare that accidents are sensational, like a broken leg or a grizzly attack. The essential things to remember in putting together a backcountry first-aid kit are that you are self-sufficient and may have to deal with all manner of unexpected maladies and that it may be a prolonged wait before you get outside medical attention.

My most complete first-aid kit was assembled when Marypat and I took our first yearlong expedition across Canada. A three-day jaunt won't require nearly the level of supplies we packed along, so adjust the list accordingly. The irony is that, even on trips that last for months on end, that bulky first-aid kit you have to wrestle across portages hardly ever comes out except for the odd Band-Aid. All well and good. When the day arrives that you really do need it, you'll be mighty grateful it's loaded in the pack.

Extended Trip Supplies

- complete wilderness first-aid manual (I like *Medicine for Mountaineering*, but there are a number of good wilderness first-aid books available)
- pencil or pen and notebook: it's important to keep a treatment record of any serious health problem
- Band-Aids (lots if kids are along!)
- adhesive tape
- gauze pads
- razor or scalpel
- scissors

- tweezers (may be the most commonly used first-aid tool)
- roller gauze
- splint material (inflatable splint or wire mesh)
- eye patch and eyewash (eye injuries are surprisingly common)
- thermometer
- elastic bandage
- safety pins
- sunscreen or zinc oxide
- sterile suture kit
- moleskin
- compress material (sanitary napkins can be handy for compresses)
- cravat bandage
- matches
- Steri-Strips (for closing wounds that might otherwise require stitches)
- a dental pick (for cleaning infected or abscessed gums)
- dental adhesive for short-term cavity repair (available in tubes)
- betadine wash for external wound cleaning
- antibacterial ointment
- aloe vera gel (good for sunburn, other burns, and general skin irritation)
- epinephrine shot kit for severe allergic reactions
- watch (not for an accurate time of day but to keep track of time elapsed during treatment and patient recovery, pulse and respiration rates, etc.)

Drugs

People should be responsible for bringing any personal drugs they are taking and should let the group know about ailments that require medication. When we've taken really long trips, we've consulted a doctor and gotten a selection of prescription drugs, with instructions for dosage, to cover common health problems. Our drug kit included prescription drugs to combat severe pain, allergic reactions, soft-tissue infections, diarrhea and constipation, urinary infections, and eye-ear-throat infections.

TWENTY-THREE

In Honor of Place: Trip Sanitation

We approach shore after a day of pristine paddling. Central Manitoba in September. Tamaracks wearing their golden fur, the wind blustery and invigorating, the sky that impossibly clear blue. There have been geese streaming south all day, talking at us from a thousand feet up. An otter popped up to watch us pass his eddy just before lunch. A moose crashed off into the forest at the edge of a quiet pond. A day full of the flaming season.

The spot we've chosen for camp is at the base of a frothing rapid. Smooth bedrock slopes down to the water. A grassy clearing extends back from shore. The site looks ideal. But when we draw near we see that we aren't the first to be attracted to the spot. Small trees have been hacked down, bits of garbage litter the ground with out-of-place splashes of color. When we get out to explore, it only gets worse. Cans and plastic lie everywhere. Several big fire pits are full of charred logs, tinfoil, and unburned scraps of food. There are rotting fish guts at the water's edge. When I walk back toward the forest, I find used toilet paper left on the ground.

It's a beautiful spot. Take away the garbage and scars and it's a place to cherish for the night, one of those camps to mark down on the map in case you ever come back. But we return to the boats and paddle away. No one says anything for a long time. The spell of the day has been choked off, and we end up settling on a marginal, but unused, campsite tucked into the bush a mile on.

Coming upon a camp like that in the midst of what you took for wild country is like finding graffiti at the altar of the Sistine Chapel. Nothing short of sacrilege. Rude and ignorant behavior in sacred places. A fouling of our communal nest. There is no excuse for it, no justification, and increasingly, no way we can afford the boorish luxury of mistreating the places we call home in the wilderness. There are too many of us to be leaving messes behind, and that patent disrespect for place is intolerable.

In town our garbage is hauled away to the dump. Our sewage flushes down the toilet. Our gray water goes down the drain. All the gritty, unpleasant refuse of life is whisked out of sight for someone else to deal with. In the wilderness, we are the garbage haulers and sanitation crews. It's our job to keep it clean, not simply for the next person who paddles up to that same spot on the shore but because it's the way we should act. Period.

End of sermon. Now for some guidance.

SEWAGE TREATMENT

Peeing and pooping in the woods is a problem. And the more people there are, the more of a problem it is. Appropriate strategies vary from peeing right into the rivers and pooping right on the ground to carting along enclosed toilet boxes and packing wastes out.

In the most remote settings, where people are few and campsites have time to recover between visitors, we can act much the way animals do. Pee well away from water sources and poop away from water and the camping area, either in shallow cat holes or exposed to the fast decomposition of air and moisture. A site has to be very little visited to warrant pooping right on the surface, but it's the fastest way to ensure decomposition. You can hasten the process even further if you smear feces around with a stick.

On trips through quiet and relatively untraveled terrain, and when campsites aren't being used for days on end, cat hole latrines are the best solution. Get well away from water (two hundred feet if possible), dig a shallow hole for each use, about four inches across and five or six inches deep, and cover up the excrement. Pee away from the water source and on unvegetated ground.

Traditional latrines made of deep trenches are hardly ever appropriate. The contents don't decompose, even over a period of years, and they become sites of point source pollution.

In heavily traveled areas, paddlers are increasingly required to pack out their solid wastes. RV suppliers and river raft companies sell enclosed toilets with sealed closures and comfortable seats that can be set up on the outskirts of camp, packed along throughout the trip, and then emptied at one of those sanitation dumps for recreational vehicles. Enclosed toilet systems start at roughly $150 for the simplest setups, often a large ammo can with seat attachment. Take along some bleach crystals or liquid bleach to add to the box after each use.

On big-volume rivers that see lots of traffic, especially in arid environments, travelers are counseled to pee right into the river. The urine is quickly diluted and does less harm as part of the watershed stream than it does on land. Although urine is sterile, on land it smells, attracts wildlife to salt residues, and harms vegetation. Western rivers like the Colorado and Green are places where paddlers are asked to overcome their entrenched aversion to peeing into the river.

Toilet paper is often as big a problem as the actual human waste. If you've ever stumbled upon wads of used paper hanging off the shrubbery and littering the ground, you know all about the gag reflex. Usually the actual wastes have long ago decomposed, but the disgusting paper lingers on. Use toilet paper sparingly, or find alternatives like large-leafed vegetation, soft moss, or smooth rocks. Whatever paper gets used should either be packed away with the garbage or burned thoroughly in the fire, not buried!

Put a bottle of biodegradable soap either in the kitchen area or next to the enclosed toilet to remind people to wash up before cooking or eating.

GARBAGE

Pack it in, pack it out. It's as simple as that, and any failure is laziness, nothing more or less. I'm always flabbergasted that people can pack in heavy canned food, gas containers, and cardboard boxes but can't take them back out when they're empty and light. They drop them on the ground and walk away. I don't get it.

Packing it out goes for everything. Used toilet paper, sanitary napkins, leftover food, and all the traditional garbage. Unless you can burn trash completely in a hot fire or can fob your garbage off on some unwitting passerby, it's yours to the end.

Garbage can be a major hassle, but you can go a long way toward limiting the amount of trash you'll be burdened with by packing smart. Get rid of cardboard boxes, glass containers, and sometimes even cans before you leave by packing supplies into plastic bags. Your garbage will consist of little more than a highly compressed wad of reusable plastic. Cook efficiently to reduce leftovers and wasted food. Burn your toilet paper and cardboard. I've spent fifty-day summers on the water and ended up with a trash bag smaller than my head!

Police your campsites before leaving to make sure you haven't left messes behind. Some garbage is really hard to keep track of. Broken matchsticks, rubber bands, and lengths of dental floss are elusive little buggers, and those twist-tie bag closures are notorious and ubiquitous campsite litter. Close bags with knots or use sealable closures instead.

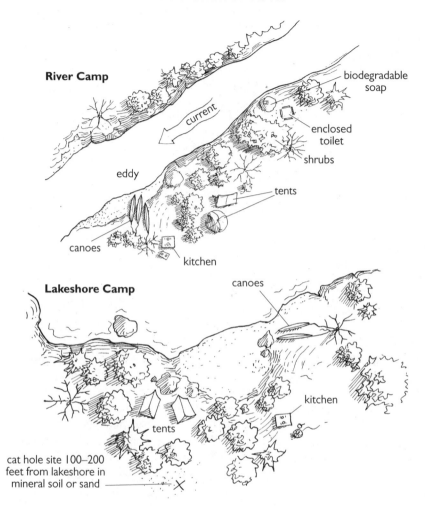

Choose appropriate bathroom sites for different camp situations.

GRAY WATER

Dirty dishwater and cleaning water should be disposed of at some distance from the water source (100 to 200 feet) in a small cat hole sump clear of vegetation. Bring along a flat screen (available in discount stores in the housewares department) to cover the pot and strain out bits of food from the water. Those bits can either be burned or added to the trash bag.

Along big-water desert rivers where peeing into the river is the norm, screen the gray water right into the river as well, where it will be diluted by the current.

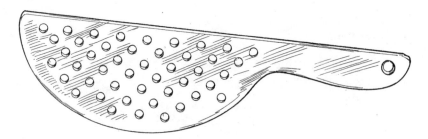

Use a sieve or screen to stop food bits form dumping out with gray water.

BATHING AND LAUNDRY

On short trips don't worry about washing up with soap or doing your laundry. You'll get a good shower when you get out, and in the meantime make do with dips in the lake. Who needs to smell like shampoo and perfume in the boonies anyway?

On longer trips, or if you're a chronic clean freak, carry a pot of cleaning water one hundred to two hundred feet from the water source and rinse out small laundry like underwear and bandannas. Get rid of laundry water the same way you would dishwater.

For washing hair or bodies, use the buddy system. Bring along a pot of water for the soap and rinse cycles and take turns dousing each other. On an in-the-river trip, use biodegradable soap and bathe right in the water or on the damp sand along the bank. Otherwise, stay clear of vegetation.

A solar shower is a great way to clean up with warm water. Fill the bag in the morning, drape it on the boat or in a sunny spot around camp during the day, and hang it from a tree branch for warm bathing in the evening. Find a private spot well away from camp if modesty is a concern, and hang the shower over unvegetated ground (or right next to the water on those pee-in-the-river jaunts). Solar showers are a good lesson in water conservation, too. You can get two people clean and shampooed with two to three gallons of water.

Consider brushing without toothpaste on shorter trips. It's the brushing that does the good, not the minty toothpaste. In any case, use unflavored brands and don't glob toothpaste onto vegetation or near camp. Walk off a ways, scrape a hole in the ground, and spit into it. Some people advocate the forceful-spray-spit method to disperse toothpaste, but I can't get over how foolish I look doing it, so I cling to the scraped-ground technique.

Solar shower camp comfort.

DRINKING WATER

Much of the world's water, and more all the time, is unfit to drink without treatment. Even the clearest mountain streams are laced with nasty concentrations of *Giardia lamblia, Cryptosporidium, Entamoeba histolytica,* and other bugs capable of bringing on dysentery, abdominal cramps, and diarrhea. I admit that I'll dip up and drink directly from streams in places like northern Canada, and sometimes from springs and sidestreams that I'm confident of, but on more civilized trips it isn't worth the risk.

The most foolproof way to ensure safe drinking water is to bring it from home. On trips that don't require much portaging, and if room allows, you can supply yourself with drinking water in large containers for up to a week. (Hard-shell five-gallon jugs are great, but difficult to pack around. Collapsible plastic containers come in two-and-a-half- or five-gallon varieties. Rinsed-out bladders from boxed wine are surprisingly rugged too.) Boil river water for cleaning and cooking when possible, and conserve the good stuff for drinking. I figure on about half a gallon per person per day, sometimes less if the weather isn't scorching.

If you use river water to drink, however, you'll need to take measures to purify it. Start by getting water from the cleanest sources possible. Find short tributaries, for example, or springs, which aren't as silty or prone to pollution as the main stream. During a rain you can use a pot to collect water dripping off the rain fly.

Next to bringing water from home, the best way to get pure water is boiling. Bring water to a boil and you've taken care of the bad guys. If you can afford the fuel, boil for a minute or two to be certain of even the most stubborn critters.

Iodine, in either liquid or tablet form, is another time-tested water treatment method. Let treated water sit for half an hour to make sure it's done

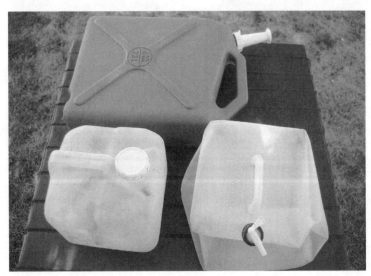

A variety of water containers.

the job, and flavor drinking water with drink crystals to mask the taste. The bad news is that *Cryptosporidium* critters aren't fazed by iodine. If they're the culprits, only boiling or filtration will do.

Water filters have come a long way in evolving lightweight and trouble-free designs. They still cost more than they should and require maintenance and replacement filters, but they do a good job of filtering out the vast majority of nasties. For long trips, buy a spare filter element and familiarize yourself with cleaning and maintenance techniques appropriate for your brand. If the water is silty, let it settle in a pot or bucket before you pump. Sediment will clog a filter quicker than you can say dysentery.

Even the most minute filter screens won't get some members of the viral community. Those tiny buggers wiggle right on through. Viral pollution is relatively uncommon, especially in more remote locations, but in more populated areas the only way to really be sure of sterile drinking water is to bring it from home or boil it.

Water filters are cumbersome but often necessary.

TWENTY-FOUR

Keeping Group Morale Afloat

O n the first day of the trip all six of us agreed to put our watches away or leave them behind. We'd travel by the sun, make our days up out of miles traveled, shoulder weariness, hunger, weather. We had the lingering daylight of midsummer to work with and an abiding desire to leave behind the civilized metronome that ordered the rest of our lives.

Only one person elected to bring her watch along. She'd stow it away in her ammo box, she said. It would be important to have a watch in case of an accident. Even if she peeked once in a while, she'd keep it to herself. OK, whatever.

For the first week we worked our way across some large lakes, over a six-portage drainage divide, and onto the main river we'd follow to the trip's end. We were on schedule, had met some of the journey's biggest physical challenges, and were doing just fine without knowing what precise time of day it was.

Most of us felt absolutely freed by our watchlessness. Within a day or two we realized how unnecessary watches were, that we could organize our days just fine by looking at the sun, reading the weather, and checking the maps to see if we were keeping to our mileage average. All of us, it turned out, except Joan, who was checking her watch pretty regularly.

The morning of day 9 was sunny and warm. Most of us slept in later than usual, then dawdled through breakfast. Joan had been up for hours. The day was well along by the time we finally got packed up. Big deal, we could paddle till dusk if we really needed to. But Joan couldn't stand it.

"Look," she exploded. "I know we aren't supposed to know what time it really is, but do you realize how long it has taken to get going this morning? It is almost eleven o'clock already!" To her the idea of lingering in camp until nearly lunchtime was appalling. She saw us slipping inexorably into a more and more lax style. Pretty soon we'd just hang in camp all day. Then we'd run into a patch of bad weather and get really behind schedule. Good Lord, eleven o'clock!

The rest of us looked at each other a bit sheepishly. Eleven in the morning did seem a bit sluggish. But we were perfectly capable of an early morning start if conditions warranted. Weren't we?

Joan's concern about time, and the group attitude, spread to a more general anxiety over our trip pace. Positions within the group polarized over the days until some people always assumed a laid-back attitude to combat Joan's fretting. One or two tried to bridge the gap and accommodate both camps. Conflict simmered just below the surface, erupting over discussions of when to camp, how far to go before lunch, whether to get an early start and beat the winds. What began as a simple difference in personal style and preference grew into a fairly profound clash.

By the end of three weeks together we were all still friends, but it was a pretty strained partnership much of the time, and a couple of us would be reluctant to go on another long trip together.

Problems within groups on wilderness trips are bound to occur. What other situations in life require us to be together twenty-four hours a day, facing physical stress, bad weather, dangerous waves or rapids along with mosquitoes, sleeping on the ground, eating less than fantastic food, and wrangling over myriad daily decisions? War is about the only condition I can think of that rivals wilderness trips for sheer unrelieved companionship under adversity.

Even marriages have breaks. We go off to work, take trips separately, work out at the gym, socialize with other friends, go to movies. No wonder wilderness trips make and break relationships. When you think about it, it's a wonder anyone ever comes back friends.

Despite the lurking potential for interpersonal strain, about the last thing anyone wants on a trip is daily rounds of feel-good group sensitivity sessions or pop psychology and psychobabble. Group solidarity is all well and good, but give me a break. Lighten up, okay?

So let's try for something in the middle. Believe me, capsized relationships in the heart of a trip are no fun, even for the bystanders. We go to the wilds to escape stress, not to be ambushed by it. Let's try for sensitivity without being cloying, honesty without encounter-group obsessiveness, and companionship at the same time that we let each other breathe. And let's be realistic. Conflicts under duress are bound to happen. Meet them when they do and then get past them.

I AIN'T NO PSYCHOLOGIST, BUT HERE'S WHAT I DO

Talk about trip goals and ambitions early on, and update the discussion as things unfold. Get together for dinner before you head off to the blank spaces on the map to talk over what everyone wants out of the trip. Is relaxation key for some? How about getting in shape? Bird-watching? Day hikes? Time to sketch and write in a journal? If people have a true sense of what motivates everyone else, they can prepare themselves to adapt and fit their own goals into the picture. If some expectations seem destined to clash, talk about compromises and strategies to satisfy both.

Periodically it may be wise to check in as the trip unfolds. Perhaps some goals will shift, or people will get into another facet of wilderness living they hadn't expected to look for. More likely the daily round will create situations that require negotiation and discussion to ensure that both individual needs and group harmony stay on track.

These discussions don't have to be formal or heavy-handed. Half an hour after lunch on a gravel bar while everyone basks in the sun. A couple of questions thrown out around the campfire some evening. The critical thing is that everyone recognize the range of expectations within the group and that, once recognized, those idiosyncratic goals be respected.

Be honest. If something bothers you, bring it up. It isn't easy to point out conflict or an annoying habit, but then it's out in the open and can be dealt with. Better that than to have unexpressed frustration fester and grow. Now, don't confuse honesty with brutal and tactless confrontation. There are ways of being up-front, and there are ways of being an obnoxious jerk. Know what I mean?

Nip it in the bud. If it becomes clear that some tension is developing between group members, talk about it early and work on coping strategies. Most of the time, simply recognizing the problem and paying some attention to it seems to do away with it.

Keep your sense of humor. Two weeks into the boonies is no time to get uptight and serious.

Respect personal space. Most of the time on a trip is spent together. We eat, sleep, paddle, portage, set up tents, cook food, and read maps together. Make sure you take some time out, and respect everyone else's need for the same. Take a little walk, sit by the river, snap some pictures, write in your journal, read a book, go fishing. Those little solitary windows, even when you don't think you need them, are incredibly refreshing.

Recognize strengths and weaknesses. The group member who couldn't portage a canoe if his life depended on it might also be the one who can cook up a quiche from heaven in the Dutch oven. Someone who drops something in the water every single time she loads a boat might also be a gifted map reader who keeps you from making a six-mile route choice mistake. And rest assured, you may think of yourself as the well-rounded, complete trip personality, but something you do is driving somebody else in the crowd crazy.

If conflicts won't go away, change the equation. Switch bow and stern paddlers, switch canoe partners, make somebody new the day's map reader, change tentmates, rotate cooking partners. A little variety in the way the days run is probably healthy to begin with, and if conflicts are brewing, shifting the dynamics might turn down the heat.

COMMON CLASHES

Besides the abrasion that results from individual chemistry, which is beyond my capacity for advice, the single most frequent source of trip tension rises out of simple, and often pretty minor, conflicts in pace and travel style.

One person is an early riser, another a morning slug-a-bed. One person insists on a somewhat militaristic adherence to daily routine, another is spontaneous and easygoing. One canoe partnership likes to get the day's mileage in early, another likes to linger through the distance and get the most out of it. People have adamant ideas, sometimes about quirky stuff— how to pitch camp, when to get going, how food gets prepared, how to fold the maps, the way packs should be loaded . . .

Strange to think these little differences in style would loom large, but they do. It's far more likely that group dynamics will run aground over something like when the morning wake-up call should be than over any actual dislike between people.

Flexibility is key in these cases. Compromise simply has to occur to keep group morale and interaction from unraveling. Take turns with the wake-up time if it's so important. Negotiate a compromise, talk it out, make jokes out of it.

Planning flexibility into the actual trip schedule is also key. If the trip deadline is absolute and distances are tight, you're almost guaranteed some problems. It's a bummer to have to hurry through the wilderness. If anything, give yourself extra days. The worst that can happen is you'll get back a bit early; you might have spare time to relax and have fun on the trail.

SOME SILLINESS GOES A LONG WAY

- Celebrate birthdays, anniversaries, life transitions. I've been on trips where people have carried cake mixes, party hats, and noise-makers over fifteen portages.

- Allocate each trip member a $5 secret treat assignment. At points in the journey when morale is low, the weather is nasty, or you just want a lift, make it a treat night. Artichoke hearts, a pint of brandy, gag gifts. Silly but uplifting.
- Bring a few games along. Miniature Scrabble, cribbage, a deck of cards. I've had windbound days pass much more quickly because of a rousing game of euchre.
- Establish a group journal that rotates each evening. People can write a paragraph or two about the day, or sketch a picture if they like. It can also be a good way to keep track of the day's logistics—weather, wildlife sightings, mileage, portages, and so on.
- Bring a small musical instrument, even if you can't play well. Harmonicas and recorders are pleasant and easy to carry.
- Bring a book to read out loud as a group. Perhaps a volume about local history or an explorer's journal.
- On a long day of paddling (like crossing a big lake in flat calm), think up a discussion question to help while away the time. Who were the most influential people in your life? What's the most regrettable thing you've ever done, the most embarrassing, the thing you're most proud of? What would you do if you were told you'd die in a year? How would you spend a million dollars? I've been in groups where the discussion question becomes an anticipated element in the daily routine.

PART FOUR

OUTFITTING

TWENTY-FIVE

Gear That Changed My Life

When it comes to outdoor equipment, I fall somewhere between a minimalist and a Luddite. My heroes are the adventurers who hike thousands of miles in tennis shoes and sleep under tarps. I still like wool and goose down and leather and Dutch ovens. Successful expeditions, in my experience, have a great deal more to do with state of mind than with state-of-the-art equipment.

Besides, if you fall prey to the seduction of outdoor equipment geekism, you'll soon be working an extra job to keep up with the latest trends and spending all your precious extra time shopping for, maintaining, and reading up on your outfit and working overtime to afford it. Most of the newest and greatest "got to have it" outdoor gear is fluff that nobody needs or gimmicks that sound spiffy as all get-out on the sales floor but then gather dust in your gear closet because they either don't work or aren't even remotely necessary.

Once in a great while a genuine equipment breakthrough comes along that makes me think two things. First, damn, why didn't I think of that! And second, I won't ever again go off paddling without one of those. It's rare, but it happens. In some three decades of paddling experience, it's happened to me about five times.

Even here, though, beware of the inevitable creeping greed inherent in the capitalist system. Once a manufacturer gets hold of a breakthrough, the next phase is to churn out all manner of spinoffs that nobody needs. Pretty soon you'll be regaled with thinner, lighter, more waterproof, less slippery, more comfortable, and inevitably, more expensive, variations on the original. Stick with the basic breakthrough article.

GEAR I HAVE TO HAVE
Bent-Shaft Paddles

The first canoe trip I took using bent-shaft paddles was in northern Québec. They were light, a little strange at first, shorter than I was used to, and I wasn't entirely sure which way the blade should face. Fortunately the company logo, a kind of idiot prompt, was on the front face, so I got around that.

We liked the paddles almost right away. They seemed efficient, and our backs and shoulders felt less fatigued at the end of a long day on the water. We didn't know how truly great they were until we met a couple of guys from Montréal and traveled with them for several days. They had all the latest gear—lightweight boat, customized spray cover, brand-new packs—but they had little better than wooden clubs to paddle with. They couldn't figure out how the two of us, in our much heavier craft, consistently stayed ahead of them.

"You ever seen these bent-shaft paddles before?" I asked them one afternoon.

"We heard about them, I guess, but they didn't seem worth it."

"Want to trade for a bit?" I asked.

We handed over the light, short bent paddles in exchange for the heavy straight-shaft boards they were using. They took a few strokes. Within half a minute their faces had assumed that pained, envious, inferior-gear-syndrome look. Suddenly they stopped.

"We have to give these back right now," the stern paddler said. "If we don't, you'll have to fight us for them."

At the time, all I knew was that the paddle had something to do with our cruising efficiency, and that I was less tired at the end of the day. It wasn't until later that I understood the mechanics of the bent-shaft breakthrough.

It's all about paddling economy. The simplest way to explain it is that the bend in the paddle shaft (commonly about 15 degrees), forces you into a more efficient stroke. The paddle automatically enters the water at the beginning of the power phase of your stroke and naturally exits at the end. Because you concentrate effort on the middle section of the traditional canoe stroke, you end up taking shorter strokes at a slightly faster pace than you do with a straight-shaft paddle. Add up thousands of shorter, more efficient strokes over a day, and it's no wonder your shoulders feel less sore.

In the old-style canoe stroke, the paddler reaches well out in front to plant the blade in the water, then pulls through in a long, steady rhythm that ends at some point well behind the hip. The problem is that the early part of that stroke is actually pushing the canoe up, out of the water. The middle part of the stroke, as the paddle blade comes past the torso, is the phase that gives power and pure forward momentum. The final part of the stroke is really pushing the canoe hull down in the water.

The bent-shaft design maximizes that middle—power—phase and does away entirely with the push-up, push-down elements of the traditional stroke. The result is more efficient cruising speed at less physical cost.

For some time I still preferred the straight-shaft paddle for sterning in whitewater. The pry stroke seemed awkward and less powerful with the bent-shaft paddle. Eventually, though, I got so I could use the bent shaft just as effectively in rapids, and these days I take a straight-shaft model along only as a kind of sentimental spare.

Fabric Spray Cover

If I had known about spray decks from the beginning, I wouldn't have nearly the fund of great near-death paddling stories to tell around the campfire. Nor would I have built up anything like the masochistic initiation dues I have from putting in dozens of wet, clammy, miserable days in canoes.

It takes about a minute to recognize the value of a spray deck on an expedition. You don't even have to get in the boat to realize what a great improvement it is over the undecked canoe.

First off, a decked boat is safer by a quantum leap. Most capsizes, especially on expeditions, are the result of swamping in large waves, either in a rapid or on an open lake. Waves come over the bow, or slurp

Traditional, straight-shaft paddle versus the bent-shaft design.

in from the side, until the canoe is a leaden, wallowing pig in the water. Capsize is almost inevitable. With decking in place, the waves wash right off and you can keep blithely on or get to shore in safety.

Second, the deck keeps you and your gear snug and dry. Load up for the day, snap on the deck, slip into the cockpit skirt, and you're as dry and comfortable as a duck. The packs and the rest of your equipment aren't sitting in a puddle of rainwater or getting periodically soaked by waves. Even in a downpour, as long as you've got rain gear on your upper body, you'll be as dry and content as possible on a gray day. The trips I took with wet, gritty gear and hypothermic paddling interludes are ancient history, gone for good the moment I found my first spray deck.

There are several spray deck designs to choose from, with all sorts of bells and whistles, zippered compartments, Velcroed sections, and cunning storage pockets. As you'd expect, I prefer the simple one-piece, no-frills model (directions for making your own are on pages 180–84). When the weather is nice and the water calm, we paddle with the middle section snapped in place over the gear and the ends rolled up underneath. If the weather deteriorates or waves come up, we roll out the ends, pull the cockpit skirts over our heads, and snap the bow and stern sections down.

Folding Chair

There were days in camp when I would have traded my canoe and everything in it for a comfortable backrest. And I've chosen camps for the sole attribute of having a log, rock, or stump that formed a natural backrest. Lack of a backrest must have done in a significant percentage our prehistoric ancestors, or at least crippled them.

Decked tandem expedition canoe.

I recognized the value of the folding camp chair the moment I saw one. I don't mean the aluminum backyard variety. I mean the lightweight, slightly padded, sit-on-the-ground models. They fold flat, pack well, add very little weight to the load, and double as extra cushioning on the canoe seat. In a pinch they even do for a kid's sleeping pad when laid flat. I've gotten to the point where I drag my chair up to the lunch spot, haul it out for map-reading breaks, and carry it along on day hikes.

They're worth every penny, which is more than I can say for all the permutations of these chairs that have come along since. Extra padding, canoeing backrests, blah, blah. Stick with the basic one.

Inflatable Sleeping Pads

You know the kind. Not the blow-up air mattresses our parents took camping to lay out inside the canvas umbrella tent. Not the old closed-cell foam pads that made you feel so spartan and pure, not to mention bruised and sore every morning.

You know. Those self-inflating backpacking pads everyone uses now, and with good reason. They actually work. They aren't, however, really self-inflating. I always need to add some air even if the pad's been lying out for hours. But once inflated, if they don't yet have a pinhole air leak, they're the best thing for sleeping outdoors since the sleeping bag. Turn and toss on uncomfortable ground no longer. Wake up cold and shivery never again. You can sleep on a set of janitor's keys and never know it.

On several trips I've paddled shoreline where the camping options consisted of cobble beaches, bare bedrock, or impenetrable bush. With the inflatable sleeping pad, no problem. Precambrian quartzite, marble-sized beach rock, lumpy root systems . . . slumber on.

The biggest drawback to these great additions to the equipment list is that they will eventually spring a tiny leak that will be very difficult to find. Take along a patch kit and hope you can find yours. If you can't, send it back for the manufacturer to find it once you get back. Truth is, even a leaky mattress will be more comfortable than the old foam pads ever were.

Cast-Aluminum Dutch Oven

Eating is really important, and eating well in the boonies is the most underrated contributing factor to group happiness, trip safety, and general harmony. In the pursuit of eating well in the wilds I've done some serious experimentation. I've packed along lightweight pressure cookers, reflector ovens, and an astonishing variety of pots, pans, and mess kits.

The single most stunning success in my quest for trailside culinary excellence has been the discovery of the cast-aluminum Dutch oven. I knew all along that Dutch ovens were great cook pots, but I wasn't willing to lug along the killing weight of the traditional cast-iron models. Sometime midway through my paddling career I found a cast-aluminum version. It weighs a fraction as much as the iron version, cooks every bit as efficiently, cleans up with ease, and doubles as a regular pot for boiling water and other cooking.

With the Dutch oven almost anything is possible. Pizza, enchilada casserole, pie, yeast bread, quiche. It's still a tad heavy to backpack with, but for canoeing it's the best cook pot I've ever found.

Honorable Mention

Two pieces of camp gear didn't quite make the life-changing category but came close enough for credit.

Bug Jackets

In bug country (see pages 131–33) the mesh bug jacket is far and away the best strategy for coping with the insect denizens. They're woven mesh with

a very loose weave, incorporating strands of cotton that wick up insect repellent. You soak the jacket in repellent, let it ferment in a plastic bag for a day, then wear it. The long sleeves and hood make for complete upper body coverage. The thing really works. Better still, it means

Dutch ovens and cast-aluminum cookware are the keys to culinary excellence.

you only rarely, and sparingly, have to apply repellent directly to your skin. There are a number of brands available, and some are commonly available in buggy parts of the world. I've seen ankle gaiters and pants advertised too, but my experience has been that the jacket is the real key to comfort. (See photo of bug jacket on page 133.)

Self-Standing, Clip-Up Tents

Remember the days when you had to take turns getting dressed, the insides of tents were always clammy with condensation in the morning, and even a moderate wind would collapse your shelter on your face?

Tent design has come a long way. The two advances that had the most impact on my camping life were the self-standing dome design and the clip-up system for attaching the tent body to the frame. The dome makes for comfortable, roomy indoor living and creates tents that are by definition stable. The clip system has done away with the monotony of threading poles through sleeves and created tents that are fast to erect and tend to have better separation between the tent and the rain fly (hence less condensation and leakage). Finally, in a wind the air flows right up and over the tent without catching against the fabric baffles that used to contain the tent poles. Result—tents that are much more stable in winds. Not immune, mind you, but far superior.

The dome, clip-tent design.

MAKING AND INSTALLING YOUR OWN SPRAY DECK

I'm not going to lay this on you as if it's the easiest thing since closing a car door—just go make your deck and put it on, no big deal. I know better. I make a point of staying a comfortable distance away from sewing machines when at all possible. If you're like me, you might want to just go buy a spray deck, or hire someone who's handy with a sewing machine to make it. My strategy was to marry a seamstress.

In any case, if you decide to take this on, you'll want access to an industrial sewing machine. It's also really handy to have a long, open cutting table, since the deck requires nearly twenty feet of material. Still with me? Here we go.

MAKING THE DECK

1. Use heavy water-locked or waterproof material for the main deck. Four-hundred-denier pack cloth works well (the stuff good backpacks are made of). Bolts of material come in 60-inch widths, which will be plenty wide. A 17-foot canoe will require roughly 6 yards of material.

2. You may be able to buy material from a local manufacturer (tent maker, pack company, etc.). Inquire in your area to find the nearest distributor of bulk fabric.

3. Lay the material out on top of the canoe and tape down the ends to hold it in place. Make sure there's some slack lengthwise, or the deck will shrink up and be too snug on a hot day.

4. Mark all the way around the boat just below the gunwales. Now go back around adding another mark 4 inches below that. The lower outline will be your pattern. The extra 4 inches is the material that will be folded under to make the hem, still allowing you roughly 2 to 3 inches below the gunwale to set snaps in the hull.

5. Accurately mark the locations of thwarts and seats on the deck fabric, since you won't want your snaps to fall where there's a thwart or seat crosspiece. (The locations of the backs of the seats are important for marking cockpit holes later.)

6. Cut out the deck pattern with scissors or a hot gun.

7. On a flat surface, outline the cockpit holes. Start about an inch behind the back of each seat. The front of the holes should allow for knee room when seated (about 28 or 29 inches from back to

front). At the middle of the seat the holes are about 22 inches wide, making the cockpit slightly oblong. Depending on the taper of your boat hull, the width of the bow hole may vary. Check the marked hole against the taper of your hull, then cut out the holes and sear the edge of the material with a candle so it won't unravel.

8. Sew a hem 2 inches wide all the way around the decking.
9. Make the cockpit skirts and attach them to the holes in the deck (see instructions below).
10. Mark the spots in the hem of the deck where you want to put snaps. At the bow the snaps should be fairly closely spaced (8 to 10 inches). Toward the center and stern they can be 12 to 14 inches apart. A 17-foot canoe usually ends up with a total of 34 to 36 snaps. Make sure you note the locations of thwarts and seat cross-pieces and avoid placing snaps there.
11. Make small holes in the hem with a leather punch (or awl) at the snap marks. Set the female sides of the snaps in place with a snap-setter tool. Make sure you face the snaps toward the hull!

MAKING THE COCKPIT SKIRTS
BASIC DESIGN

1. Use much lighter fabric than for the main deck, approximately 200-denier cloth. You'll need 3 yards for a pair of skirts.
2. Cut out the pattern according to the illustration on page 183 and mark the center of the fabric, both top and bottom.
3. Measure down 5 inches from the top center mark and cut a slit.
4. Sear the bottom edge and the sides of the slit.
5. Roll the edges of the slit and sew in a narrow hem.
6. Take a square piece of webbing and sew it at the base of the slit using a box stitch. This will reinforce the fabric and keep it from ripping.
7. Sew the back in a covered (French) seam (wrong sides facing together first in a ¼-inch seam, then right sides facing together in a ½-inch seam).
8. Turn the top over to make a hem, or casing, 1 ¼ inches wide and sew the elastic cord inside (easier than threading it through later).
9. Put on the pull toggle. (continued next page)

MAKING AND INSTALLING
YOUR OWN SPRAY DECK

(continued from previous page)

10. Sew the skirts to the main deck, starting at the front center mark and sewing one way to within 4 inches of the back center mark, pulling and easing the material to make the fit exact. Then start again at front center and finish the skirt in the opposite direction to within 4 inches of the back center. Finally, sew down the last 8 inches in back, making any final adjustments.

11. Waterproof the seam with seam-seal goop where the skirt attaches to the deck.

DELUXE DESIGN

1. Follow steps 1 and 2 of the Basic Design.

2. Refer to the illustration and mark the placement for the webbing, Velcro, grommet, and top and bottom center marks.

3. Sear the bottom edge.

4. Use a leather punch to make the grommet hole, and set the grommet (this is where the elastic cord will emerge).

5. Sew the Velcro on, carefully following the marks. The top strip should be ¼ inch down from the top of the pattern so you leave yourself enough edge to turn under. The bottom Velcro strip can be almost flush against the top strip.

6. Sew the back in a covered (French) seam (wrong sides facing together for a ¼-inch seam, then right sides facing together for a ½-inch seam).

7. Sew down the end of the elastic cording to the ends of the Velcro strips (no cording runs through the section of the skirt with Velcro) and make a casing around the top of the skirt, enclosing the elastic as in the instructions for the Basic Design.

8. Fold the Velcro section of the skirt closed, matching the two sides as closely as possible. Punch a hole in the webbing strap ½ inch out from the sewn-down end. Match that hole with the corresponding spot on the casing and make a hole in the casing. Pound the female side of the snap into the webbing and the male side of the snap into the casing. (This is your quick-release handle.)

9. Follow the final two steps of the Basic Design to attach the skirts to the deck.

(continued page 184)

Deluxe Deck Skirt

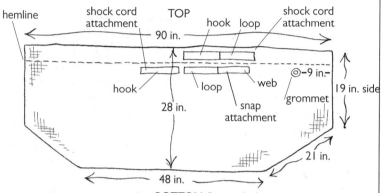

Supplies needed:
6 yards 400-denier pack cloth
2 66-inch shock cords
8 12-inch Velcro strips, 1-inch wide
2 6-inch webs, ¾-inch wide—burn edges
2 toggles
2 grommets, ⅝-inch
2 snaps

Basic Deck Skirt

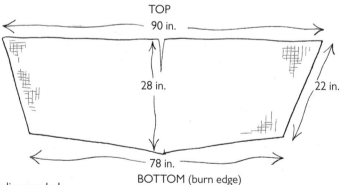

Supplies needed:
3 yards 200-denier pack cloth
2 90-inch shock cords
2 toggles
2 web squares—burn edges

MAKING AND INSTALLING YOUR OWN SPRAY DECK

(continued from page 182)

INSTALLING THE DECK ON YOUR CANOE

1. Lay the deck on top of the canoe (you may want to tape down the ends to free your hands) with plenty of slack lengthwise. If the deck is taut when you install it, it will shrink up on a hot day and become impossible to snap on! Make sure the cockpit holes are positioned correctly over the seats (with about an inch to spare behind the seats). Also, check that the deck is centered side to side.

2. Go to the center snap, pull the fabric down the desired distance below the gunwale (again, don't stretch it too tight), and mark the spot under the center of the snap. For boats with gunwales that extend significantly from the side of the hull, you may want to take the deck farther down the hull to reduce the angle of fabric and lessen the chance of popping the snaps loose in rough water. Do the same on the other side (it helps to have two people working on this), and make sure the deck is roughly centered.

3. Drill ⅛-inch holes at the marks and attach the male sides of the snaps with pop rivets. Remember to put the washers on the inside of the hull. Most canoe hulls will require ½-inch rivets. Kevlar or aluminum hulls will need the shortest rivets you can get and may still require extra washers, or spacers, for a snug fit. (See illustration below.)

4. Snap the deck to the hull at the center, move toward the bow to the next snap, and repeat the process on both sides. Remember to maintain some slack in the deck, especially lengthwise, as you go. Repeat all the way to the bow, snapping the deck on, and then do the same toward the stern until all the snaps are in place.

5. In the field, the fabric has a tendency to shrink up lengthwise on a warm day, occasionally making the snaps hard to fasten. As soon as the deck gets wet it will loosen up. If the deck is tight, try fastening the end snaps first, then doing the rest. In extreme cases you may have to wet the deck to loosen it up.

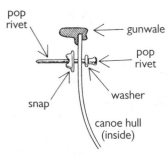

pop rivet — gunwale — pop rivet — washer — snap — canoe hull (inside)

Pop rivet assembly on a canoe hull.

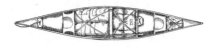

TWENTY-SIX

The Gear List

It's nearly midnight, and my living room looks like a paddling retailer's showroom after a terrorist attack. There are little winding paths through piles of packs, food, plastic bags, duffels, ammo boxes, trash heaps, fuel canisters, cameras, dry bags, wet-suit booties, scraps of foam pads. Overflowing, duct-taped card-board boxes are coded with cryptic hieroglyphics in indelible marking pen. There have already been several nervous discus-sions about fitting this sprawl of food and equipment into the sleek hulls of our canoes. That moment of truth will have to wait.

Departure is slated for before dawn, a few hours away. Some-where buried in the rubble is the equipment list. It's time for the final check. It's been time for the final check for twenty minutes, but nobody can find the damn list.

"Aha!" A voice comes out of the kitchen. "Here it is on top of the fridge. I wonder how it got there? Maybe I set it there when I got out the cheese a while back."

"Oh, brother! OK, OK, let's just do it and get to bed."

It's nearly 1:00 A.M. by the time we work our way down through the clothing, the group gear, the kitchen equipment. In each category there are the inevitable little essential items nobody thought of—the spare batteries, the journal, the extra tie-down, the bug dope. We make a short list of the things we need to buy on the way to the put-in, people make forays into the gear room for this and that, there's the usual round of "I'm pretty sure I packed that already, but I better check." Five minutes of serious rummag-ing. Then, "Yup, here it is. Just wanted to be sure."

The list is very complete and targeted for long-haul trips where the temperatures can dip below freezing any month of the year, where biting insects are expected company, and where help is days and days away. Adjustments are made, things skipped, to fit the trip at hand, but everyone feels assured by the end that nothing has been left to chance. If we forget anything, it isn't because we weren't thorough. And nobody begrudges the lost hour of sleep.

When we finally go to bed the room still looks like the aftermath of an earthquake, but we know everything is there, somewhere, and the piles are organized into a system that at least someone understands, I think.

ULTIMATE EQUIPMENT LIST
Personal Clothing

- comfortable camp shoes: tennies, moccasins, light hikers (if day hikes are planned, bring shoes that will work for walks as well as in camp)
- boat shoes: treated leather boots, hiking boots, canvas high-tops, slip-on river shoes—shoes that are either waterproof or quick-drying, that will work for portaging and lining and shallow wading

Rubber boots *and* ***warm socks*** *are terrific remedies for cold-weather foot care.*

- rubber midcalf boots (optional): good on trips without many portages and for cold water
- wet-suit booties or neoprene socks (optional): necessary only if you plan to do a lot of wading in very cold water
- four pairs of socks (several thicknesses—wool, wool blend, synthetic)
- quick-drying lightweight pants
- heavy pants (canvas, wool, fleece)
- long underwear bottoms (polypropylene/Capilene—moisture-wicking material)
- wind pants of 60–40 fabric or similar material (these can substitute for the light pair of long pants)

- rain pants (I prefer the bib overall style, but they aren't always the most convenient for women when it comes time to pee in a rainstorm)
- light, quick-drying shorts (good to wear under wind pants)
- three pairs of underpants
- two or three T-shirts
- quick-drying long-sleeved shirt
- wind jacket with hood and good cuff closures to keep bugs out
- long underwear top (wicking fabric)
- rain jacket
- vest or turtleneck
- bug jacket (optional, see pages 132, 133 and 178–79)
- warm long-sleeved shirt
- sweater or fleece jacket (for cold weather destinations, you should have three warm layers for your torso)
- two bandannas
- visor or brimmed hat
- head net (optional)
- gloves or mittens
- warm hat (wool or fleece)

General Personal Gear

- toilet kit (include personal medications)
- waterproof packing bags for food and clothing, maps, books, fishing tackle, etc. (dry bags and packs are one option, and so are duffels lined with heavy-mil plastic bags, regular packs with plastic liners, etc.)
- sleeping bag
- sleeping pad (see page 177)
- insect repellent (see pages 132–33)
- cup, bowl, and spoon (you can get fancier when it comes to utensils, but these do the trick)
- waterproof match safe (pack matches in several waterproof

A **wind jacket** that fits well might be the most-worn item on the clothing list.

containers in different places in the outfit—with the kitchen gear, in the repair kit, in the ammo box, etc.)

- knife
- life jacket
- sunglasses (optional)
- personal water bottle for drinking during the day (optional)
- ammo box or other waterproof container for things you want access to in the boat (journal, camera, bug dope, binoculars, maps)
- book or journal and pencil or pen (optional)
- fishing tackle (optional)
- camera, lenses, and film in waterproof containers (optional)
- binoculars (optional)
- flashlight, headlamp, or candles (may not be necessary in midsummer, northern latitudes)
- day pack or hip sack (for short hikes and easily accessible lunch pack) (see page 116)
- playing cards or compact board games (optional)

General Group Equipment

- tent with rain fly (see page 121)
- ground cloth
- cooking or gear tarp (large enough for group to get under in a rain and to cover the gear with—10- by 12-foot works adequately for groups of four or fewer)
- gear packs or duffels (packs are best if portaging is involved—I like internal-frame packs with plastic liners, but there are lots of

The **ammo box** and contents.

dry bags with shoulder straps on the market, too—on long trips,
I usually take three large packs per boat; only really long journeys
with lots of food require more than that)

- canoe (see pages 191–200)
- paddles (one spare per boat)
- canoe spray deck (see pages 175–76)
- bow and stern lines (three-eighths inch by twenty-five feet at each
  end should cover most circumstances for lining and tying up)
- tie-down cord/straps for securing gear in boat (see pages 117
  and 118)
- plant, bird, or animal identification guides (optional)
- toilet paper (optional)
- boat bailers (make out of half-gallon juice containers)

Kitchen

- hatchet or small folding saw (if building fires)
- grill with adjustable legs (if cooking over fires)
- backpacking stove
- stove fuel
- small metal trowel (for moving coals in the fire, digging sump
  holes, digging cat hole latrines)
- water container or containers (a collapsible 2½-gallon container
  is nice in camp and takes up
  very little space; large, rigid
  water jugs are good on trips
  where you need to carry
  large quantities of drinking
  water)

- large pot or Dutch oven (10-
  or 12-inch Dutch ovens work
  well for two to four people)
  (see pages 177–78)
- pot lifters
- pot scrubber and biodegradable soap
- fry pan or griddle
- medium pot (2-quart)
- wooden spoon
- small metal spatula
- fillet knife (optional)
- small cutting board (optional)

Various solutions to the need for a morning coffee fix.

- coffee filter or pot (some filters don't require extra liners and eliminate the need for an additional pot just for coffee)
- extras (see pages 145–46 for luxury kitchen items to take on portageless trips)

Navigation

- one set of topographic maps per boat (1:250,000 scale is adequate, but consider 1:50,000 detail for confusing terrain) (see pages 33–36)
- one compass per boat
- waterproof bags for maps (see page 100)
- map wheel (optional)

First Aid

(See pages 156–57 for complete list.)

Safety

(See pages 131–39 and 147–53 for discussion.)
- throw rope and three or four carabiners
- bear spray canister (for travel in bear country)
- emergency location transmitter (ELT) (for very remote travel, see page 137)

Repairs

- sewing kit: needles, thread, stitching awl, variety of patch material, snaps and snap-setter, zippers (especially for tent door—see pages 112–14), Velcro, buttons, drawstring, elastic, webbing, Fastex buckles, extra zipper sliders
- boat repair: spare center thwart, appropriate nuts, bolts, and screws, patching kit to match hull material, touch-up paint (especially for ABS boats—see pages 196–97), oil for gunwales and thwarts
- general repairs and maintenance: stove repair parts and small tools, extra cord, wire, waterproofing or seam seal, spare pack straps, pliers, screwdriver, small crescent wrench, duct tape, whetstone, epoxy glue, bicycle patch material, spare tent stakes, extra rubber gaskets for fuel bottles, spare match safe, lighter, small knife

TWENTY-SEVEN

Trip Canoes

My first trip canoe was a 17-foot aluminum lake canoe I borrowed from my parents on long-term loan. You know the kind—big, honking keel, no rocker, bow and stern air tanks, almost indestructible; you could hear it banging through a rock garden from half a mile away. Pretty serviceable, if not the sexiest thing on the river. And the price was right. That canoe got me through the scary early part of my paddling learning curve. It still sits in my parents' yard, with a few dents and battle scars, some twenty-five years later. It even gets wet once in a while.

With the next boat I made a quantum leap in quality and materials. On the way to an expedition in Québec, I stopped off at the Old Town Company headquarters in Maine and arranged to purchase an ABS-hull tripping canoe, one of the first of its kind. It was still 17 feet long, but this boat had no keel, enough rocker to be maneuverable in rapids, lots of capacity for gear, and a hull that seemed to me then to be absolutely frictionless. We glided through the water so smoothly, so quietly, that I kept catching myself holding my breath in awe. Beyond that, the boat was a cosmetic-defect second with a price tag about half what the canoe normally retailed for. I never did find the defect.

Since then I've paddled a great many trip canoes of every stripe, color, hull material, shape, and length, outfitted with all manner of gadgetry. I now own three canoes, which cover my paddling needs for the moment, and any one of them performs admirably on expeditions.

I think of those three canoes this way. One is the boat best suited for cruising journeys on pretty flat water. The shortest of the three, a sixteen-footer with fairly pronounced rocker, is the craft I pick for trips on moving water with rapids. It doubles as our slightly bulky solo canoe. The third canoe, a deep-hulled beauty a tad over seventeen feet long, is the family station wagon, the boat I trust my children to.

THINGS TO CONSIDER WHILE SHOPPING

Price

Most of us have a bottom line that keeps us in check. Some are higher than others, but they're present nonetheless. So we have some vague target price range our boat needs to fit. It's often as good a way as any to limit the field. Just look at boats in your financial window and do away with all the rest. With canoes, as with most things, you get what you pay for. Anything really cheap, unless you've worked out some scam, is probably not going to be particularly noteworthy when it comes to performance, durability, or craftsmanship. But most of the boats made by reputable manufacturers, from midprice range up, are pretty solid craft. You certainly don't have to go to the high end of the price spectrum to get a boat that will be serviceable and even modestly elegant.

For some of us, and during some periods of our boating careers, price is a pretty constricting reality. At those times you may simply have to make do with a boat that requires a fair amount of forgiveness and forbearance. So be it. I don't resent the trips I took with that aluminum clunker. I feel a very real fondness for that first boat, the kind of fondness I felt for my garage-sale first bicycle. Some gear you grow up with.

Also, don't assume you can't get a nice boat for a reasonable price. Check out paddling stores and canoe liveries at the end of the season and ask about sales of rental boats. Look in the classified ads. If you live in a town with any respectable population of outdoorspeople, canoes will show up in the want ads now and again. Ask manufacturers about cosmetically blemished seconds. Often as not they'll be willing to deal, especially if you can drive to their factory and pick the boat up. What's a tank of gas if it cuts the price in half?

Performance

The way a trip boat handles is a matter of compromise. You want, essentially, an all-around craft. A canoe that will track reasonably across broad reaches of open water, that won't be blown sideways like a leaf in a crosswind. At the same time, you want some maneuverability in moving water and rapids, the ability to ferry and sideslip and pivot when you have to. You want a boat that will handle a whopping load but that isn't so heavy you need three grownups and a teenager to portage the thing. In short, a

(continued on page 196)

CANOESPEAK

Every pastime and hobby has its lingo, its version of jive. Paddling is no different. It isn't all that complicated, though. A short glossary of common canoespeak terms will get you through that first paddle club potluck, even if your tripping résumé ends back at that scouting overnight you did when you were twelve. Whenever the conversation gets a little shaky, just throw out a few of these:

Rocker. The extent to which a canoe hull is shaped like a banana. Most tripping boats won't have a pronounced, or even very discernible, rocker—maybe a couple of inches end to end. Rocker gives you pivoting maneuverability for things like eddy turns. The more rocker, the more a boat turns on a dime. What you give up with lots of rocker is the ability to go straight on flatwater or in a wind.

Tracking. A canoe's ability to follow a line across flatwater and to hold that line against the forces of wind and current. The ultimate tracking feature is a keel that extends down the center of the hull. Most modern tripping canoes make do with a V-shaped hull rather than an actual keel. In addition to tracking, that V-shaped feature makes holding a ferry angle in current much easier and more effective.

Freeboard. The amount of the hull, at midships, that stays above water even with a load inside. Most paddlers like to have six inches or more out of the water at the center of the canoe.

Stability. The beamier a canoe is, the more stable it tends to be. Stability is good, but the wider your canoe is, the more volume you have to push through the water with every stroke. Narrower generally translates into faster but less stable. As usual, you find a comfortable compromise. Canoes with a rounded hull profile tend to have "secondary stability" when the boat is leaned to one side, as you would do when running whitewater.

Tumblehome. An inward curvature of the canoe hull just below the gunwale, generally intended to increase paddling efficiency.

Chine. The degree of curve in the canoe hull where the bottom turns up into the sides of the hull. A hard chine refers to an abrupt, almost angular curve, and a soft chine is a more rounded corner.

Downriver canoes. Built for straight-ahead river cruising with little maneuvering. These hulls are usually long and narrow, with vertical ends, meant to maximize speed and paddling efficiency.

(continued next page)

(continued from previous page)

Tripping canoes. Large-volume, deep-hulled boats that tend to have minimal rocker and a slight V in the hull profile, a compromise between maneuverability and tracking.

Canoe Parts and Design Features

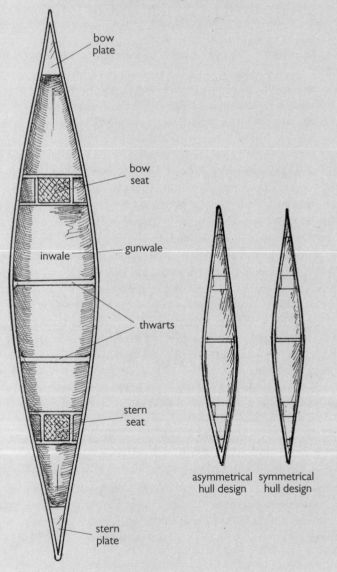

bow plate

bow seat

inwale — gunwale

thwarts

stern seat

stern plate

asymmetrical hull design   symmetrical hull design

Hull Types

straight

straight, with rise at bow and stern

slight rocker

dramatic rocker

Hull Cross-Sections

flat

flared sides

rounded V

straight sides

pronounced V

pronounced tumblehome

Bow Profiles

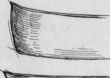
plumb stem

raked stem

recurved stem

(continued from page 192)
tripping canoe should be ready for flatwater, big lakes, waves, current, and whitewater.

There are exceptions to any rule of thumb, but the generalizations I operate from in looking at a tandem tripping canoe include these:

- a length of at least 16 and not more than 18 feet
- some modest rocker in the hull for pivoting maneuverability in whitewater
- center width of about three feet
- load capacity of 1,000 to 1,200 pounds, with at least 6 inches of freeboard
- hull depth at the bow of at least 12 inches (to avoid shipping water in standing waves); some canoes with what looks like borderline hull depth are designed to shed water away from the hull and do a surprisingly good job of staying dry
- enough of a V-shaped hull so that the canoe will track moderately well on flatwater (not a keel, but at least a hint of that V contour that will help nail the boat down to a course)

Durability

When I go away into those blank spots on maps far from roads and towns and fences and condos, I do not want to break down. I'm perfectly willing to portage some extra weight between lakes in exchange for the security of knowing my canoe will withstand the hard knocks and accident potential of expedition life.

That was one of the beauties of the aluminum era. Those boats could really take a beating, and even if you wrapped the canoe around a rock, when you got it off you could jump up and down inside and hammer on it with large rocks until it resumed something approximating its original shape, then carry on.

More recently I've made a habit of the ABS hulls, largely out of a bias for durability (*ABS* stands for *acrylonitrile butadiene-styrene*, a plastic laminate). Partly this is the result of honest self-appraisal. I'm not a handyman. I'm not a fussy, meticulous, careful gearnik either. I tend to treat my equipment with a certain casualness. Not neglect, usually, but not always reverence, either.

If you're handy and meticulous and welcome the maintenance and upkeep of fine equipment, you may be just the person for hull material that is less forgiving and more demanding. Wood and canvas, for example. Paper-thin, extremely light Kevlar perhaps.

I like the way ABS takes wear and tear without complaint. I like its ability to pop back to its original shape when dented (a property known in the industry as *memory*). I like the fact that, other than some touch-up paint now and again, I don't have to do a thing to maintain the canoe. I'm willing to tote some extra weight and give up a small amount of cutting-edge performance in exchange for the confidence and security of paddling a canoe that is nothing if not durable.

I'm not saying that Kevlar or generic fiberglass or polywhatever or wood or even inflatable boats aren't durable. It's that ABS is what I started with when I began my tripping career, and it has never let me down. Let's just say I'm loyal, have limited imagination, and feel no interest in getting into high-maintenance, unforgiving materials.

Comfort

This may sound odd, but I want a canoe that fits me right. When the paddling is going well, when you've been out awhile, it starts to feel as if the boat is an extension of you, that you're in some way wearing the thing. That's a good feeling, and it will come more readily if you start in a boat that fits well right off the bat.

Admittedly, there are few cut-and-dried guidelines for ascertaining this: it's ultimately subjective. The only real way to test it is to get in a canoe, load it up, and paddle a ways. But here are some things to pay attention to when you go test-driving:

- You feel comfortable in either the bow or the stern seat. Some canoes are too beamy in the bow for small paddlers to reach out and stroke comfortably. Others are constricted enough in the bow that anyone in the six-foot realm is going to feel cramped.
- Seats that wear well. I prefer cane or webbing seats because they give a bit, drain water, and seem to adapt to my rear. Over days and days of sitting, a seat matters a lot! Try a few types to see which fits you best. Manufacturers are sometimes willing to customize boats with the seats you prefer.
- Stability. Get in the boat, loaded the way you'll most likely load it, and see how stable it feels. It's a bummer to always be on guard. By the same token, some hulls feel tippy when you first step in but settle down with a load and have great secondary stability when they heel over a bit.
- Some minor, but not unimportant, features. I look at things like thwart placement, which affects the sturdiness of the hull, the way you'll have to pack your gear, and the amount of leg room you may have in the stern. I check for extra room under the seats and in the bow and stern for packing niches (rain gear, the spray deck bag, an ammo box). I kneel in the boat to make sure my feet fit comfortably under the seats and that the hull configuration isn't

uncomfortable for my preferred stance (for example, a canoe with a pronounced V hull may make you feel as if your knees are on slopes instead of solid, flat surfaces). I try paddling in the boat to feel how comfortable my strokes are, bow and stern. Some hulls just work better with some bodies. Finally, I try to get some vague, aesthetic sense for the craft. I strive for some bit of canoe aura— essence of boat. I close my eyes, let the canoe drift along, and take its pulse. Weird, I know, but there it is.

THE WAY YOU PADDLE

It comes down, really, to three factors. What sort of water you prefer. Who you generally go off on trips with. How long you stay gone.

Water

I understand that it's difficult to be categorical about this, but most people have their preferences. Some like the big, open vistas of lake country with only occasional connections of river water. Some like moving current and see lakes as the necessary, and they hope infrequent, exceptions along a route. Some like whitewater. The more thrills per mile the better.

Pick a boat that does it all, but cheat a little on the side of the water you like best. So if it's fast water you crave, cut a bit off of the boat length and go for a more pronounced rocker. If it's fast water you avoid, get a long, sleek, open water cruiser that will track a line like a train on the rails.

People

My preferred group is my family. For a time that was just two of us, and we tended to gravitate toward 16- to 17-foot tandem boats designed to handle everything from 200-mile lakes to class III rapids. More recently the group has expanded to include children, so we've gone to longer, beamier, deep-hulled boats with a preference for stability. Solo paddling, tandem, three-in-a-boat, whatever it is you do, think about who will be there, consider their preferences and comfort zones, and choose accordingly.

Also, if you and your partner differ dramatically in body weight, you'll want to consider how to distribute your weight in the canoe. Consider a boat with a sliding bow seat. It can be a problem in terms of how you pack and for the placement of spray deck cockpit skirts, but it's the most effective method of compensating for weight differences. It is also smart to shift the load in the boat in accordance with who's in the bow and stern (see page 119).

Length of Trip

With some exceptions, you carry the same stuff for a three-day weekend as you would for a monthlong expedition. The big difference, mostly, is

FOLDING CANOES

One of the biggest hassles on longer expeditions is transporting the silly canoe. Here's this 17-foot, 70-pound rigid monstrosity that has to perch on top of your car, get strapped onto plane floats, fit inside a freight car, whatever. It's like taking the piano along.

So it's very tempting to go with something inflatable, foldable, something that packs down into a duffel and can be reconstructed at the put-in. Problem is, until lately the easy-traveling alternatives have compromised a lot when it comes to performance, handling characteristics, hull speed, and durability. For the most part, despite the convenience, it hasn't been worth the risk.

There's one canoe in this category, however, that I would recommend. It's called a PakBoat, and it comes in a variety of lengths and styles to suit varied trip demands. The 17-foot PakBoat weighs 50 to 60 pounds packed in its duffel and can be checked as airline baggage, thrown in the back of a station wagon, and treated like more trip luggage.

At the put-in, it takes about half an hour to assemble the thing, and you're off. The truly good news is that the tough hull (made of raft material) is extremely durable, the boat is surprisingly fast, and the paddling characteristics are remarkably comparable to those of a hard-shelled boat. The hull has a little more wobble here and there, and it's light enough that you really want to tie it up when you stop, but it actually is a bona fide trip canoe that travels well. You can even change the hull configuration to adapt to the paddling conditions—for example, put more gear in the center and you suddenly have some rocker.

At the take-out, clean the boat, tear it apart, roll it up, and throw it on the bus. (See appendix 2 for a contact for the PakBoat.)

A PakBoat on the riverside assembly line.

the food you have to cart along, and drinking water if you need to take big jugs of fresh stuff. In an honest appraisal of your vacation flexibility, get some grasp of how long most of your canoe trips will be. If it's a week or less for the immediate future, you can probably afford to go with a sleeker, faster hull, less load capacity, and more performance characteristics. If a month or more is a possibility, you'll pick a fairly beamy, big-load boat with some of the qualities of a trusty mule. Mules don't have to be clumsy and plodding!

In the end, it's very much like buying a car. You factor in your preferences, your budget, the logistics of your needs and requirements; you quench your passion for bells and whistles and color preference. You sit in there and see if it feels and smells good and moves pleasantly, if it seems solid and well made. Then, with all the tangibles lined up, you add a big dollop of pure subjective, intuitive gut feeling and make the leap.

TWENTY-EIGHT

Overhyped Equipment

I won't be getting any endorsement money after this chapter, but I've lived this long without it. I might as well do away altogether with that wan hope of a financial windfall.

So. Don't you think it strange how some equipment develops incredible sales, gets all manner of exposure, even becomes generally known by its brand name, as in, Do you have any _____ here? when it's either demonstrably flawed or patently frivolous? Some of this stuff is outlandishly expensive to boot, so you aren't just stuck with junk—you'll be making payments on it long after you've discovered the fraud.

It can only be another example of marketing overpowering objectivity, or more evidence of our simple gullibility. Maybe these equipment scams tap into the wellsprings of insecurity we're all so vulnerable to. When gear doesn't work, we think it must be our fault. We're doing something wrong. I'm the one who's strange and defective. I don't know what I'm doing in the wilds anyway, and this is just further proof of my incompetence.

Well here's the short list of paddling gear that is useless, defective by definition, or harmful to the user.

WATERPROOF, BREATHABLE RAIN GEAR

You all know the brand name this stuff is known by, but in the wake of that business success, all manner of look-alikes have appeared, each claiming to be truly waterproof and also breathable. Not only do these manufacturers have the temerity to make this assertion without blushing, but they have the gall to charge hundreds of dollars per garment and put the material to uses that are so ridiculous they'd be laughable if people weren't dropping their paychecks on the stuff. Waterproof, breathable boots! I mean, really. Is there no shame?

Sorry, but it doesn't work. It is really good wind gear, and nice in dry snow, but who needs a $600 wind suit? Pay no attention to the showroom demonstrations that supposedly mimic rainstorms and the rigors of outdoor use. They're smoke and mirrors. Take it on a trip, clog a few pores with sweat and dirt, subject it to real-life activity, and about three rainstorms in you'll be looking for the plastic garbage bags and working up a good angry sweat thinking about the salesperson who sold you the miracle suit.

The bitter truth is that staying dry in the rain without working up a sweat inside your suit is an age-old conundrum we won't be solving anytime soon. It's one of those dilemmas of the human condition, no matter how much money you throw at it.

Put your faith and hard-earned money into rain gear that doesn't claim to breathe and keep you dry at the same time. Coated nylon with sealed and treated seams remains the standard. As far as the sweat part goes, look for designs with good ventilation features like openings at the armpits and then don't work too hard in the rain. Don't expect the impossible; it's going to be a bit humid inside.

STRAP-ON RIVER SANDALS

Another whopping example of inexplicable outdoor retailing success. I got suckered in, myself, but only once. Those strap-on sandals with neon detailing look great on models in bathing suits, and they even work pretty well for evening strolls in the sand.

Beyond that, though, there are problems. Put them to work on real trips and their shortcomings come out of the woodwork. To begin with, they're uncomfortable. Maybe I have gnarled feet, but I've found the hard buckles and straps rub painfully, especially when they get wet and gritty, which they certainly will. Second, as soon as you start really scrambling around somewhere slippery and uneven, the sandals slide around on your feet and turn into treacherous little dance shoes. Finally, in river current when it really matters, like when you're working to retrieve a boat or lining a set of rapids or going to help someone, the sandals bend back on themselves, catch all kinds of painful gravel, and snag on sharp objects. You're better off barefoot. At least then you don't wade in assuming you have foot protection.

You'd be much better off wearing slipper-style wading shoes with good friction soles. They don't look nearly as neat as the fluorescent sandals the volleyball beach set will be wearing, but on a river trip, who cares?

PADDLING BACKRESTS

A classic example of a great idea taken too far. The same people who made the fantastic folding-chair discovery took hold of their good thing and went a couple of steps across the boundary into the land of the frivolous.

A backrest is a terrific idea, but the ones sold as attachments to your canoe seat are not—unless you plan on not paddling. If you actually paddle, you simply can't lean back. The kinesthetics just don't work that way. You'll either be sitting up straight or leaning slightly forward. The backrest will tickle your lumbar region once in a while, making you dwell on that insidious lower-back ache, but it will come in handy only when you stop paddling. At that point you could just as easily lie back against the stern plate of the canoe or on the packs loaded behind the bow seat. Save your money for a better paddle and the folding camp chair.

GLOBAL POSITIONING SYSTEM (GPS) UNITS

I'm going to get in trouble here, because these things are all the current rage. People think of them the same way they think of the Internet or e-mail. There's no going back. This is the wave of the future. Get on or get left behind. Well, bye-bye. Send a postcard from Techweenie Land.

I've been on several paddling trips with people using a GPS unit. They inevitably have the fervor of a revival tent preacher. Problem is, in my experience using the thing is like trying to get an uncooperative computer to do what you want. People are always muttering and pushing buttons. Minutes go by, punctuated with exasperated little outbursts like "Oh, yeah, I've got to punch in my access points" or "Well, that's the distance in air miles, it doesn't account for all the river bends" or "Just a second, I think it's almost got us." Minutes that could be spent pulling out the map, taking a look, and getting back under way.

The only application on canoe trips that I'll admit to enjoying is the feature that will tell you your ground speed as you sail across a lake with a tailwind. Now that's pretty heady stuff, but it's hardly worth the expense and wasted time of bringing the gizmo along.

There are places and times when I understand that a GPS unit would be handy. Bushwhacking across confusing desert terrain, for example, when knowing your precise location would be a real godsend. Or flying a bush plane through fog. Problem is, very few situations where the GPS unit is useful crop up on canoe trips.

Get good at map reading and using a compass instead. Even if I haven't talked you out of buying a GPS, at least you'll have the navigational skills to fall back on when the batteries die.

My beef with GPS goes beyond its backcountry efficacy. I have a philo-
sophical bone to pick as well. It smacks of the growing tendency to bring
cell phones everywhere we go. Excuse me, but don't we go to the wilderness precisely to escape the grasp of gadgets, technology, and the other
claptrap of civilization? Don't we go there to get *out of touch*? What are
we doing bringing our laptops, our phones, and the other toys of the modern era to places full of loon calls and canyon wrens and lapping water?

TWENTY-NINE

The Sentimental List

P romise you won't laugh. The piece of equipment I feel the most sappy about, and that I'd be the most devastated to lose or break, is a pair of pot-gripper pliers.

But they're great pot grippers! Not those wimpy, untrustworthy tweezers you get when you buy a set of nesting pots. These are one-of-a-kind, last-a-lifetime bomber grippers that grab your attention the first time you lift a twelve-pound stewpot off the stove. I've never seen another set like them, and everyone who uses them takes a hard second look and asks where to find a pair.

"What are you going to do when you lose those things?" Marypat once asked me.

"I don't know," I said. "I might have to quit camping."

I found them in an army-navy surplus store in Cincinnati almost thirty years ago. It was that period in my outdoor career when I was just beginning to amass my gear and had almost no discretionary income.

Crammed onto a shelf full of dusty canteens, mess kits, shovels, and canvas gaiters was a little cardboard bin full of these pliers. They were very light, but they felt sturdy and had a hooked handle with flat-surfaced grippers that seemed like they'd work well for lifting pots. They cost 59 cents. Even I could afford that, so I bought a pair.

One trip with those pliers and I realized what a find I'd made. Why didn't I buy a dozen? Ever since, I've searched surplus stores in vain.

Almost three decades later, I've gotten so attached to the silly things that I won't let anyone under age fifteen handle them. They have their precise storage niche in the equipment room. On trips a specific pocket in the kitchen pack is reserved for them. When I get around to making my will, those pliers will have their own category, and choosing a beneficiary will be excruciating.

I'm not a gear freak. I don't spend my time poring over equipment catalogs and reading up on the latest materials and design breakthroughs. I do, however, feel sentimental about some pieces of the outfit. When we're young we have our favorite blanket. When we get older we have our cherished pot grippers. What can I say?

My first sleeping bag is the same way. I bought it about that same time, through a college outdoor program that sold them at cost. A down-filled, three-season, contoured model. Pretty cutting edge for the time, but back then I snapped it up just because it was a good deal.

Thirty years have gone by. That bag has been all over the continent, stretched out on desert hardpan, alpine tundra, unstable talus slopes, Arctic riverbanks. It has kept me cozy through raging thunderstorms, two-day deluges, freezing nights, and sandstorms. Over the years it lost some of its loft—about half in fact. After two decades the zipper gave out. It got so I could take it only on trips to warm places or during one or two months in the summer.

Then I thought about seeing if the company would recondition a bag like that. I packed it up, wrote a note saying how much it meant to me, and sent it off. Three weeks later I got the bag back. It had been absolutely restored: cleaned, patched, refilled with new down, outfitted with a new zipper. All for about $30. So now I'm stuck with the bag I love, and it might well outlast me.

My wind shirt rests in this hallowed category too. It's nothing special to look at, but I've worn it for twenty years now. It's been pretty well everywhere and is the piece of clothing I pull out of the pack more than any other. It's 60–40 material, with a fitted hood that actually fits my head, a cargo pocket at belly level that my hands rest in nicely, a Velcro-closed chest pocket for a map or journal, and a drawstring at the waist. It keeps the bugs at bay, sheds wind, and provides that in-between layer when a jacket or rain gear is too much and a shirt too little. If I had to pick the single invaluable piece of outdoor clothing in my gear room, it would be that, hands down.

Years ago, when the material had faded to a dusty shadow of its original red, pocked with ember holes and various abrasions, Marypat took it on herself to make me a replacement. She's a talented seamstress. She made me a beautiful shirt. To all appearances it was an exact replica of the original. But it didn't fit the same way. It just wasn't right. Something intangible didn't work. I wore it for her, but she could tell something was wrong.

Then, in a true outburst of love, Marypat painstakingly took apart the old jacket to make an exact pattern. She made me a new one, copying the original down to the last feature. The only piece of the old jacket she retained was the hood. Somehow, she knew, the hood was the key, and almost impossible to reproduce. And it worked. It feels just like the old one.

OK, I won't take this much further. Just one more special piece of gear.

When Marypat and I moved in together, a long time ago now, she introduced me to the fine art of garage-saling. Even then she was a veteran. She could go into a driveway full of clutter—boxes of old clothes, rusty tools, broken lamps, scratched records—and zero in on the set of glasses we needed in twenty seconds flat. She could sniff out a dud sale in less than a minute and be on her way. And she was a master at bargaining—Turkish carpet salesmen had nothing on her.

One of the first Saturdays in my education, we pulled up at a subdivision house with the usual scatter of junk strewn around. I was still navigating the fringes when Marypat called to me from inside the garage. She had found a vintage two-burner gas stove. She talked to the owner and assessed him as one of those meticulous types you cherish when it comes to secondhand stuff. He wanted $12. Seemed like a good deal to me. We got it for $7.

It's now seventeen years later. That stove still goes on our portageless trips (see pages 145–46). It's got its quirks, but what camp stove doesn't? It cooks like a champ. Hasn't ruined a meal yet.

Not long ago I was camping with some friends who had a brand-

The author with his sentimental collection.

new model. I kept comparing it with our old one. I watched carefully in terms of performance, upkeep, sturdiness, reliability. I wasn't even slightly tempted to turn ours in.

This sentimental business is mysterious. I don't know, really, why I get so attached to one piece of equipment and couldn't care less about another. Time has something to do with it—sheer number of days out together. Reliability certainly does. Gear that lets me down is gear that gets left behind. Shared experience. The places we've been together.

I don't understand what it's all about. Just don't get between me and my pot grippers.

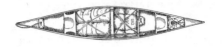

THIRTY

The Human Fuel

The part of the trip outfit that you have most power over, and that has the greatest impact on your experience, is your food. Nothing else comes remotely close. It's literally the fuel that runs the expedition machine. If it's inadequate, scanty, unvaried, boring, or lacking in nutrition, the expedition bogs down like a car with sugar in the gas tank.

Nothing turns a trip sour, and potentially scary, like poor food. People get testy with each other, group morale heads south, and that festering growl in the belly is always lurking in the background. Often it becomes more than a sore point. Poor food over a long period is fundamentally dangerous. Without adequate nourishment, people won't operate at full potential against the challenges of long portages, windy paddling days, and big lakes. Bodies won't be as capable of battling hypothermia or recovering from fatigue.

bad food = bad trip

It's a simple equation and a danger that there's no excuse for falling prey to.

The good news is that food is the sector of the trip package you can do the most about. If you take the time to think through the menu plan, you can overcome all manner of shortcomings by having a well-nourished, content, and strong crew. With strong bodies and full bellies, who cares about slow boats, heavy paddles, poor weather, and hard portages? On the other hand, the most expensive, cutting-edge gear won't matter a whit when the human engines are grumbling for higher octane.

Whether you head off for a three-day weekend or a month in the wilderness, your gear list doesn't change much. A few clothes more or less, a luxury item here and there, but the core equipment list remains largely the same for short or long stints. The whopping variable in the outfit is food.

When you pile up all the food a group will eat in a week, it's staggering. Hard to believe we're capable of cramming it all into the boats, not to mention into our bodies. It's positively obscene, the mound of fuel it takes to keep a working human animal going. What's more incredible is that at the end of the time all that food is really and truly gone, and there were probably meals when you wished you had more!

As a culture, we tend to overeat. Something about the neurotic, obsessive-compulsive round of our capitalist forty-hour-workweek frantic lives leads us to find comfort and diversion in food we don't really need.

On the trail, however, it's hard to be a glutton. I always lose weight on trips, and it isn't because I'm not eating. I'm eating plenty. I pride myself on good trip food. But the truth is that it's hard to keep up with the environmental demands. You're paddling steadily all day, with stints of adrenaline-driven labor in whitewater or headwinds. You heave packs in and out of boats and wrestle with heavy gear several times each day. You're out in the weather, dealing with heat and wind and drizzle and cold. You may be portaging heavy loads across rough trails, lining boats, wading in frigid water, scouting trails, taking day hikes.

Outdoors, under the demands of strenuous activity, we can gobble up 4,000 to 6,000 calories a day and not gain an ounce. In fact it's pretty hard to keep up with the caloric demands of a really rigorous journey. You'd have to gorge on energy-rich foods almost nonstop to stay ahead. Luckily, most trips aren't that rigorous, at least not on a sustained basis. And most of us have a tad of extra weight to donate to the cause. Losing a few pounds, getting buff, isn't the end of the world.

Still, by being efficient and thoughtful about the trip food you can have the greatest effect on the weight and bulk of your supplies. Putting some work into food preparation also has a major impact on the cost of your journey.

EDIBILITY FACTORS
Variety

Same old, same old is not the refrain you want to be hearing around mealtime a week into the boonies. Same old, same old is a total bummer a week into the boonies.

It's seductively simple, back in the comfort of your living room and within reach of the refrigerator, to reduce the burden of planning and prepa-

FIGURING YOUR METABOLIC RATE

We know that a variety of factors will affect how much fuel you'll need in a day. But we also need someplace to begin our figuring from.

To compute your basal caloric requirement (the minimum fuel you need, even on a sedentary day, to metabolically tread water), multiply your body weight by fourteen calories. If you weigh 200 pounds, your basal daily requirement comes out to about 2,800 calories. Your 125-pound paddling partner would need more like 1,750 calories.

Now, on an average paddling day, during which you stroke steadily perhaps six or seven hours, do camp chores, lift some heavy packs, and so on, you're apt to boost the basal requirement by 50 percent, so the big guy will be up to 4,200 calories and the smaller member of the team will need 2,625 calories. On a really strenuous day, when the headwinds are up, two or three portages bar your path, and you have to keep warm in hypothermia weather, you could easily double your metabolic needs— 5,600 calories and 3,500 calories, respectively.

Remember, this isn't a hard-and-fast rule. The equation has some serious wiggle room, but it's a good starting point and a good reminder that body type and size really do make a difference when it comes to planning trip food.

On one long and strenuous summer trip Marypat and I cut our food supplies to the bare minimum to keep the load down. We each ended up eating about the same portions of food every day, even though I outweigh her by seventy-five pounds. At the end of the trip she had lost about five pounds while I shed almost thirty!

ration by taking shortcuts with the food. A week of instant oatmeal packets for breakfast—why not? We can stand anything for a week. Wrong! Variety is not that hard to plan into a menu, and it will keep people humming along, literally and metabolically.

Variation Tips

- Pack a complete spice kit. Spices are light and relatively inexpensive and let you broaden the menu to include chili meals, curry meals, Italian meals, and so on. Spices bought in bulk are invariably fresher and more flavorful than the supermarket varieties. Take along salt, pepper, garlic, curry, oregano, basil, chili powder, cinnamon, nutmeg, dill, bay leaves, thyme . . .

- Variations on a theme: So what if some of your staples and meals are the same? You can still vary the components. Some examples: cheese for lunch—make it cheddar one day and Swiss the next; trail snacks—gorp one time, sesame sticks the next; dried eggs for breakfast—complement them with refried beans one morning, hash brown potatoes another; bannock recipes—make one with garlic and dill and another with cinnamon and raisins. Get the drift? Instead of oatmeal packets all week, throw in Cream of Wheat one time or Malt-o-Meal or grits. It isn't that hard to make hot breakfasts a tad different.

- Condiments. Another easy strategy for variety is to include some lightweight, compact condiments in the pantry. Hot mustard, dried salsa, tamari or soy sauce, Mongolian fire sauce, horseradish. Whatever floats your taste buds. Why not?

- Selective fresh foods. Some foods will keep quite a while and withstand the rigors of outdoor life. They add immeasurably to the flavor of trip food. Fresh cheeses will last weeks, especially if you leave them in the plastic, vacuum-sealed wrap they're sold in. A head of fresh garlic in the spice kit. Carrots, cabbage, onions, and some other hardy vegetables add zest to meals. Put a slice of onion or bell pepper on the lunch sandwich. Add a fresh onion to the dinner pot. Munch carrots for the first few days. Fresh food means extra weight and bulk, but a few indulgences are worth it.

- Meal rotation. I like to plan dinners around a rotation of at least seven days. If you repeat more frequently than that, it's going to get old. (See one-week menu, chapter 31.)

Expense

Food is the biggest cost variable, once you get your basic equipment needs under control. This is also one category that defies the axiom "You get what you pay for." In the case of food, the cheapest strategy has the potential to also be the best in terms of trail nutrition and culinary excellence.

To start at the expensive end of the spectrum, simply run to an outdoor retailer's showroom and buy all your meals from the racks of the dried and freeze-dried, ready-made selection. Don't forget your checkbook and charge card. Unless you have a lot more money than I do, you'll be broke about five days into the menu. Not only that, but packaged trail meals start to all taste the same a few days down the road. The products have come a long way since the early days of dried eggs and repackaged military rations, but it's still a far cry from home-cooked. More to the point, for the price of a single dinner entrée for two, you can supply that same couple with food for a day by taking charge of your own menu and food preparation.

The next rung down the expense ladder involves shopping for staples at grocery stores and health food outlets and then packaging your own meals. It used to be that mainstream stores had a couple of bins of gorp, brown rice, and some starchy whole-wheat noodles, and that was about it for selection. Nowadays you can get couscous, cracked wheat, powdered refried beans, nutritious dried soup mixes, quick-cooking rice and noodle entrées, healthy cereals, on and on. It can still be expensive, but nothing compared with the boil-for-three-minutes pouches at the outdoor store.

Even if you choose not to go the grocery store route completely, at least have a look and sprinkle in a few items as an experiment. My bet is that when you discover how easy it is and how good it tastes you'll never buy another expensive pouch.

Down there at the inexpensive, but labor-intensive, bottom rung is drying your own food supplies. Here's where you can really save money and get a varied, nutritious, lightweight menu to boot.

Buy a good-quality dehydrator with a thermostat, round trays, and an electric fan (see photo page 21). The expense is worth it. Besides, you'll pay back the cost of the unit with your savings in the first couple of weeks of food shopping. Pick up food throughout the year and dry it as you go. Get cheap fruits and vegetables in season and dry them in quantity. Dry game meat, eggs, sauces, whole dinner entrées, fresh berries, garden produce. Pick up a good book on drying techniques and go to work.

You'll save a tremendous amount of money over the prepackaged meals, and you can assure yourself of the nutritional quality of your food. Best of all, you'll be able to program as much variety in your trail food as you do at home.

I've dried food for very long trips, up to fourteen months of wilderness living. It's been the most important strategy for making those trips affordable and for getting the food down to a manageable weight and bulk. By drying food and packing efficiently, I've paddled as long as sixty days without needing a resupply and have kept my food expenses at rock bottom.

Responsibility

Food prep and packing easily constitute the biggest grunt job in gearing up for an expedition. Best to get on it early and stay on it. If you leave it to the last week, you'll be swamped and it will take you days on the water to regain your equanimity.

Assign one or two people in the group to supervise handling the food. That doesn't mean they have to do it all, but they'll have the overall scheme under control and can delegate jobs.

Start by surveying the group for food allergies, vegetarian habits, preferences and dislikes. While you're at it, encourage trip members to brainstorm meal ideas and recipes to get the menu planning rolling. Decide what the ballpark food budget needs to be. Trip length, ability to resupply, expected weather conditions, and demands of the route will all affect the selection of trip foods.

Once the parameters are set, it's nothing more than a matter of time, labor, and nitpicky attention to detail. Once you've penciled in the trip menu, circulate it among the group for final input and reaction.

On trips of a week or less it can work well to rotate meal responsibilities among couples or individuals. Each couple might assemble a dinner and a breakfast, while you all take care of your own lunch food, for example. Or each couple might take complete charge of one day. An odd person out can handle the drink selection, or desserts, or trail treats.

Once the food supplies are amassed—dried, purchased, or picked from the garden—the job of packing looms. Often this is the final big chore of the preexpedition phase and takes place until about two o'clock on the morning of departure. It's best to share this bit of logistical drudgery if at all possible. Get everyone together, buckle down, and get through it. It's way too much to ask of any one trip member unless you're going solo, in which case you might as well get used to doing things alone.

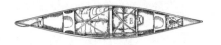

THIRTY-ONE

Menu Planner

ONE-WEEK EXPEDITION-STYLE MENU OVERVIEW

Day 1

BREAKFAST: granola with dried fruit; hot drinks

LUNCH: bannock (see page 218); dried fruit; cheese; sesame sticks

DINNER: rice and beans casserole with cheese and salsa (see page 219)

Day 2

BREAKFAST: oatmeal with brown sugar, raisins, and butter; hot drinks

LUNCH: crackers; dried fruit; peanut butter and jelly; gorp

DINNER: macaroni and cheese with touch of dried tomato sauce and dried green peas

Day 3

BREAKFAST: dried eggs and hash browns; hot drinks

LUNCH: bannock; dried fruit; salami; spicy trail mix

DINNER: lentil stew with bannock

Day 4

BREAKFAST: cold cereal with milk; dried fruit; hot drinks

LUNCH: crackers; cream cheese; canned green chilies; dried fruit; sesame sticks

DINNER: spaghetti with dried sauce; small bag of Parmesan

Day 5

BREAKFAST: bulgur hash (see page 217); hot drinks
LUNCH: bannock; hummus (see pages 218–19); dried fruit; gorp
DINNER: chili made with dried ingredients (dried meat optional)

Day 6

BREAKFAST: seven-grain hot cereal with brown sugar and butter; hot drinks
LUNCH: crackers; cheese; jerky; dried fruit; Oriental trail mix
DINNER: Dutch oven quiche with fresh Swiss cheese, dried eggs, and dried veggies

Day 7

BREAKFAST: dried scrambled eggs with cheese; dried refried beans; hot drinks
LUNCH: bannock; meat spread; dried fruit; sesame sticks
DINNER: curried rice and dried veggies

Remember that the menu can be spiced up according to taste by bringing along a complete selection of spices and that condiments like hot mustard or dried salsa can enliven the lunches. A few canned goods like a meat spread or whole green chilies don't add that much weight and pick up a meal considerably. It may also be possible to live off the land a bit by picking berries in season or by catching fish.

OTHER EXPEDITION ENTRÉE IDEAS

- Dutch oven pizza
- Cauliflower-mushroom-rice-cheese casserole
- Noodles and dried pesto
- Corn chowder and bannock
- Spanish rice or bulgur

FIVE-DAY LUXURY MENU
(ASSUMING FEW PORTAGES AND SPACE FOR A COOLER)

Day 1

BREAKFAST: fresh eggs; sausage; hot drinks
LUNCH: bagels; cream cheese; canned green chilies; fresh fruit; nut mix
DINNER: chicken and rice casserole

Day 2

BREAKFAST: pancakes with butter and syrup; hot drinks
LUNCH: bagels; salami; mustard; fresh fruit; nut mix
DINNER: burritos with flour tortillas, beans, meat, fresh tomatoes-onions-olives, cheese

Day 3

BREAKFAST: corned beef hash and poached eggs; hot drinks
LUNCH: pita bread; fresh hummus; sliced red onion; fresh fruit; nut mix
DINNER: beef stew with fresh ingredients; garlic bread

Day 4

BREAKFAST: hot cereal with sugar and butter; dried fruit mix; hot drinks
LUNCH: sandwich bread; cold cuts; cheese; mustard; fruit; chips
DINNER: spaghetti with fresh veggie sauce; French bread

Day 5

BREAKFAST: cold cereal with dried fruit; hot drinks
LUNCH: crackers; peanut butter and jelly; fruit; jerky; nut mix
DINNER: Dutch oven enchiladas

Don't forget a bottle of wine here and there, a dessert or two, and snack treats.

WHAT'S IN THE PANTRY

Think of the pantry pack in the same way as a closet space off the kitchen where you keep the bins of flour, bags of sugar, and other cooking staples that might be required for any meal. My expedition pantry usually includes the following:

- extra bag of flour or bannock mix
- powdered milk
- cooking oil or margarine
- spice kit
- selection of hot drinks
- cold drink crystals
- daily treats
- selection of condiments
- extra matches in a plastic bag
- desserts
- beef and chicken (or veggie) bouillon

THIRTY-TWO

Favorite Recipes

Over the years the meals get fine-tuned. Some you eat so many times you swear off them forever. Split-pea soup comes to mind. Others I never tire of. Macaroni and cheese, spiced up with some salsa and with green beans or peas added, I've probably eaten several hundred times by now, and I'm happy to find it in my bowl every time. Recipes evolve, the ingredients shift, preparation techniques adapt. Some of my favorites are the recipes listed here (amounts are for hearty helpings for two), but use them as a starting point and feel free to experiment. Soon enough you'll have your arsenal of expedition meals guaranteed to get you down the river and over the portage to the next meal.

BULGUR HASH

I know, I know, *bulgur* rhymes with *vulgar*. Get over it. This is the best expedition breakfast recipe ever, period.

> *1 c. bulgur*
> *1 T. dried onion*
> *2 ½ c. water*
> *black pepper, basil, garlic powder to taste*
> *1 T. cooking oil*
> *1 T. tamari or soy sauce (or to taste)*
> *¼ lb. sharp cheddar*

In a saucepan, add water to bulgur and onion and bring to a boil. Sprinkle in spices and simmer until liquid is absorbed (15 minutes). Heat oil in skillet and sauté bulgur mixture until it starts to brown. At the end, sprinkle on the tamari or soy sauce and add the cheese, cut into small chunks. When the cheese is melted, breakfast is on. (Sautéing a fresh onion slightly before adding the bulgur makes this even better.)

BANNOCK

Bannock, or fry bread, is traditional in some form or another in pretty well every corner of the world. It's surprisingly easy to make and much more satisfying than crackers at lunch. Premix batches of the dry ingredients before you leave home.

> ½ c. white flour (brimming)
> ½ c. whole wheat flour (brimming)
> 1 t. baking powder
> ½ t. salt
> 3 T. powdered milk
> water

If you haven't premixed the dry ingredients, stir them together in a bowl. Add careful dribbles of water until the dough is slightly sticky in your hands. Form into four patties ½ to 1 inch thick. Fry over medium heat in a lightly oiled pan until browned on the outside and cooked through. There's no end to the variations you can concoct: garlic and dill; Cajun; cinnamon and raisin; cheese. Also, you can experiment with different flour mixes or add seeds or nuts, wheat germ, etc.

DRIED HUMMUS

I like hummus because I'm not a particular fan of peanut butter and jelly. It makes a nice change in the lunch menu even if you do like pb&j.

> 1½ c. dried garbanzo beans, soaked overnight and cooked until
>   mushy—drain water off
> 3 cloves fresh garlic, minced
> 1½ t. salt
> pinch of cayenne pepper
> dash of tamari
> juice of 2 lemons
> ¾ c. tahini
> ½ c. fresh minced parsley
> half an onion, chopped

Throw everything into a food processor and zing it into a thick paste. Spread on dehydrator trays and dry at 130°F until crumbly. Powder in a blender. On the trail, reconstitute with warm water. Be sparing with the water or you'll end up with hummus soup. I take a small container on trips just to mix the hummus in, but you can mix it in a plastic bag.

RICE AND BEANS CASSEROLE

4 c. water
½ c. black-eyed peas (these cook in about 20 minutes)
1 4-oz. can green chilies
1 T. dried onion
1 c. long-grain rice
4 T. dried salsa, rehydrated
3 cloves fresh garlic (or powdered)
1 t. salt
pinch of ground cumin seed
1 package dried sour cream mix
½ lb. Monterey Jack, cubed

Boil water and cook peas, chilies, and onion until peas start to soften. Add rice, cover, and simmer until tender. Drain any excess water. In the meantime, rehydrate salsa with the garlic and other spices and mix the sour cream package with water in a cup. When the rice is done, mix everything except the sour cream and bake briefly (if cooking on a fire), or heat over low flame until cheese melts. Garnish with sour cream.

ALL-IMPORTANT COFFEE STRATEGY

In my existence, coffee is a pretty essential part of every day. Canoe trips are no exception. That morning cup might even be more important while paddling than in civilized life. In any case, if it doesn't matter to you, or if you're a tea drinker, skip the discussion.

There are several ways to deal with the coffee question in the wilds. The main variables in deciding which will work best for you are whether everyone drinks coffee, whether you can afford to carry a separate coffeepot, and how you like your morning cup prepared. Here are a trio of solutions.

SEPARATE FILTERS

This method is particularly appropriate if you have coffee, tea, and cocoa drinkers all dipping into the hot-water pot come morning. Coffee

(continued next page)

(continued from previous page)

drinkers can bring one-cup filters made to sit on the cup. Many of these require a separate paper filter, which makes for additional trash and cleanup. You can find filters with built-in screens that do away with paper inserts; these work best on trips. Using one-cup filters keeps everyone happy no matter what the drink of choice is, and the communal pot of water serves all.

PRESS-POT THERMOS

It's hard to beat the quality of press-pot coffee. But until recently most press pots were made of glass, so you had to wrap them in wool socks and treat the equipment pack as if you were transporting plutonium. Now, though, you can get a combination press pot and thermos in virtually indestructible stainless steel. The drawbacks are that the pots are expensive ($40) and that they're bulky. On trips with plenty of storage space and not too many portages, a press pot is tough to resist. Ask Santa for one.

COWBOY COFFEE

The coffee solution most steeped in history and trail lore, not to mention a certain amount of controversy, is cowboy coffee. It's an inexact science, prone to strident opinions, but the tradition runs deep and wide.

The technique for settling the coffee grounds is at least as contentious a topic as the best way to brew cowboy coffee. I've heard of everything from dropping a raw egg into the pot to putting in a pebble or two to floating eggshells in the pot to swinging the brew around your head in an alarming demonstration of centrifugal force. Here's my recipe, for what it's worth.

Start with a 2-quart pot of cold water. Add about five fistfuls of ground coffee beans right at the start (I said this was inexact stuff). Cover and bring to a strong rolling boil, then turn off the heat and remove the pot. If you're patient, simply let the pot sit for a few minutes, then tap the side sharply a couple of times with a spoon to encourage the last grounds to settle. It you're not patient, and I'm usually not, add about half a cup of cold water to drop the grounds to the bottom, tap the side of the pot, and serve up.

THIRTY-THREE

Disciplining the Pile

IT WON'T EVER FIT!

Marypat and I straighten up simultaneously from opposite sides of the mound of gear and food in our basement. It's a pretty big basement, but right now it's remarkably lacking in clear floor space.

"There's no way this will all go in a canoe," Marypat says.

"It has to. We've done it before, for crying out loud! It just looks big now, all spread out the way it is." I sound confident, but I'm not at all sure Marypat isn't right this time. The mass of stuff is just too big. I think about the tapered hull of the canoe resting next to the garage, then survey the sea of stuff around me, all of it somehow essential to the success of our journey. Impossible!

This moment comes every time, no matter how many trips we take, no matter how often we accomplish the magic act of stuffing a basement full of gear and edibles into about half of a canoe seventeen feet long and three feet wide. Sometimes the instant happens late at night in the living room. Sometimes it's at the put-in parking lot. Sometimes it's at the checkout at the grocery store. No way. We're doomed.

START PACKING

The only way to move past the crisis in confidence is to begin putting things in packs and condensing the load into the parcels that will soon go inside the boat. Ignore the doubting little voice in the background. Pick up something, anything, and put it where it belongs. Then keep going.

Big Packs

Start with the three big packs (per tandem canoe) that the basic outfit, including food, will have to fit into. By big, I mean packs with capacities of at least 5,000 cubic inches of storage space, and perhaps as commodious as 8,000 cubic inches.

Designate two packs for personal gear, one for each paddler, and the third for group equipment. Food will be crammed in wherever there's room. A large pack designated wholly for food would be too heavy to get off the ground.

Line the personal packs with heavy-mil plastic bags or some other waterproofing layer and lay in your sleeping bag and then your clothes. Try to bury clothes you likely won't need, or won't need often, at the bottom (wool hat, long underwear, etc.). If there isn't room for sleeping bag and clothes in a single waterproof bag, waterproof the sleeping bag stuff sack separately and pack it solo.

Now store the miscellaneous personal items you may need to get at throughout the day in side pockets and lid pockets. The headlamp, for example—your water bottle, the toilet kit, that sort of thing. There will probably be room for other gear too: fishing tackle, spare film, extra journal . . .

By rights you should still have plenty of room in the pack. This is where you start cramming in the food bags (see pages 224–25). In the interest of efficiency, try to put food of one type, such as breakfast food, in the same pack.

Now for the third big pack, set aside for group gear and food. Again, pack things you're least likely to need, or need in a hurry, at the bottom. This pack holds the kitchen gear, stove and fuel, kitchen tarp, water filter, first-aid kit, folding saw, repair kit, and so on. Again, there should be extra room for the rest of the food.

It's likely there will be some bulky items of gear that won't conveniently fit inside the packs—inflatable sleeping pads, commonly, or folding chairs, or the tent. These can usually be strapped down under the pack lid or cinched onto the sides of the packs. I usually don't bother waterproofing the tent or pads because they dry so quickly. If you'd feel better stowing them in dry bags and then strapping them on, it's up to you.

It's also a distinct possibility that you'll end up with odds and ends of food lurking around,

The ominous mounds of expedition gear.

kitchen tarp
tent
water bottle
food
toilet kit
clothes
sleeping bag

Personal packing scheme.

especially on long trips without resupplies. An extra duffel or small pack may be needed to handle the overflow for the first week or so.

Loose Stuff

An amazing quantity of items need to be either left out of packs or stowed in a more accessible way.

DRY BOX I use an ammo box, but there are any number of dry box arrangements. Inside go all the little things you may want to get at quickly as the day goes by. Mine has at least the following: pencil, pen, journal, map, insect dope, sunscreen, binoculars, compass, camera and film, and match safe. The design of the canoe will dictate the best place to tie in the dry boxes. I generally put them between my feet or under the seat in the bow, and just behind the back thwart, in front of my feet, in the stern.

WEATHER GEAR Even when the sky is clear and the temperature warm, I'll keep out the stuff sack or medium dry bag with my wind shirt and rain gear. If you don't, you're sure to bring on a storm. When bad weather strikes, the clothing you need is close to hand. I prefer to store the rain gear bag behind or under the stern seat.

LUNCH AND SNACK FOOD We designate a hip sack for the day's food. It doubles as a small pack to carry on day hikes, and you can clip it in somewhere handy on top of the load. Every morning we repack it with the lunch du jour, whatever snacks are allocated, and odds and ends of leftover food.

LOOSE BUT NOT FORGOTTEN A lot of gear needs to be handy for use during the day.

- paddles, life vests, and the spare paddle
- throw bag (clipped to seat or thwart)
- water bottles and big jugs (on trips without good drinking water)

- spray deck bag
- map and map case
- fishing gear (perhaps)
- pocketknife
- sunglasses
- boat bailer
- plant and animal guides

All of it will naturally find its best niche as the days pass and you shake out the travel system.

At this point the gear pile is looking at least more contained and, hopefully, a good deal more compact. By now Marypat and I have regained our equanimity and confidence a bit, except that there's still the appalling stash of food we seem to need to maintain basic metabolic function.

DEALING WITH THE FOOD

Unpackage

We're a society of overpackagers. Food comes wrapped, double-wrapped, boxed, and shrink-wrapped. We're three layers deep before we reach anything edible. Start by getting rid of the excess layers. That step alone can diminish the volume of the pile by a third. The only thing to watch for are those essential directions that are generally printed on the packaging; without them you'll be doing the trial-and-error culinary thing down the trail and losing the group popularity contests. When you find important directions, just cut out that part of the package and store it in the bag with the food. Not only will unpackaging reduce your load, it will minimize the garbage you'll have to deal with along the way.

Repackage Efficiently

Now that all the redundant wraps have been tossed, put everything back together in a way that will make sense on day 20. Combine meal ingredients that can cook together—dried veggies, for example, dried tomato sauce and onions, rice and lentils, all the stuff in a meal that can be poured into a pot together and cooked up simultaneously. Even when you can't combine ingredients, you can still put all the parts of a meal together in a larger bag.

Do some of the preparation ahead of time. Premix the dry ingredients for bannock batches, add the powdered milk right into the cold cereal bags, put spices into dried eggs. Package the premeasured ingredients for meals in separate bags so you don't have to mix and match in the field. The more you can reduce steps before you leave, the more thankful you'll be that day when it rains from dawn to dusk.

I generally use cheap plastic bags to pack the food in, double thickness and knotted (twist-ties are impossible to keep track of and probably constitute the greatest category of wilderness microgarbage). Occasionally I'll succumb to heavier reclosable bags for more substantial food or for a handful of smaller, bagged-ingredients that all go into a single meal. You can get fancier with more expensive bags, home vacuum-heat-seal outfits, and the like, but you don't need to. A food scale that measures accurately to a quarter pound is handy, especially when you're cutting up and weighing things like bulk cheese.

Color-Code Bags

I've been on trips where each day's food was packaged in a separate numbered bag. I don't usually get that organized. It's enough for me to know that each meal is in its container and that I can browse through the dinner sack to pick the evening's entrée. I like the flexibility of matching food with the conditions of the day.

What I do instead is to separate the main food categories by the color of the stuff sack they go into. Breakfast food will be in red sacks, lunch in blue, dinner in yellow, and the pantry supplies in silver. Something along that line. If you don't have, or don't want to make, quantities of extra stuff sacks, you can code the bags with different colors of yarn or tape.

If you don't have some of that inner confidence back by now, maybe you really *are* in trouble. It still may seem like a helluva pile to fit inside that trim paddle-powered unit, but it's at least conceivable. Besides, you can always leave a few luxuries behind in the shuttle vehicle if it gets really and truly too snug.

MAKING YOUR OWN STUFF SACKS

This is one sewing project I might even take on myself. That is, if I hadn't married a seamstress. It's easy, and you can always use more stuff sacks.

Pick out some material, or use scraps—any kind of coated nylon works well, sometimes cotton or canvas is nice, or even lightweight Cordura. Anyway, find the material that works for you. These directions make a medium-size sack, the sort of bag you'd use for packing food, for example, or a really compact sleeping bag. To make bigger or smaller sacks, just adjust the initial dimensions. (continued next page)

MAKING YOUR OWN STUFF SACKS

(continued from previous page)

1. Cut a rectangle 27 by 15 inches.
2. Sear the cut edges in a candle flame to seal them (nylon).
3. Fold the material in half with the right (coated) sides together to make a rectangle 15 by 13½ inches and sew down the side and across the bottom with a ¼-inch seam (make sure you back-tack at the ends).
4. Cut a piece of cord (parachute cord works well) 3 to 4 inches longer than the circumference of the sack; sear the ends of the cord.
5. Make a drawstring casing at the top by turning the top edge of the bag toward the inside into a hem about ½ inch wide. Lay the cord inside the fold, with the ends sticking out, then fold the rough edge of the top under again into a ¼-inch hem and sew the casing down with the cord inside. Be careful not to catch the cord as you go, and be sure to back-tack the start and finish of the circle. Leave about an inch open where the cord ends come out. Tie the cord together in an overhand knot, or add a toggle if you want to get fancy.
6. Now, with the sack still inside out, lay it flat. Pick up one of the bottom corners and pull the sides apart to create a triangle, with the bottom seam in the center. Sew across the bottom of the triangle about three inches in from the corner. Repeat on the other bottom corner. This will make a stuff sack that will stand up (see illustration).
7. Turn the bag right side out and you've got it, a stuff sack roughly 11 inches tall and 13 inches wide.

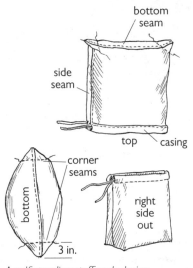

A self-standing stuff sack design.

PART FIVE

FAMILIES AND CANOES

THIRTY-FOUR

Why It Works

I was one of those idiots who thought life wouldn't really change just because I had kids. Sure, I knew there would be diapers and sleepless nights and two-year-olds fishing in the toilet bowl, but I was sure I wouldn't have to capitulate on my adventurous leanings. The kids would come along; we'd just adapt our style a bit. The children, hardy beings every one, would rise to the occasion.

Serious denial. I mean, what was I thinking? Helloooo!

About one week into fatherhood I saw the incredible error in my calculations and expectations. No. Things are never the same. In some ways they're better, in some ways harder, in pretty well every way more stressful. The same? Wrong.

Okay. Let's talk about plan B. We're on the unalterable road of family life, stuck with a deep well of ambition for outdoor adventure and with kids along for the ride. We have no interest in putting our passion for adventure on hold for a couple of decades. We see the error in our rationalization that life won't really change. What are the options?

Well, there's car camping. There's bowling. There's bridge night. And then there's canoeing.

Why not? Put the kids in a boat and float off downstream. Camp out, travel to wild places, carry plenty of gear, don't be saddled with heavy backpacks *and* kids to carry.

In short, canoeing as a family salvaged a faint glimmer of my naive and obtuse hope to remain active and adventurous even with young children. Don't be fooled; it isn't the same. Never was, never will be. But it *is* a great way to get outside, stay comfortable, and have the boat and river do the work.

Canoes succeed for the same reason cars and horses do. A vehicle besides the parental pack mule carries all the gear and human cargo. Locomotion comes, at least from time to time, as a gift of current. A canoe is better than either horses or cars because it needs very little maintenance and upkeep, doesn't consume food or fuel, requires essentially no investment beyond the initial purchase, and gets you to spots as remote and wild as you can stand.

Each one of our three children went on a canoe trip in utero and again within the first year of life. During one ungainly stage we maxed out the capacity of our largest seventeen-foot canoe with all five of us, the full complement of camp gear, and two weeks of food. One boat! We did that more than once, in fact.

We've spent two weeks on the Rio Grande in Big Bend, Texas, with two toddlers and another kid seven months along in the womb. We took our eight-month-old firstborn down the entire length of the Yellowstone River in Montana—a month of river life with a diaper-clad infant. Our kids had been down more rivers and across more lakes in the first decade of life than lots of adults can claim.

These achievements sound boastful, but that isn't it at all. What I am is immensely relieved—relieved to have found an outlet for my adventurous leanings along with a means to initiate our children into the joys of outdoor life.

Even at a tender age, children and canoe journeys go together.

A FEW FAMILY CANOEING CAVEATS

Paddle a boat you feel completely comfortable in. If you're still in the early, tippy stages of learning to canoe, you might be better off taking family raft excursions or getting your own skills up to snuff before loading up the kids. Even if you're adept, when choosing a craft for the family, err on the stable, beamy side.

Paddle water where you feel completely confident. Anything can happen on any water, just as bad things can happen on the sidewalk in front of your house, but pick routes that you feel unquestionably competent to handle. There is a huge difference between the sorts of runs I'll make with Marypat, in a canoe outfitted with a spray cover, and the ones I entrust my children to.

Pad your itinerary with extra days. Choose a route, figure how long it would take you to paddle it without children, then double it. Really. If the weather turns bad you can lay over and play games or go exploring. When the kids are restless, it's no big deal to pull in to shore and let them play in the sand for an hour. Extra time in the schedule translates into happy campers and safe travel decisions.

Invite friends and relatives. Adults who are willing to take turns sharing the burden of kid entertainment and care are a major asset. Bring along grandparents, other families with children, the neighbors. Kids enjoy the diversion of playmates and different adults, older children can go off

Relatives are great family trip partners, if they're willing.

together or paddle their own canoe, and adults can take turns getting time without kids clamoring for their attention.

Plan diversions. With infants and toddlers diversions often take the form of food treats and drinks. Older kids like to have companions, sketch pads, books to read, games to play.

Don't worry too much about carting along toys. A pail and shovel will be about all you'll need. Who cares about Barbie when there's no end of sand and rocks and water and sticks?

Think carefully about access points along the route in case of emergencies. Begin your family canoeing career with fairly short suburban outings and push the wilderness envelope more as you get comfortable and seasoned.

As much as possible, involve the kids in the trip. Give them tasks appropriate to their age—let them read the map, help set up tents, collect firewood, keep a bird list, paddle the boats. The more they're in the expedition loop, the more satisfaction and ownership they'll feel.

From an early age, get kids comfortable with water. Go to the pool, get them in swimming lessons, take them to swimming holes. Once they're beyond the toddler stage, swim with them in unobstructed river current with life vests on. It gives them a visceral sense of what moving water is all about. When they're comfortable, try swimming some riffly water.

Swimming in moving water is a visceral and important lesson in how current behaves.

THIRTY-FIVE

Parental Judgment

JUST SAY NO

It's raining hard when we first see the river. We sit in the car and look over the scene from a muddy turnout at a fishing access. Windshield wipers slog away, and the heater blunts the spring chill.

This section of the upper Madison River is normally a pleasant, steady float, the kind of mild descent where you can recline with your legs stretched out on the gunwales, watching the Montana scenery coast past.

Today it's a brawny flow just below flood stage, full of standing waves and river flotsam. The boat ramp is half under water. Every few minutes another big log comes bobbing downstream like a bumpy, slow-moving torpedo.

"This river is bookin'!" are my first words.

My river-running adrenaline immediately kicks in. The pedestrian float suddenly looks like it might be pretty exciting. This stretch is more float-fishing stream than whitewater run, no matter what the water level, but right now it looks like there are plenty of small riffles, strong eddies, and nice little rollicking wave trains.

We've been planning this outing for weeks. It's to be our shakedown cruise for a summer of paddling with two little boys. Eli's a year and a half and tough to restrain. Sawyer's not quite three months, still a chubby infant. Another couple plans to join us with their year-old daughter. The idea was to do a docile float and concentrate on kid containment and diversion strategies.

Every weekend for a month we've made plans, only to have something come up and postpone them. Finally we're here, loaded down with tiny life vests, harnesses, toy buckets and rubber ducks, crackers and dried bananas for those teething gums.

We have all afternoon before meeting our friends at the river campsite that will be our put-in, so we dawdle along upstream, pulling out at every access, every bridge, for another view of spring-swollen current.

"Look at that," we keep saying. "This thing is goin' like hell!"

Back there niggling away in whatever part of the brain the center of judgment occupies there are faint little questioning voices. "Don't forget the kids," they say. "Is this really what you had in mind?"

But the urge to run this fast river is powerful. Weeks of frustrated attempts to go paddling have steeled our resolve. There's no question we can handle this water.

Once in a while a stubborn image of a mishap worms out of my sub-conscious. Capsize in snowmelt water, babies adrift in current that isn't shy about its captives. But I lock these images back up, conceal them under a lust for fun and the simple, ponderous inertia that has built up behind this jaunt.

Our buddies pull in to camp around dinnertime. The weather has cleared and warmed; looks good for the morning. Within minutes they stroll down to look at the Madison. They're gone a long time.

"What do you think?" Scott asks, when they come back.

"Looks like fun," Marypat says. "It's higher than we've ever seen it, but it still is pretty mild whitewater."

"Yeah," Sue agrees. "It does look like fun, but what about the kids?"

Nobody says anything for a bit. "Still seems doable," I venture, finally.

We have a nice little fire in camp, share a bottle of wine. The kids all go down. Distant thunderheads bump over the Madison Range, far-off lightning stitches the night sky. The hurrying river is clearly audible several hundred yards off.

I don't sleep all that well. The sound of the river is always there, intruding, and the small voices are more insistent in the dark, the visions more vivid. I hear Marypat stirring too. And I listen for minutes at a time to the soft, quick breathing of our two little boys.

I'm first up in the clear morning, working on coffee. By the time it's ready Marypat is getting dressed, primed for her first cup.

"I think Scott and Sue are pretty concerned," I say, when I hand her coffee to her. "Actually, I'm kind of concerned too."

"Let's not do it, then." Her words are abrupt, out of the blue. "Why don't we go do that stretch lower down, the one we said we'd never do again?"

"Perfect," I agree. "I'll go ask those guys."

Scott and Sue leap at the new option. "We were thinking of plan B, too," they say.

The mood in our camp is suddenly lighthearted and energized; relief is palpable. The new objective is a bit of river always crowded with those silly yellow rafts, peopled by beer-drinking floaters who wouldn't know an eddy from a hot dog. Even at high water the current is barely thigh deep, with hardly a riffle. Normally it's a float we'd disdain, the last place we'd ever go. But this morning it's exactly right, just the kind of thing we were thinking of for the kids. All it took was for one of us to say it out loud.

There's a truism in the world of risk sports that goes something like this: "Never let desire overwhelm your better judgment" (see pages 151–52). Whenever someone recites it everyone else automatically nods in agreement. We've all heard the tragedies of folks who ignored that advice. Some of us have had friends who died ignoring it.

We all nod automatically, but in those moments of adventure lust, when all the effort of preparation, built-up desire, expense, and resolve is bunched up behind you with the momentum of a freight train, the toughest thing of all is to turn away and go home, even when it's only a weekend float on a neighborhood stream.

STAY FLEXIBLE

Flexibility is a condition of parenthood. Kids force us to become adaptable. Without some give, family life is a very long lesson in frustration.

On the water with a family, flexibility is pretty close to a survival necessity. Children don't have the same agenda as parents most of the time, and travel together is a fairly constant exercise in compromise and negotiation. Being open to suggestion, and to the needs of offspring, is a major part of succeeding in the watery wilds.

Flexibility in the overall plan is also critical. If conditions change, water comes up, weather goes to hell, a child gets sick, it's time to reconsider. It helps to have a few other options if things don't go as planned. Another piece of river, going for a walk instead, visiting some friends, finding a beach and never getting on the water. Kids don't know they should be disappointed. Likely they'll be just as happy playing in the mud on the riverbank as in the canoe—maybe happier.

It's one thing to inflict misery on yourself or on a few adult companions, but kids are a different matter. More than once we've called off a trip and headed home because the weather turned awful or conditions weren't what we thought they'd be. There's nothing shameful in saying no, and there's too much to lose by taking chances.

Trust your intuition. If those little voices are sounding the alarm, listen up. Chances are other people in the group are hearing the same doubting chorus and will be tremendously relieved when someone has the courage to bring it up.

THIRTY-SIX

Infants

It's the first time I've set my firstborn in a canoe, and it isn't going well. We're high up on the Yellowstone River in Montana. Eli is eight months old. The river is busting along with snowmelt. Eli seems particularly vulnerable and helpless when I hand him to Marypat in the bow. He hates the life jacket we strap him into. His lungs are in fine working order and operating at top volume when we shove off from shore for a twenty-five-day jaunt down the entire navigable length of the river, to the confluence with the Missouri, just across the North Dakota border.

I'm thinking, What are we doing? The river jostles us along. Eli continues his complaints. I look around to see if anyone is watching this peculiar form of child abuse from the banks.

What we are doing, I remind myself, is starting our child's career in boats and on water. Great start. He'll go on to be a real estate agent or stockbroker for sure, with this visceral memory simmering in his subconscious. He'll move to the biggest city he can find as soon as he can escape our clutches and never again leave the security of pavement and air conditioning. What *are* we doing?

It takes us about two miles to start to cope. Eli is teething, and it turns out that the bananas we brought along, dried in long strips, are fantastic teething equipment. He's busy masticating bananas for half an hour at a time, drooling all over himself, completely lost in the experience. The rhythm of the current eventually lulls him to sleep. Marypat lays him on a piece of foam between her feet in the bow, and he naps to the tune of rocking river.

By this time both of us are exhausted with the stress of insecurity and self-doubt, and we just drift along, letting the river do the work, avoiding even the little standing waves, relishing the quiet.

That shaky beginning isn't the last moment of doubt—not by a long shot. There's the sudden hailstorm, pellets of ice the size of marbles beating down on us while we cower on the shore and shelter Eli under our ponchos. There are accumulating diapers. There are days of unrelenting sun, way out in eastern Montana, when heatstroke seems like a fifty-fifty proposition. There's the rattlesnake swimming the river down near Sidney, Montana. Handfuls of sand going into Eli's mouth. A minor burn at the evening campfire. Long nights in the tent with a squalling infant.

Wilderness challenges. Not all that much different, when I thought about it, from the obstacles we faced at home. At home there were stairs to tumble down, table corners to fall against, bugs to eat in the yard, bad nights in the family bed. The stage setting is changed, but the problems are the same.

Eli, we discover, is at a pretty ideal age to go on a trip. We don't know that at the start. We've gone because it's the window of summer that works for us. He's on the verge of his first step. He can hold himself up by the gunwale of the canoe, for instance, but he can't climb out or really walk. He's still breast-feeding, so he can eat our leftovers mashed up and chew on dried fruit, but most of his nourishment is carried inside Mom. He's little enough to sleep between us without needing his own sleeping bag.

Our eldest son and his first wilderness baptism by canoe at eight months.

Logistically, the biggest problem is that he's still in diapers. Our solution is to bring a diaper pail and about thirty cloth diapers. We have a small stash of disposables in reserve, but we never have to use them.

When diapers are only wet, we rinse them out in the river, then drape them over the packs to dry. The canoe looks like some sort of gypsy rig with

BABY FOOD

When you think about it, what a great thing breast-feeding is. Talk about self-contained! Not only that, but nursing is as sure a pacifier as there is when babies are unhappy.

Bring along some diversionary food treats, too. Crackers are good, and bananas dried the long way are fantastic, both as long-term sucking material and as a good teething food.

Take one of those old-fashioned hand-crank food mills. On the Yellowstone trip we'd just grind up some of our dinner (as long as it wasn't too spicy) and feed it to Eli.

Instant baby cereal is a nice filler around or between meals.

Bring a backpack kid carrier, the kind that stands up on its own, and use it at mealtime as a kind of high chair.

*Backpack and **feeding station,** all in one.*

laundry hanging out, but we're not that proud. Soon as the breezes start picking up corners of the diapers, we know they're dry. The rinse and dry cycle can be repeated four or five times before the diapers start feeling more like cardboard than cloth. Then we retire them.

Poopy diapers (that's how you'll talk when you have babies, too) are a different matter. The contents we dispose of the same way we do with adult poop. On the Yellowstone we dig shallow cat hole latrines (see page 159). Soiled diapers go into the diaper pail in a plastic bag.

The Yellowstone River is, it so happens, a perfect cloth diaper sort of river. We didn't know this at the outset, mind you, but it seems that a riverside town always turns up just when the diaper pail on board is brimming full and turning a tad toxic. We pull in to town and make our way to the coin laundry. About once a week we need to stop and refresh. About once a week a town like Columbus or Miles City or Glendive looms above the banks, and we try not to look sheepish with our sack of doodoo on the way to the washing machine.

Vanity is pretty tough to maintain once you have children. A run to a riverside laundry with a sack of dirty diapers will bludgeon that personality trait into submission within about two blocks. I guarantee it.

The other good thing about the Yellowstone is that it has fresh current without much in the way of whitewater challenge. Most of the watercourse flows along at a steady, strong pace, so we can stroke enough to stay on course and maneuver when we have to, but even just drifting along we cover twenty or thirty miles a day without much effort. Good thing, because whoever is in the bow with Eli tends to be pretty occupied with him. The stern paddler does most of the paddling each day, while the bow person pitches in when needed or when Eli succumbs to a nap.

For nearly a month we coast across the state of Montana. Eli becomes adept at standing in the bow, hanging on to the sides of the boat and exhorting the world. He points to geese and pelicans, leans over to touch the water, jumps up and down in the canoe hull. Once or twice bad weather keeps us in camp, but we have time, so we wait it out.

My parents join us for a five-day stint and give us relief with baby duty in camp and at lunch stops. Another friend with older kids comes along for part of the time too, and his ten-year-old daughter immediately takes on entertaining Eli in a series of riverside camps. The most consistent challenge is to keep sand and rocks and goose poop out of his mouth. Kids are pretty oral at that age, and Eli seems exceptionally so.

We're alone, just the three of us, when we finally slide into the Missouri River, some 550 miles downstream. It's a victorious, and also melancholy, moment. We've done it. We don't want to end it. We paddle into an eddy at

BABY TIPS

A folding camp chair works as a pad for the baby to sleep on in the canoe and a sleeping pad in the tent at night.

The backpack kid carrier is nice in camp because it allows you to carry your baby while you do chores or go for walks and keeps your hands free. Eli was quite content to hang out in a pack, but if we set him down on a blanket and went to do chores, he'd squall.

In warm weather, babies don't need their own sleeping bags. Lay them on the camp chair between adults and drape your sleeping bags over them, or zip two adult bags together and keep the baby in the middle.

Haul the canoe into camp upright, throw a few toys inside, and use it as a playpen as long as your child can't climb over the gunwale.

Bring a picnic blanket along to spread out for a crawling space.

Invite friends or relatives who like kids or who have their own and will share some of the chores.

Insects can be a real hazard with babies. Try to avoid high bug season. Dress young'uns in long-sleeved shirts, and if it gets bad, retreat to the tent.

Tents with sleeping bags laid out inside are fun playpens for infants as long as it doesn't get too hot.

When shopping for the family canoe, think about having enough room in the bow for your legs and a baby, either standing up or napping.

In camp, a canoe becomes a playpen (right). Bring a picnic blanket along for safe crawl space (below).

the confluence of the two great rivers and just sit there in the midday sun, feeling the currents swirl past.

A fisherman is in a boat nearby, fishing higher up on the same eddy. He asks what we're doing, where we've been. We tell him we've been a month on the river with our kid. Started up by Yellowstone Park, came all the way down without stopping.

He doesn't say anything for a long time. He sends another cast into the quiet water, sits back, looks at us for a minute.

"Just your little family, huh?" he says. "All the way down the river." He shakes his head. "That's pretty neat. Just the family, all the way down," he says again. "Pretty darn neat."

INFANT SAFETY

Infant life jackets have a great deal in common with torture devices. In the interest of creating bomb-proof, head-up flotation, manufacturers make tiny life vests that could double as cervical collars. Ask yourself, when you go shopping, "Would I wear that thing?" My preference is to pick a vest that fits comfortably rather than one with great flotation and uncomfortable snugness. What good is a fantastically buoyant vest if your baby won't wear it? Pick one the child will tolerate. One of the problems with little kids' life jackets is that they can slip over the baby's head in the water. Make sure it has leg loops! On the life jacket it should list the range of body weight it can handle. Flotation near the top of the vest, a head flap, or both is more important for infants than for older kids.

We added a body harness and tether rope on Eli. The tether is tied to the adult in the bow with the baby, who is wearing a life jacket, always. That way, if you go over, you can reel your child to you and get to safety. The only warning is to be careful not to make the tether too long (six to eight feet of slack between you and your child is plenty), and beware of getting entangled in brush or deadfall. It's a good idea to wear a safety knife on your own life vest so you can cut the tether free if it gets tangled.

Remember that kids are much more susceptible to environmental stress than adults. It's the surface area–body mass ratio. They get cold quicker, hot quicker, hypothermic quicker. And they aren't working the way you are, so just because you aren't feeling the cold doesn't mean they

(continued next page)

INFANT SAFETY

(continued from previous page)
won't be. Dress them warmly and bring plenty of spare clothing. Protect them with sunscreen and good sun hats (ones with neck flaps are nice). Shade them while they nap, on board or on shore. If they get wet, change them into dry clothes right away. Plan plenty of extra time in your itinerary so you won't feel pressured to push on in bad weather.

At least until you're comfortable with your abilities, plan trips with escape routes (bridge crossings, towns, road access) at fairly frequent intervals.

Include infant supplies in the first aid kit (baby aspirin, Band-Aids, diaper rash cream, etc.).

Tether and harness systems *allow you to retrieve an infant and get to safety together.*

THIRTY-SEVEN

Toddlers

Picture this. The Subaru, laden like a gypsy caravan, comes to a stop in front of the muddy Rio Grande, at the upstream end of Big Bend National Park, Texas. Doors fly open as if a bomb has gone off inside, spewing children's books, garbage, toys, packs, paddles, and people—some quite short and exhibiting the frenzied energy stored up over the 2,500 miles between Montana and Mexico.

While Marypat and I start organizing the bomb debris, the boys, ages two and three, work on their own agendas, with the dialogue going something like this:

"I gotta go pee."

"Where's my bear?"

"Can I have a sucker?"

"I gotta go pee, now!"

"Just a second, Eli."

"I wanna take all these books."

"Don't touch that, Sawyer! It's a cactus. Remember, we talked about that."

"Dad, I want new pants."

"Why?"

"Cause I peed in these ones."

"Where's my bear?"

And so on.

Before we escape onto the river, Eli has sunk to midcalf in riverside mud, Sawyer has had his first close encounter of the cactus kind, and Marypat has the same hopped-up look as the patients in *One Flew over the Cuckoo's Nest* right before they got their daily dose of Thorazine.

The good news is that if you survive the drive to the put-in and the leap over the transitional abyss from vehicle to boat, time on the water will be pretty blissful. Believe me, days in the canoe, or in waterside camps, are nothing compared with sibling warfare in the back seat, motel meltdown, or herd containment between car and canoe. If you don't believe me, try four days in a small, overloaded station wagon with two young children.

OK, blissful might be stretching it a tiny bit. Canoeing with toddlers is probably the most difficult family paddling stage. They're mobile enough to be big trouble, but not coordinated or focused enough to help. Oh, they'd like to help, but their idea of helping requires more supervision than feeding time at the pigsty. They're young enough to need a great deal of attention and energy, but old enough to strike off on their own in alarming ways.

Parents end up doing everything for everyone. You tie all the shoes, stuff all the sleeping bags, put toothpaste on every toothbrush, pack every duffel, cook every meal, paddle every stroke.

Languid mornings with journal and sketch pad, energetic excursions up side canyons, social evenings around the campfire—all are relegated to nostalgic memories and distant hopes. But then life with toddlers, even at home, isn't exactly stress free. The same frenzied pace and nonstop demands are right there front and center in civilized settings too. Life with toddlers is labor intensive, period. Canoe trips are no different.

And if you wait till they're old enough, you've lost the bet. By the time they've graduated physically to the point of relative self-sufficiency, you'll be competing with soccer practice, dentist appointments, and birthday parties. If you haven't established a tradition that the kids embrace, a tradition that includes tents and boats, you'll be lucky to get one weekend a year.

Paddling as a family is different from paddling with other adults. Face it and get on with it. Besides, the kids will surprise you with how readily they take to outdoor life, with their exuberance about the small adventures in a day, and with how much they reveal to you about the wonder and magic around you. When was the last time you were amazed by an ant carrying a leaf? Remember how much fun it was to build dams across a little creek or race sticks down a side channel? Here's your chance.

The trip on the Rio Grande was nearly two weeks long. It took three or four days to really get into the rhythm. Kids, like adults, need a transitional window. They're adjusting to the pace, adapting their worldview, getting used to sleeping in a tent and eating outdoors the same as we are. If you go only for an overnight, none of you make the leap to the trip cadence. By the same token, too long is too long. I think ten to twelve days is about the outside limit for kids under six. You can go longer, but the few times we have it's seemed like pushing things, and the kids have been overjoyed to get back home and reacquaint themselves with their toys and their rooms. It's been clear that they were more than ready to return.

The toddler stage is also the one that requires the most flexibility, the most distractions, and the greatest patience. Break up the day's travel with a long lunch break. Make stops to explore and scramble and chase lizards. Build sand castles. Make up stories and sing songs. Short days with plenty of breaks work better than either long days paddling or entire days spent in camp.

The single most failproof distraction is rocks. Toddlers love to throw rocks into the water. It's universal. Eli and Sawyer would stand on the riverbank and heave rocks for hours on end if they had the chance. During the day, we'd fill their buckets with little stones and they'd plunk them over the side as we paddled. Mostly they were content to play with sticks, rocks, and mud, but a few cars and plastic animals were valuable, and we trailed a couple of inflatable toys alongside the canoe that they could reel in and toss out again.

Food diversions were critical. Suckers, fruit candies, licorice, jerky, dried fruit, mixed nuts, lemonade. Once a day, at some critical juncture of family duress, we'd hand out one of those caramel suckers that last forever and make an incredibly sticky mess. The half hour of relative peace was worth it.

Inviting other families with children is another valuable strategy. The kids interact, at least from time to time, so parents are free from constant demands for attention. Couples can also play tag team, taking turns watching the kids and going off on adult excursions.

Several seating scenarios are possible with two kids aboard. Most of the time we put the boys in the center of the canoe, one ahead of the other, in small, low-slung director's chairs we picked up at a local discount store. Dry bags and duffels surrounded them, and they each had a small backpack full of diversionary material. Usually we offset their seats so they could lean over the side and retrieve their inflatable toys or throw rocks overboard.

When they were getting along and wanted to play together, we turned their seats to face each other, and they'd sometimes go for miles inventing games with their animals or coloring. When separation was critical, one of the boys sat on an ammo can in front of the bow paddler while the other held sway in the center of the boat.

Canoe seating arrangement with two toddlers aboard.

Once Ruby was born, and until she turned about two, we crammed all five of us into one beamy seventeen-foot canoe. The two boys ran rampant in the center of the boat while Ruby stayed tethered to the bow parent. Our longest stint with five aboard was a twelve-day cruise down the Yellowstone River. That was plenty. Don't get me wrong. We had fun. It was worth it. But twelve days was plenty.

The good news is that the toddler stage doesn't last forever. In fact, two or three years after the kids are out of diapers, they're ready to move past the passive, sit-in-the-boat gig. By the time they turn six they want to paddle, can actually be of some minor help in camp, and might even be tricked into doing a few chores for fun.

TODDLER TIPS

Most of the same safety advice holds true for infants and toddlers (see page 241). But with toddlers containment is much more of a problem.

Little ones love to play at the water's edge and throw rocks and sticks into the current. It's a good policy to insist they wear life jackets near the water.

Bring lots of Band-Aids in the first-aid kit. Also a small container of eyewash, as well as tweezers to get out splinters or cactus spines.

Bring a few bird, animal, and plant books along. Young kids like to keep a list of exciting things they see and start to identify species.

Work hard on getting kids water-safe. Get them in swimming lessons, go to the pool, take them to local ponds and creeks.

Until children are about five, they don't require lots of extra food at mealtimes. We usually padded the meal plan we used for two adults by about one small portion, and it covered the two boys. The major difference in the menu is the treats and food diversions.

Even at a pretty young age the boys liked to help in camp. They could do some small things like collect firewood and carry the sleeping bags to the tent, and the routine of camp chores is a good ritual to introduce early.

Leg loops on life jackets are still critical at this age. If anything, skinny youngsters with little body definition are even more prone to having life vests slip over their heads than infants are.

Break up a trip with varied activities. Follow a long travel day with some day hike explorations. Stop at a beach to swim and get the kids tired, then they might nap long enough to make some miles.

THIRTY-EIGHT

Subadults

We meet Grant and his two kids, ages thirteen and ten, at a riverside campground along the Yellowstone River in Montana. We have already been afloat for ten days, and Grant will paddle along with us for the next week.

Carolyn, his ten-year-old daughter, immediately adopts the role of Eli's caretaker. Eli is practicing walking while holding on to things, and Carolyn takes on the challenge. She walks slowly behind while Eli hangs on to her thumbs and cruises down the beach. It's a pose that becomes standard over their days together.

Ben is a big kid, physically capable, socially awkward the way all thirteen-year-olds are, able to help when reminded but not particularly focused on the agenda. The adult agenda, that is.

When we get under way, Grant is soloing his canoe for the most part, despite having two passengers. Because Ben is a big teenager and the load can be shifted to trim the canoe, Grant can paddle the boat facing bow downstream. Carolyn and Ben take turns sitting in the bow and ostensibly paddling or seated in the center of the canoe on a duffel with the load heaped around them like bulky armrests.

During her passenger stints, Carolyn dives into her books. White pelicans fly overhead, lovely badlands scenery sweeps past, a mule deer bounds up a slope. Carolyn glances up momentarily, murmurs something vaguely appreciative, and submerges again. Her books' covers show clusters of young girls on sidewalks in front of school buildings.

When he's a passenger, Ben exudes boredom. He drapes himself in the middle of the boat and needles Carolyn about her lack of

Two older kids switch off in paddling and reclining positions.

paddling ability until he finally gets to her and she lets out a frustrated squeal that flushes game for half a mile around. Mostly he just hangs out, talks about Michael Jordan, participates the way teenagers do in groups they've been cajoled into joining. That mixture of disdain, forbearance, and occasional enthusiastic involvement.

Ben is actually a talented and strong paddler when he puts his mind to it. Every so often Grant gets tired of pumping along alone, trying to keep up with the two of us in our canoe, and he gets Ben into a rhythm that's really impressive. Their canoe shoots ahead for a time, but then something happens, the cadence breaks, and it's back to a solo job.

In camp the kids are freer and more involved. Carolyn devotes herself to Eli. Ben gets into hunting for river agates to the point that he fills a duffel with about three hundred pounds of rock and Grant has to do some serious winnowing each morning. They love to swim in stretches of fast water with their life jackets on. We take hikes up side canyons.

One night I ask Carolyn what her favorite foods are. She thinks for a long moment, then says, "Mostly the hot dog family, I'd say." This out of a vegetarian, health-food upbringing. So much for our influence as parents.

There are really fantastic moments too. An evening on a gravel bar where Grant plays his recorder under a twilight sky and Carolyn makes up modern dance routines in the sand. Ben running up with a beautiful moss agate the size of his fist, beaming with discovery. Camp tableaus with the three children arrayed in ways that make adults' hearts swell with tenderness.

Good stuff. The kinds of times we fervently hope will stick through all the other adolescent influences, that will lodge somewhere in the subconscious to be hauled out and awakened as adults.

Other children are the best diversions you can bring along.

On the last night together we camp at the take-out fishing access where Grant had his car shuttled. Since we're near a road, we cruise into town to get some hot-dog-family food. Eli, at eight months, is thoroughly seduced by Carolyn's mystery-meat affinity, and he gobbles down two dogs in about three minutes.

When we paddle on all alone the next morning, there's a palpable sense of loss. I don't miss the sibling squabbling, or Grant's parental pestering, or Carolyn's piercing screams of protest. But they were great company, good companions for Eli, fun to share the adventure with. As I paddle on under the Big Sky, I conjure up images of my own older children, envision trips we'll take together, imagine the paddler Eli might become. They're realistic images, given weight through another man's children, and they're hopeful ones.

TIPS FOR PADDLING WITH SUBADULT COMPANY

Subadult is a category that's hard to pin down exactly. Depends on the kid to a very large extent. I put the brackets at about ages six to sixteen. At age six kids can paddle a bit. They have their own agendas, are physically mobile and energetic, can be seduced into diversionary activities, can sort of entertain themselves. Once past age sixteen, either you have them hooked or you've lost the battle, at least for the time being.

At the young end of this spectrum, you'll probably be paddling solo almost always. Because of the weight disparity, it works best to turn the canoe around and situate yourself near the center of the hull (see page 91). Younger kids fit well in the stern seat turned backward, and they can paddle when moved or stridently requested.

Once children gain a more adult weight and size, somewhere around a hundred pounds, you can turn the canoe back around and at least have a real chance at recruiting a bow paddler.

Older kids are much more pleasant when they have friends along. If they have to put up with an exclusively adult group, there will be tough moments at regular intervals. Invite buddies, or another family with kids, and they can go off and do whatever it is that occupies adolescent and youthful energies.

As with toddlers, it's important to make stops and use up energy with explorations and other activities.

Bring journals, books, sketch pads, small musical instruments, and fishing gear to provide alternative stimulation.

Older kids are capable of getting involved with camp chores and can be a real help, but by that age they've lost the youthful motivation to try adult jobs. It takes some nagging, and it may come down to assigning certain tasks that have to get done before anything else happens, but it's worth establishing the precedent.

Along with the drudgery in camp, let older kids start taking responsibility for some of the more fun daily routines. Give them a turn in the stern on easy stretches of water. Let them navigate for a day. Encourage them to learn safe campfire construction. Have them take part in cooking. Maybe they can have their own tent in camp. If there are a couple of strong paddlers in the younger group, let them paddle their own canoe for part of a day.

Get them involved with some of the trip preparation too. That way they'll know what's in the outfit and how it's packed, they'll have had some say in the menu, they'll have seen the maps and thought about the itinerary. That pretrip engagement gets them that much further along in being involved with the journey.

THIRTY-NINE

Kids' Gear

You'll find out within days of their birth that children have their own unique and pressing requirements in the world and that, from the moment of emergence, they have no trouble at all voicing their needs. It's up to us to interpret and address their problems and frustrations. Being on the water with kids is no different. At every stage they exhibit strong preferences and desires that, often as not, aren't shared by their adult companions. Having the right gear can make the difference between a contentious and exasperating journey and one during which negotiations come to equitable solutions and generations coexist as happily as is ever possible.

Check the full equipment list (pages 186–90) and then add appropriately from this kid checklist to address the needs of your children.

CLOTHING

- water shoes—slip-on mesh shoes are best, and old tennies that don't take an age to dry are second best
- two pairs of dry shoes for camp and day hikes—kids are really good at getting shoes wet
- a full set of extra dry clothes, from socks to hat, just in case
- rain gear that really works—kids' ponchos aren't a bad option, and they cover a fairly broad age range
- diapers for infants (about twenty-five cloth diapers should handle a week on the water, or you can go disposable and deal with the mounting toxic garbage bag)
- good sun hats (neck flaps are nice for infants and toddlers)

PERSONAL GEAR

- small sleeping bag (infants can sleep with parents without a separate sleeping bag or in a lightweight liner envelope made of flannel)
- sleeping pads (you can get away with folding camp chairs laid flat until kids are six or seven)
- sippy cups (cups with lids keep spillage down when kids are little)
- life jackets (make sure they fit snugly but comfortably, have enough buoyancy for the weight range, and have leg loops—it doesn't hurt to have a trial float in the swimming pool to make sure the life jacket works the way it's supposed to)
- books, sketch pads, journals, field guides (especially for toddlers and older kids)
- buckets, shovels, a few floating toys (infants and toddlers)
- books for reading out loud
- simple fishing tackle (older children)
- camp games (Yahtzee, for example, or some card games)

GENERAL EQUIPMENT

- diaper pail (on infant trips that don't have portages)
- picnic blanket (especially with infants and toddlers)
- small day packs for kids' toys and treasures
- paddles (toy ones for the young set, but ones that actually work for kids six and older)
- training potty (for toddlers those plastic, bowl-style potties are really convenient—kids don't have to hover over the latrine, and you can rinse them out after use)
- backpack kid carrier (infants and early toddlers)
- plenty of extra Band-Aids in the first aid kit, along with kid-specific health supplies like baby aspirin, diaper rash ointment, children's sunscreen and insect repellent, and children's allergy medicine
- small folding chairs for kids to sit in on board and in camp
- hand-crank food mill (infants)

FORTY

Trip Activities

I f you think taking to the water will be a panacea against whining and boredom and the other pitfalls of travel with children, you're delusional. You know how on a five-hundred-mile car trip, about six miles in, one of the kids will start the "When will we be there" chant? Well, on canoe trips you might delay the inevitable with backcountry novelty, but the inevitable is just that. Pretty soon kids will want something to do besides sit in their folding chairs and watch the water go by. Pretty soon you'll be pressed into inventing trip sidelines to occupy those eager, peripatetic, and largely uncontainable energies you've given birth to.

In camp, and during stops, it won't be quite as difficult because there are things to get into and movement isn't constrained. The main challenge then may well be containing the explorations. The most difficult times will generally be paddling stints, when children are cooped up and largely unoccupied.

Bring friends. Especially when kids get past the infant stage, bringing other children along is the best diversion. Groups of kids will occupy themselves to a tremendous extent, and they have the passion and energy to stick with each other, whereas adults tend to fizzle after an hour or two of mud play.

Keep lists and journals. Even at a young age, it's fun to catalog things on a trip. Have kids keep track of birds and wildlife they see, make lists, draw pictures, look things up in natural history guides. They can practice writing by keeping journals and making sketches. Bring colored pencils so they can draw as you travel.

Tell stories and sing songs. Kids will sit still and listen to stories pretty well endlessly. Make up tales out of the landscape you're traveling through. I once told a whopper with cowboys and mythical bulls because we were floating past a butte called Bull Mountain. With older kids, start a story and pass it along so everyone creates a chapter. Sing songs to pass the time and perhaps even lull kids to sleep.

Kids need activities on trips, the same as at home.

Make exploratory stops. Break up a long travel day with stops at side canyons, beaches, gravel bars. The stop doesn't have to be long. Kids will immediately start scrambling around, digging in sand, climbing over log-jams, skipping rocks, taking dips, wallowing in mud. A couple of half-hour stops over the day won't slow you down that much, and it will make life inside the canoe much more tolerable.

Read out loud. Reading a chapter of a book makes time fly. One adult can keep paddling while the other reads the story. At night in the tent, it's just like bedtime reading at home.

Have treasure hunts. Rock collecting, picking up pretty driftwood, finding butterflies and lizards and feathers—kids will devote hours to wandering around and finding treasures. The only problem is in winnowing down the stash to the "keepers."

Go swimming. In stretches of benign current, kids who are water-safe love to trail along behind the canoe in the water. They can hang on to the stern line and bob downstream, cooling off and playing in the water. In camp, if a minor bit of current is rolling past, it's fun to wade out with kids and float down through small waves and current, practicing floating on your back with feet downstream to fend off obstacles. It's also a good way to begin teaching the skill of reading water: identifying eddy currents, tongues of deep water, pillows over rocks, and such.

Have stick races. Make little rafts, or race sticks in the current in small streams and side channels.

Fish. A simple spin-casting setup and a couple of lures (make sure you pinch down the barbs) create a huge diversion for kids six and older. If they actually catch a fish, they'll keep at it for hours in hopes of another shot of that electric excitement.

Bring camp toys. A few simple games or toys can enliven camp time tremendously. A soft football, a Frisbee, a soccer ball to play with on beaches; Yahtzee, Go Fish, card memory, a travel set of Battleship for time in the tent or before dinner. Kids will make use of trees and sand and water for most of their play, but having a couple of options to fall back on is good insurance.

Teach trip skills. Kids want to get good at being outdoors and paddling boats too. Challenge them to master the techniques as they become capable. Have them read the map for the day, try paddling in the stern, set up the tent, help cook dinner, figure out how to take a compass bearing, practice tossing a throw bag to someone in the water. Make games out of valuable and useful techniques.

PART SIX

EXPEDITION DESTINATIONS

FORTY-ONE

An Expedition Medley

I never meant this book to be a destination guide, and it isn't. But when the discussion turns to trip lore, the seduction of places hovers in the background—or at least it should. It's what fuels this business, after all, those bodacious swatches of geography. Behind the lists and techniques lie the expanses of open lake, the roar of rapids, the quiet canyons, the misty dawns with a canoe wake drawn through them. Without them, what's the point? What's a garage full of gear and file drawers crammed with paper without places to explore?

Willpower has never been my strong suit, so why should I resist the temptation to throw in a few great places to set canoes in the water and stroke off toward adventure? Take my ideas and massage them to suit your needs. Make them longer or shorter, easier or more difficult, add another stretch of river, connect to a nearby drainage, throw in a portage, and keep going. My guess is that if you really are made in the canoe tripping mold, you'll prove my point. You'll take one of these jaunts and come up with six more you need to get to.

You'll go to the Big Bend of the Rio Grande and realize there are more canyons both upstream and down that you have to do. Or you'll paddle the Pictured Rocks shoreline of Lake Superior and the North Shore will beckon. Or you'll do some of the Missouri River in Montana and the headwaters will pull you their way. Pretty soon you'll have a life list to bequeath to your descendants along with whatever else your estate has to offer. To have more trips lined up than a life span can cover is wealth no bank account can match.

BIG BEND OF THE RIO GRANDE

Immerse yourself in the exotic spell of Big Bend country in Texas. Chihuahuan desert cactus, sheer limestone canyons, remote Mexican ranchland to the south. Birds not found anywhere else in the United States, hot springs alongside the river channel, slot canyons to explore with pools draped in maidenhair fern, peregrine falcons on airy cliffs.

The Rio Grande winds for 130 miles along the border of Big Bend National Park, between Lajitas and the highway bridge at La Linda. Three major canyons—Santa Elena, Mariscal, and Boquillas—break up the float, separated by open desert stretches. Several major rapids warrant caution, most notably the Rock Slide in Santa Elena, rated class IV at moderate and high water. Several other rapids can reach class III difficulty.

Plan ten to twelve days for a leisurely pace along the entire park

Big Bend National Park.

boundary. Winter is a great time to do the float, and fall or spring can be nice as well. Midsummer is brutally hot, with daytime temperatures over 100°F.

TRIP PLANNER

ROUTE. Lajitas to La Linda—130 miles. Shorter trips down one or more of the canyon sections are easily arranged, and longer trips can be added to incorporate canyons both upstream and down.

SKILL LEVEL. Intermediate to expert.

SEASON. October to May is best in terms of weather. Check with local sources to research water levels and drought conditions.

CONTACT. Big Bend Natural History Association, P.O. Box 68, Big Bend National Park TX 79834; 915-477-2236, www.bigbendbookstore.org (river maps, shuttle and outfitter contacts, park information).

LAKE SUPERIOR'S PICTURED ROCKS

Lake Superior is oceanic, a body of water with purity and power unmatched by any other; and Pictured Rocks is one of the most stupendous sections of coast on a lake renowned for stupendous shorelines. Sheer faces of sandstone, waterfalls pouring straight into the lake, miles of pristine beaches, trails to walk inland.

For roughly fifty miles, the shoreline is quiet wilderness, most of it protected as National Lakeshore. Put in at Grand Marais, Michigan, or at one of several access points nearby and paddle to Munising, at the western end of the park. The route is split roughly fifty-fifty between long sand beaches on the eastern half and sheer sandstone cliffs on the western half. Designated campsites are spaced at convenient intervals along the way, with trails that wind along the shore or penetrate inland through forests.

Pictured Rocks National Lakeshore.

Lake Superior is vast open water, so paddlers should beware of sudden storms and winds. Outfit canoes with spray decks and plan extra time in the itinerary for weather delays. Sections along cliff faces with few safe places to land are particularly dangerous. Pick your crossing moments with care.

TRIP PLANNER

ROUTE. Fifty miles from near Grand Marais to Munising. Or make a loop along the sand beach section and back to avoid the danger of cliffs.

SKILL LEVEL. Beginner to intermediate.

SEASON. July is the best bet for calm winds and pleasant weather.

CONTACT. Pictured Rocks National Lakeshore, P.O. Box 40, Munising MI 49862-0040; 906-387-3700; www.nps.gov/piro.

RANGELEY LAKES, MAINE, AND THE NORTHERN FOREST CANOE TRAIL

Rangeley Lakes lie on the border between Maine and New Hampshire, nestled in the beauty of the White Mountains. The 40-mile established water trail was the first dedicated section of the 740-mile Northern Forest Canoe Trail (NFCT). It incorporates a lovely bit of lake and stream country, full of quiet campsites, moose and loons, and New England beauty. Much of the trail follows lakeshores, but there are several sections of small streams to navigate as well. Portages are available around rapids, some of which can reach class IV difficulty. Do the entire 40 miles, putting in at the town of Rangeley and taking out below the Errol Dam portage, or take on a shorter portion of the route and arrange a shuttle at one of several access points.

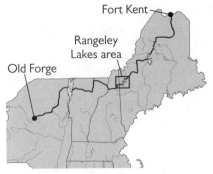

Northern Forest Canoe Trail.

For a much more extensive challenge, try the entire NFCT, which connects Old Forge, New York, in the Adirondacks, with Fort Kent, Maine, on the Canadian border. Although sections of the route cross through settled land, the NFCT demands the entire gamut of a paddler's skills—open water crossings, upstream travel, portages, whitewater—and takes about eight weeks to navigate.

TRIP PLANNER

ROUTE. The 40-mile Rangeley Lake trail extends from Rangeley, Maine, to the Androscoggin River below Errol Dam. The 740-mile Northern Forest Canoe Trail goes from Old Forge, New York, to Fort Kent, Maine.

SKILL LEVEL. Beginner to intermediate for Rangeley Lakes; expert for NFCT.

SEASON. May through September.

CONTACTS. Northern Forest Canoe Trail, Inc., P.O. Box 572, Waitsfield VT 05673; 802-496-2285; www.northernforestcanoetrail.org (maps and guidebooks).

 Rangeley Lakes Heritage Trust, P.O. Box 249, Oquosoc ME 04964; 207-864-7311; www.rangeley.org/rlhthome/ (maps, interpretive guides, outfitter, and shuttle contacts).

WILD AND SCENIC MISSOURI RIVER, MONTANA

The 150-mile section of the Missouri River between Fort Benton and James Kipp Bridge is without question the piece of Lewis and Clark's trail that remains the most unchanged since they traveled through in the summer of 1805, and the most evocative of their grand expedition. The river makes great loops through the semiarid land of central Montana. Sculpted sandstone formations rise away from the river, badlands "breaks" offer chances to explore, and you can camp in the same cottonwood groves as Lewis and Clark. Bring a copy of the expedition journals to read from as you paddle.

 The Missouri along this reach is easy water with no rapids. The biggest challenge is occasional upriver winds that can be a struggle. Desert bighorn sheep are sometimes sighted along the lower reaches, and white pelicans are common all along.

The route can be broken roughly in half by taking out at the Judith Landing Bridge. Trips can run two to three days or cover the entire distance in five to eight days. Camp in cottonwood groves or on islands, or take advantage of several established sites at scenic points along the way. Plan to allow plenty of time for exploration.

Missouri River between Fort Benton and James Kipp Bridge.

TRIP PLANNER

ROUTE. It's 150 miles from Fort Benton to James Kipp Bridge on Highway 191. Shorter trips can put in at Coal Banks Landing, downstream from Fort Benton, or at Judith Crossing, roughly halfway.

SKILL LEVEL. Beginner to intermediate.

SEASON. June through September.

CONTACT. Bureau of Land Management, Lewistown District, Airport Road, Lewistown MT 59457; 406-538-7461.

EVERGLADES WILDERNESS CANOE TRAIL, FLORIDA

Water is what makes the Everglades what they are, and water trails are the best way to explore this strange and lovely environment. Several paddling loops are available throughout the park, but the 100-mile Wilderness Waterway, established and maintained by Everglades National Park, has the most expedition-like quality. It meanders through swamp, river, and lake at a slow pace while you take in the sights of alligators, egrets, and mangroves.

Campsites are like none you've probably ever experienced. Since solid ground is pretty well nonexistent, platforms called "chickees" have been built at intervals along the entire route, complete with picnic tables, fire grates, and tent spots. The Everglades have an almost imperceptible gradient, so water flows very slowly. The biggest challenges are mosquitoes in the summer and the disorientation that comes from long periods of not walking on solid ground.

TRIP PLANNER

ROUTE. One hundred miles from the Gulf Coast Ranger Station to the Flamingo Visitors' Center. Shorter sections can also be done.

SKILL LEVEL. Beginner to intermediate.

SEASON. Winter is best for bird and wildlife viewing and for a tolerable level of mosquitoes. Summer is hot, muggy, and buggy.

CONTACT. Everglades National Park, P.O. Box 279, Homestead FL 33030; 305-242-7700; fax 305-247-7728; www.nps.gov/ever/.

LAKE ATHABASCA CIRCUMNAVIGATION

Sometimes big lakes are worth a trip just for their own sake. Lake Athabasca is very remote northern wilderness, but it has road access at the western end and varied scenery and paddling conditions that keep the route interesting. The circle route begins and ends at Fort Chipewyan, Alberta. Paddle the north shore first for an experience of glaciated bedrock and convoluted shoreline that offers protection from winds, islands full of blueberries, and impressive headlands. Uranium City, almost a ghost town, sits at the halfway point, and where the lake finally narrows down, roughly 150 miles later, the Chipewyan town of Fond du Lac offers the chance for resupply and contact with the outside world.

Turn around there or continue all the way into the narrows to Stony Rapids, Saskatchewan. You can end the trip there and fly out or come back along the more exposed southern lakeshore. Sand dunes, beaches, and tributaries like the MacFarlane River offer diversions along the return, which ends at the vast Peace–Athabasca delta.

It's worth exploring Fort Chipewyan, Fond du Lac, and Wood Buffalo National Park, since you've come that far. Add on the Athabasca, Peace, or Fond du Lac Rivers to make an already extensive trip a true expedition.

Lake Athabasca is vast and prone to fickle weather. Spray covers are really an asset, and windbound delays are almost certain. Pad the itinerary with some extra time and use the breaks to pick blueberries, fish for lake trout, or explore the country.

TRIP PLANNER

ROUTE. From 300 to 450 miles, depending on where you decide to turn around.

SKILL LEVEL. Intermediate canoeing skills, expert wilderness skills.

SEASON. Ice sometimes doesn't go off Lake Athabasca until mid-June, and by mid-August fall is already in the air. July is the most dependable travel month.

CONTACTS. Travel Alberta, 5th Floor, 999 8th St. SW, Calgary AB CANADA T2R 1J5; 403-297-6574.

SaskTravel, 3211 Albert St., Regina SK CANADA S4S 5W6; 306-565-2300.

Wood Buffalo National Park, P.O. Box 750, Fort Smith NT

CANADA X0E 0P0; http://parkscanada.pch.gc.ca/parks/nwtw/
wood_buffalo/Wood_buffalo_e.htm.

GREEN AND COLORADO RIVERS, UTAH

Stillwater and Labyrinth Canyons of the Green River provide the experience
of big-wall, high-desert canyon country without the rapids associated with
so many of the river canyons in that region. Put in at the town park in Green
River, Utah, and float 123 miles to Spanish Bottom, just downstream of
the confluence of the Green and the Colorado and just upstream of Cataract
Canyon. Alternative put-ins at Ruby Ranch and Mineral Bottom allow for
shorter trips.

Camping is lovely in side canyons and on sand beaches. Along with the
experience of floating through the grandeur of these tremendous canyons,
the potential for hiking is unlimited. Some people just float down as a
means to get to great hiking country. At the very least, hike to the Doll
House from Spanish Bottom at the end of the trip.

The only downside to this trip, as I see it, is that you are saddled with paying for a jet-boat shuttle up the Colorado River to Moab at the end. The only
other ways out are to paddle up the Colorado or portage out through Canyonlands National Park. Neither option is very workable for most people.

Take a copy of John Wesley Powell's journals and read aloud, imag-
ining what it must have been like to be the first known explorer to
encounter this awesome, compelling desert landscape with great rivers
coiling through it.

TRIP PLANNER

ROUTE. It's 123 miles from
Green River to Spanish
Bottom, 100 miles if you
put in at Ruby Ranch,
and 55 miles if you start
at Mineral Bottom.

SKILL LEVEL. Beginner to
intermediate.

SEASON. Early summer and
fall are best. Midsummer
is very hot, and the lower
river is full of rafts. Early
in the season you get high
water for better floating
conditions, but fall allows
more campsite choices and pleasant temperatures.

Green and Colorado Rivers.

CONTACTS. Canyonlands National Park, 2282 SW Resource Blvd.,
   Moab UT 84532; 801-259-5277; www.nps.gov/cany/.
      Bureau of Land Management, San Rafael Resource Area,
   900 N. 700 E., Price UT 84501; 801-637-4584.

YUKON RIVER

It's hard to imagine a trip more steeped in history, more redolent of the Far
North, than a paddle down the Yukon River. It's fairly brimming with arti-
facts and stories from the gold rush era. It whispers with Jack London stories and the poetry of Robert Service.

Besides which, the Yukon is a big, wild flow with plenty to offer even
without its rich history. The water in this stretch is fast but very straightforward, a perfect trip for families or a first wilderness expedition. The
camping is best on islands and gravel bars, where a breeze keeps the bugs
down and the fishing can be fantastic.

The entire 270-mile jaunt between Dawson, in the Yukon, and Circle,
Alaska, takes one to two weeks, depending on how much you want to dawdle and explore, or you can take out at Eagle, Alaska, after 100 miles and
three to four days. The Yukon has carved itself a massive valley, full of
islands and channels and rock bluffs, where distances are deceiving. It's
very much a river-centered trip in that few hiking trails offer themselves,
and side excursions for the most part are limited to checking out old min-
ing cabins here and there.

TRIP PLANNER

ROUTE. Start at the riverside campground just below Dawson, in the
   Yukon Territory, and paddle 270 miles, crossing the United States
   border along the way, to Circle, Alaska. Alternatively, take out at
   Eagle, Alaska, 100 miles along.
SKILL LEVEL. Beginner to intermediate paddler with strong wilder-
   ness camping background.
SEASON. June through September (August and September are best
   for campsite selection and fewer bugs).
CONTACTS. Yukon-Charley Rivers National Preserve, P.O. Box 167,
   Eagle AK 99738; 907-547-2233; www.nps.gov/yuch/.
      Eagle Canoe Rentals, P.O. Box 4, Eagle AK 99738;
   907-547-2203.

Off-Season Boat Puttering

A long about the middle of February in Montana, the restlessness starts up. Daylight is slowly oozing back north, and there's been a thaw or two already. Winter seems to have gone on long enough, thank you. I keep waking up late at night thinking about rivers, about lazy afternoons floating along the Yellowstone with the Absaroka Mountains looming over the valley and bald eagles hovering in search of one of those blue ribbon trout.

Problem is, it's too early by a solid couple of months. In the morning the yard will still be full of crusted snow, the canoes will be mantled with a quilt of the white stuff, and the rivers will still be clamped in that icy vise of season. But the restlessness won't go away, not entirely.

So I do the next best thing to paddling. It's a very distant next best thing, but so be it. I get the canoes down from the rack, pull them into the garage, and start puttering.

Just being around them, running my hand over the rounded hulls, feeling the wood gunwales, touching up the paint job, is a temporary antidote to the restless doldrums. Not a cure, mind you. Only being out again, dancing downstream, will cure that seasonal angst, but boat puttering is at least a couple of aspirin for the soul.

BOAT INSPECTION

Begin by taking stock. Start at the stern and work slowly around the entire boat, then turn it over and go round again. Abrasions and gouges? Dried-out wood? D-rings coming unglued? Ropes frayed or worn?

As you take this first inventory, things from the last paddling season will start popping into your head. You'll remember the frustration in white-water at not having adequate knee pads. Then there's that lash tab you wished you had to tie in gear. And the portage pads you vowed to put on and then never did.

If you're a list maker, make a list of the obvious chores. If you don't have my short-term memory problem, keep the list in your head and gather yourself for the work.

START SLOW AND EASY

Sneak up on the bigger jobs by taking on the simple, mindless tasks first. Replace the bow line with the worn spot, tighten a few screws, sand down the rough spots on the wood trim, reglue the corner of D-ring that's come loose. Maybe there are some paddling accessories that need similar care— a paddle that cries out for another coat of wood varnish, a dry bag that could use a patch, the zipper slider on your tent that ought to be replaced. By the time you've warmed up on the little jobs, you'll be in the proper frame of mind to take on more important work.

TENDING THE WOOD TRIM AND GUNWALES

Wood is aesthetic stuff, a beautiful accent to any canoe. Besides, it tends to be lighter than other trim materials. The only real downside is that wood requires maintenance to stay beautiful and functional.

When you go through the initial inspection, check for dings, gouges, splinters, and other rough spots in the wood. Your job is to keep these vulnerable spots from getting worse and protect them from moisture. Smooth any rough places, using 180- to 220-grit sandpaper. Clean away excess dirt with a damp rag and repair splinters or cracks with yellow wood glue. Clamp the glue jobs in place for at least six hours.

A couple of times every year, and mid-February is as good a time as any, give the wood trim a good oiling. Use a penetrating oil such as marine-grade Watco or Deks Olje and apply with a clean soft rag. A couple of coats may be warranted if the wood is particularly dry. Pay particular attention to screw holes. These are prone to cracking, moisture penetration, and dry rot. Check around the holes for the gray staining that signals mildew. If you find any, back the screw all the way out, drip in some oil, and reseat the screw.

HULL REPAIRS

Preventing hull damage, and quickly repairing any problems, is the most important aspect of extending the life of a canoe. Ultraviolet rays are the big culprit. Sunlight will fade the gel coat or vinyl layer over time, but that's largely a cosmetic fact of aging. More important, sunlight will break down exposed core material and even make the entire hull brittle over long years of unprotected storage.

If years of bumping over ledges, bashing rocks, and scraping through shallows have worn away the protective coating and revealed the core layers of Royalex, Kevlar, or fiberglass, you'll need to deal with it, and the sooner the better. Here's how.

Royalex

In most cases the easiest way to treat wear spots is to simply apply another coat of paint. Canoe manufacturers carry vinyl paint to match hull colors, though any fading your hull has already done will make a perfect match unlikely. You can also buy flat acrylic primer, the kind auto body and marine shops use. Match your color as closely as you can, clean the surface, rough up the area lightly with sandpaper, and paint the worn spots.

For the rare deep gouges, clean the area with an acetone-moistened paper towel, let it dry, then fill the gouge with an epoxy putty. Canoe companies sell patch material, or you can get the same stuff at building supply stores. Usually it's called epoxy ribbon or epoxy putty, and it comes in a two-toned stick that you mix before using. Spread it with a putty knife so the fill is slightly raised. When it dries completely, sand it down smooth and apply a coat of paint.

Fiberglass

Small scratches in the gel coat are often more trouble than they're worth to repair. Sometimes you do more damage by trying to fix them and they're better off just left alone.

Larger, deeper scratches should be cleaned out and slightly enlarged with a knife blade, cleaned with acetone, and then surrounded by tape. Fill the scratch level with the surface with colored gel resin mixed with catalyst (available through canoe dealers). Before the resin dries, remove the tape and carve off any excess with a knife. It's best to set up the repair outside, but in the shade. In direct sunlight the resin hardens in minutes.

After the repair has set for several hours, sand it smooth with 300- to 400-grit wet-dry sandpaper and then rag polish the repair with some rubbing compound.

For big gouges and abrasions, clean the area, tape it, and carefully pool the resin-catalyst mixture without overfilling. Carve down any excess before it hardens, then finish off the repair as you would with scratches.

Kevlar

Kevlar hulls (especially with clear gel coats) should be waxed with good-quality car wax once a year to mitigate ultraviolet damage. The most common wear spots on Kevlar hulls are at the ends, where the material gets fuzzy when worn. This isn't a problem until you wear through several layers. Until then it's enough to sand down the fuzzy material with 300-grit wet-dry sandpaper, reapply gel coat if necessary, and then polish it up. After long use and several repairs, it might be time to consider grunch pads (see below).

GRUNCH PADS

If you're like me, which is to say not always obsessively careful with my gear, you'll eventually need to add grunch pads to those vulnerable ends of your canoe. My experience is that the common lot of an expedition canoe, which includes fairly regular scraping and hauling over sand, rock, wood, and whatnot, will wear away the protective coating at the bow and stern in surprisingly short order. It's usually the stern that goes first, but if you're installing one grunch pad, you might as well do two.

I used to routinely add grunch pads as soon as I got a new canoe. More recently, though, I've waited until the boat's been used enough to warrant protection before adding the weight, and changing (ever so slightly) the paddling characteristics, of my canoe.

Installing grunch pads to the worn ends of a canoe hull.

It's best to go to a boat retailer and buy a kit. They cost roughly $50 and include two Kevlar felt pads, epoxy resin, hardener, and instructions.

The instructions will explain the process better than I can, but in a nutshell what you'll be doing is this. First, cut the pads to fit the wear pattern on your boat hull. Rough up the hull with sandpaper and clean the area with a damp rag. Mix up the epoxy and hardener, soak the pads, and lay them in place to cure. Make sure you work in a shaded, well-ventilated spot. This resin mixture is particularly potent.

EXPEDITION OUTFITTING

The three most useful bits of boat customizing for longer trips, in my estimation, are these:

Bow and Stern Lines

Use rope that is easy on the hands and that will hold a knot. (In other words, not that slippery colored nylon stuff you see attached to the bows of sailboat dinghies!) I like a tightly woven, ⅜-inch diameter rope between 25 and 30 feet long. Some people advise lines up to one hundred feet to help with particularly difficult lining propositions, but I've paddled thousands of miles and never needed more than 30 feet. Besides, excess rope has a way of getting tangled up and in the way. If you're really concerned about it, throw some extra line in the repair kit or use the throw rope for reserve.

Knee Pads

I kneel only sporadically on long trips, but when I need that lowered center of gravity in rapids or waves, it's nice to be comfortable. Besides, knee joints are notoriously vulnerable to injury, and when you get to that creaky, arthritic time of life, padding is not just nice, it's essential.

The 3-inch-thick pads advocated for whitewater paddling are, I think, overkill. I like ½-inch closed-cell foam cut in two rectangles with rounded corners, roughly 9 by 12 inches per pad. Kneel in your canoe the way you would when paddling and position a pad under each knee. Outline the rectangle with a marker. Clean the area and rough it up slightly with sandpaper, then install the pads using Vynabond (an epoxy-based glue) or two-part polyurethane glue.

Lash Points

I'm adamant about tying in my gear, and I sometimes need more tie-down points than the thwarts and canoe seats allow for. Pick up metal or plastic lash loop kits from a boating retailer. They're easy to install on wood gunwales. If you don't have wood trim to attach to, glue in a couple of small D-rings (¾-inch should do it) on the hull, just below the level of the gun-

In rough water, it's important to kneel to lower your center of gravity. Knee pads provide comfort and protection.

wales. Some folks even add a D-ring or two on the floor to tie in smaller loads or really cinch down the gear.

WINTERIZING

Now, if you've waited until mid-February to do this, either you are a very bad boat owner who should consider some time-management counseling or you live someplace like Florida, where winter is only a less balmy version of summer.

In temperate climates like Montana, winter can be the toughest season on your boat even though it never comes near running water. Moisture, sunlight, and extreme temperature fluctuations are patiently wearing down your trusty craft the same way they wear down mountains.

If you're lucky, you can keep your boats inside and avoid the season. If not, at least do the minimum—pamper the woodwork (see above), keep your boat off the ground, and patch or paint the hull to prevent ultraviolet damage.

In parts of the world that get large accumulations of snow each winter, remember that canoes (especially fiberglass hulls) can be crushed and dented by snow and ice buildup or when a snow load slides off a roof. A protective roof is ideal. Barring that, store boats away from steep roofs and remember to shovel snow off the hull when it gets thick.

Where temperatures get well below zero during the winter, canoes with wood gunwales and Royalex hulls are prone to "cold cracking." At extreme temperatures, the wood and Royalex expand and contract at radically different rates. The pressure created can crack the canoe hull, sometimes severely.

Cold cracking is easy to prevent. Simply back off the screws that hold the gunwales to the hull so the two materials aren't rigidly held together. The sections of the gunwales nearest the ends of the boat are particularly critical. Screws near the bow and stern should be substantially backed out. At the end of the winter, before tightening the screws again, dribble a drop or two of oil around the screw holes to prevent moisture damage.

MAKING A SIMPLE BOAT RACK

OK, so you've done all the puttering you can think of, even the bigger jobs, and you're still restless and irritable. This level of boater's angst might just require an additional project. Let's try building a two- or three-boat storage rack. (Dimensions used here work for boats between 16 and 18 feet long.)

Materials

two 8-foot two-by-fours
four 3-foot two-by-fours
eight 3-foot two-by-twos
six 4-inch lag screws
sixteen 2½-inch lag screws

eight 4-inch nails
eight metal plates and sixteen
    screws
one quart wood stain or paint

Tools

drill with bits
saw
hammer

crescent/socket wrench
screwdriver
paintbrush

Construction

1. In the 8-foot two-by-fours (the uprights), drill holes for the 4-inch lag screws at 2½ feet, 4½ feet, and 7 feet, measuring from the ground up.

2. Using 4-inch nails, attach the 3-foot two-by-fours (the shelves) to the uprights, one at 3 feet and one at 6 feet from the ground, hammering the nails in from the back of the uprights.

3. The weight of the boats will tend to pull these nails out, so anchor each side of the 3-foot shelves to the upright with a metal plate and screws. (You could even add some right-angle metal plates and screws below and above each shelf for extra support.)

4. Use the two-by-twos (two per shelf) as angled support pieces. Measure 17 inches down from the top of each shelf along the edge of the 8-foot uprights, drill a hole, and loosely attach one end of the two-by-two there with a 2½-inch lag screw. (Allow the two-by-two to extend slightly past the upright and cut it off flush after you've finished.) Swivel the two-by-two up until it

Three-boat storage rack.

rests beside the outside of the shelf, about 25 inches out from the upright. Another 2 ½-inch lag screw goes there. Tighten the screws and cut the two-by-twos flush. Repeat this on both sides of all four shelf pieces.

5. Stain or paint the rack and let it dry.
6. Attach the rack to your outside wall with the four-inch lag screws. From outside edge to outside edge of the uprights, my rack measures 9 feet, 8 inches.

You've just made yourself a two-boat rack, with room for a third to rest on blocks below the bottom shelf.

Wilderness Paddler's Resource Center

BOOKS

Some of these books may be out of print but still available through interlibrary loan or used-book sources.

American Canoe Association. *Introduction to Paddling: Canoeing Basics for Lakes and Rivers.* Birmingham AL: Menasha Ridge, 1996.

Cassady, Jim, Bill Cross, and Fryar Calhoun. *Western Whitewater: From the Rockies to the Pacific, a River Guide for Raft, Kayak, and Canoe.* Berkeley CA: North Fork, 1994.

Conover, Garrett. *Beyond the Paddle: A Canoeist's Guide to Expedition Skills: Poling, Lining, Portaging, and Maneuvering through the Ice.* Gardiner ME: Tilbury House, 1991. A thorough and engaging treatment of less common canoe tripping skills.

Davidson, James West, and John Rugge. *The Complete Wilderness Paddler.* New York: Vintage Books, 1983. A classic in how-to literature, using a trip tale to hang the information on.

Geiger, Beth, ed. *Paddle Sports.* Bethesda MD: Discovery Communications, 2000.

Getchell, Annie, and Dave Getchell Jr. *The Essential Outdoor Gear Manual: Equipment Care, Repair, and Selection.* 2nd ed. Camden ME: Ragged Mountain Press, 2000. Good overview of how to deal with and care for all manner of outdoor equipment.

Jettmar, Karen. *The Alaska River Guide: Canoeing, Kayaking, and Rafting in the Last Frontier.* Anchorage: Alaska Northwest, 1998.

Kellogg, Zip, ed. *The Whole Paddler's Catalog.* Camden ME: Ragged Mountain Press, 1997.

Kesselheim, Alan S. *Going Inside: A Couple's Journey of Renewal into the North.* Toronto: McClelland & Stewart, 1995. A second trans-Canadian expedition tale, this time with a baby along in utero.

Kesselheim, Alan S. *Threading the Currents: A Paddler's Passion for Water.* Washington DC: Island Press, 1998. A collection of water-based stories drawn from some twenty-five years of paddling experiences.

Kesselheim, Alan S. *Trail Food: Drying and Cooking Food for Backpackers and Paddlers.* Camden ME: Ragged Mountain Press, 1998. My own guide to drying food for wilderness trips, with more than fifty recipes.

Kesselheim, Alan S. *Water and Sky: Reflections of a Northern Year.* Golden CO: Fulcrum, 1989. My adventure tale of my first yearlong journey across Canada.

Kraiker, Rolf, and Debra Kraiker. *Cradle to Canoe: Camping and Canoeing with Children.* Erin ON: Boston Mills Press, 1999.

Manley, Atwood, and Paul F. Jamieson. *Rushton and His Times in American Canoeing.* Syracuse NY: Syracuse University Press, 1968. The story of one of America's most notable canoe builders and the birth of recreational paddling in North America.

Morse, Eric W. *Fur Trade Canoe Routes of Canada: Then and Now.* 2nd ed. Toronto: University of Toronto Press, 1979. A great source of northern trip ideas, with lots of historical information.

Niemi, Judith, and Barbara Wieser, eds. *Rivers Running Free: Canoeing Stories by Adventurous Women.* Seattle: Seal Press, 1992. A nice collection of paddling adventures undertaken by North American women.

Olson, Sigurd F. *The Singing Wilderness.* Minneapolis: University of Minnesota Press, 1997. Perhaps the best work by this Minnesota nature writer, wilderness paddler, and conservationist.

Patterson, R. M. *Dangerous River: Adventure on the Nahanni.* Erin ON: Boston Mills, 1999. A reissued version of the rollicking tale of a season spent in the wilds of northern Canada. Told in great style.

Powell, John Wesley. *The Exploration of the Colorado River and Its Canyons.* New York: Penguin, 1997. The best rendering of one-armed John Wesley Powell's account of his first descent of the Green and Colorado Rivers in 1869. A true adventure.

Ray, Slim. *The Canoe Handbook: Techniques for Mastering the Sport of Canoeing.* Harrisburg PA: Stackpole, 1992.

Ross, Cindy, and Todd Gladfelter. *Kids in the Wild.* Seattle: Mountaineers, 1995.

Seidman, David, and Paul Cleveland. *The Essential Wilderness Navigator.* 2nd ed. Camden ME, Ragged Mountain Press, 2001. For those who want to dive into the intricacies of map and compass.

Sevareid, Eric. *Canoeing with the Cree.* St. Paul MN: Minnesota Historical Society, 1968. A classic piece of inspiration and adventure, originally published in 1935, based on the story of two young men who put a canoe in the water in their home town and paddled north to Hudson Bay.

Stelmok, Jerry, and Rollin Thurlow. *The Wood and Canvas Canoe: A Complete Guide to Its History, Construction, Restoration, and Maintenance.* Gardiner ME: Harpswell Press, 1987. A book devoted to the wood and canvas canoe, complete with instructions on how to build, repair, and maintain your own.

Walbridge, Charles, and Wayne Sundmacher Sr. *Whitewater Rescue Manual: New Techniques for Canoeists, Kayakers, and Rafters.* Camden ME: Ragged Mountain Press, 1995.

Wilkerson, James A. *Medicine for Mountaineering and Other Wilderness Activities.* 4th ed. Seattle: Mountaineers, 1992. This remains the authoritative wilderness first aid and treatment guide. Get the most recent edition and put it in the trip first aid kit.

PERIODICALS

Backpacker
33 E. Minor St.
Emmaus PA 18098
610-967-8296
E-mail:
    editor@backpacker.com
www.backpacker.com
Leading outdoor recreation journal, with some emphasis on paddling stories.

Canoe and Kayak
10526 N.E. 68th St., Suite 3
Kirkland WA 98033
800-829-3340, 425-827-6363
Fax 425-827-1893
E-mail: subscribe@canoekayak.com

www.canoekayak.com
The leading periodical of paddle sports. The annual buyer's guide is especially valuable.

Che-Mun: The Newsletter of Canadian Wilderness Canoeing
P.O. Box 548, Station O
Toronto ON
CANADA M4A 2P1
416-789-2142
Fax 416-789-7553
E-mail:
    mpeake@rogers.wave.ca
www.gorp.com/chemun/alex2.htm
The best, and most interesting, publication devoted to wilder-

ness trips in the North and the
issues that relate to northern
expeditions.

Kanawa
P.O. Box 398
Merrickville ON
CANADA KOG INO
888-2KANAWA (888-252-6292)
Fax 613-269-2908

E-mail: staff@crca.ca
www.crca.ca

Paddler
P.O. Box 775450
Steamboat Springs CO 80477
970-879-1450
E-mail: circulation@paddler-
    magazine.com
www.paddlermagazine.com

WEB SITES

www.acanet.org

The American Canoe Association is the granddaddy of paddling clubs
in North America. The Web site includes affiliate clubs, publications
(books and magazines), conferences and events, and general information for paddlers.

www.amrivers.org

American Rivers is a nonprofit conservation organization dedicated
to the preservation and enhancement of rivers. Publishes a newsletter,
promotes advocacy and political action.

www.americanwhitewater.org

The Web site for American Whitewater, an organization devoted to
whitewater paddling, with special emphasis given to boating safety
and rescues and to issues involving river access.

www.gorp.com

A general outdoor site, with some attention given to paddling.

www.nativetrails.org

The Web site for Native Trails, Inc., a worldwide nonprofit geographic
and educational organization that traces major historic travel routes.
The Web site has information on canoe trails, particularly in the Northern Forest.

www.thebackpacker.com

A site maintained by *Backpacker* magazine, devoted to general recreation, including paddling.

www.tourism-canada.com

The general tourism and travel site for all of Canada. From here, link
to specific topics of recreation or go to the province or territory
you're interested in.

www.usgs.gov

Use this site to get into the main site maintained by the United States Geological Survey. The two most useful features found here are the Current Streamflow site, which maintains an up-to-the-minute record of water levels on all streams and rivers with gauging stations. They are organized by state and also show historical records for stream flows, which can provide useful comparative data. This site also links to map ordering information, online or off.

www.wcha.org

Site for the Wooden Canoe Heritage Association, a nonprofit group working to preserve the history and heritage of traditional canoes.

PADDLING SCHOOLS

Adventure Quest
P.O. Box 184
Woodstock VT 05091
802-484-3939

Bear Paw Outdoor
Adventure Resort
N3494 Highway 55
White Lake WI 54491
715-882-3502
E-mail:
   bearpaw@newnorth.net
www.bearpawinn.com

California Canoe and Kayak
Jack London Square
409 Water St.
Oakland CA 94607
800-366-9804, 510-893-7833
E-mail: calkayak@aol.com
www.calkayak.com

Madawaska Kanu Centre
P.O. Box 635
Barry's Bay ON
CANADA KOJ 1BO
613-756-3620, 613-594-5268
   (winter)
E-mail: paddle@owl-mkc.ca
www.owl-mkc.ca/mkc

Nantahala Outdoor Center (NOC)
13077 Highway 19 W.
Bryson City NC 28713
888-662-1662, 828-488-2175
E-mail: programs@noc.com
www.noc.com

New England Outdoor Center
P.O. Box 669
Millinocket ME 04462
800-766-7238
E-mail: info@neoc.com
www.neoc.com

RiverRun Paddling Centre
P.O. Box 179
Beachburg ON
CANADA KOJ 1CO
800-267-8504
E-mail: riverrun@renc.igs.net
www.riverrunners.com

Rocky Mountain Outdoor Center
University of Whitewater
10281 Highway 50
Howard CO 81233
800-255-5784
E-mail: rmoc@rmoc.com
www.rmoc.com

Saco Bound
P.O. Box 119
Center Conway NH 03813
603-447-2177

Fax 603-447-6278
E-mail: rivers@sacobound.com
www.neoutdoors.com/sacobound

WILDERNESS FIRST AID AND SAFETY

National Association for Search and Rescue
4500 Southgate Pl., Suite 100
Chantilly VA 20151-1714
703-222-6277
www.nasar.org

Wilderness Medicine Institute
P.O. Box 9
413 Main St.
Pitkin CO 81241
970-641-3572
www.wildernessmed.com

Stonehearth Open Learning Opportunities (SOLO)
P.O. Box 3150
Conway NH 03818
603-447-6711
www.stonehearth.com

Wilderness Medical Associates
189 Dudley Rd.
Bryant Pond ME 04219
888-945-3633, 207-665-2707
E-mail: office@wildmed.com
www.wildmed.com

MAP ORDERING

Topographic Maps for the United States

United States Geological Survey Information Services
P.O. Box 25286
Denver CO 80225
888-ASKUSGS (888-275-8747)
E-mail: infoservices@usgs.gov
http://ask.usgs.gov

Topographic Maps for Canada

Canada Map Office
615 Booth St.
Ottawa ON
CANADA K1A OE9
800-465-6277, 613-952-7000
Fax 800-661-6277
www.mapsnrcan.gc.ca

SOURCE FOR FOLDING CANOES

ScanSport, Inc.
P.O. Box 700
Enfield NH 03748
888-863-9500

Fax 603-632-5611
E-mail: scansport@connriver.net
www.pakboats.com

INDEX